OPEN SKY PRESS

ANNOUNCES

Premananda has decided to go back
to his given birth name, John David.

john david
(formerly Premananda)

"This change comes after 10 years of having the name
Premananda, given by my friend Swami Satchitananda,
master of Anandashram in Kerala. The unconditional
love pointed to in 'Premananda' has become embodied
in my life and continues to expand.

The name change reflects a recent inner shift and the
expansion of my outer work in the Open Sky House
Communities in Ukraine and Spain."

www.openskypress.com

Arunachala
SHIVA

Commentaries on
Sri Ramana Maharshi's Teachings
Who Am I? (Nan Yar)

Premananda

OPEN SKY PRESS
www.openskypress.com

Arunachala SHIVA

Published by Open Sky Press Ltd.
483 Green Lanes, London N13 4BS
office@openskypress.com

First edition

© Open Sky Press Ltd. 2009

ISBN 978-0-9555730-6-4

Photographs from Time Life / Getty Images by Eliot Elisofon: pp 71, 139, 203
Photographs from Magnum Photo by Henri Cartier Bresson: pp 279, 313, 315
Arunachala photographs from G. Boyd: pp 113, 228, 245, 280
Arunachala photographs from Dev Gogoi: pp 44, 175
All other photographs from Ramana Ashram Bookshop
and Open Sky House archive.

Printed in China

OPEN SKY PRESS
www.openskypress.com

Bhagavan Sri
Ramana Maharshi

*I dedicate this book to
Bhagavan Sri Ramana Maharshi,
the Sage of Arunachala. He came into my life
quietly, imperceptibly, through a photograph
twenty years ago, and has become a central
inspiration in my life.*

*Thank you for the exemplary life you led
and for the simplicity and clarity with which
you guide us. The question, 'Who am I?' has
provided a golden key to all who wish to know
their essential nature.*

Bhagavan Sri Ramana Maharshi

The Sage of Arunachala, born in 1879, is one of the most famous and most recent of India's wealth of sages, saints and spiritual Masters.

As a young man of sixteen he had a spontaneous awakening. He left his home in Madurai and made his way to Tiruvannamalai and the holy mountain, Arunachala. He lived for many years, alone and in silence, on and around the mountain, which he never left. In the 1920s the present ashram was constructed. Here he lived and taught until his death in 1950.

Many of this *Maha Rishi's* (great seer) students and devotees, who through him gained Self-realisation, passed on to their own students Sri Ramana Maharshi's practice of Self-enquiry, using the question, 'Who am I?'

The cover's background image is of Sri Ramana's original Tamil handwriting.

Bhagavan Sri Ramana Maharshi

Bhagavan	Living God
Sri	Honorific meaning illustrious
Ramana	One who knows he is the Self One who revels in the heart of all
Maha	Great
Rishi	Wise One / Pure Awareness

The illustrious Saint who dwells in the heart of all.

Sri Ramana Life Events

1879 Dec 30 .... Born in Tiruchuzhi, Tamil Nadu, South India,
as Venkataraman

1896 July .... Spiritural Awakening aged sixteen

1896 Sept 1 ..... Arrived at Arunachala aged sixteen

1897 Feb .... Moved to Gurumurtham

1898 .... Moved to Virupaksha Cave aged twenty

1902 .... Gave first recorded teaching *Who Am I?* aged
twenty-two

1906-07 .... Recovered his speech

1907 .... Given the name Bhagavan Sri Ramana Maharshi

1916 .... Mother arrived to live at Virupaksha Cave

1916 .... Moved to Skanda Ashram age thirty-seven

1922 May .... Mother died and later Bhagavan moved down
the hill

1920s .... Bhagavan rewrote and published *Who Am I?*

1920s .... Simple bamboo ashram buildings constructed

1927-1942 ...... Stone ashram buildings constructed

1930s .... Paul Brunton visited

1940s .... New granite Hall built in front of Mother's Shrine

1949 .... Cancer appeared on Bhagavan's arm

1949 .... Moved very ill to live in Samadhi Room

1950 April 14 ... Bhagavan passed away at 8.47pm

Other books by Premananda
Papaji Amazing Grace
Arunachala Talks
Blueprints for Awakening – Indian Masters

DVDs by Premananda
Blueprints for Awakening – Wisdom of the Masters
Arunachala Shiva

Forthcoming books by Premananda
Blueprints for Awakening – Western Masters
Songs of Silence

Acknowledgements

I owe an enormous debt of gratitude to my two direct Masters, Osho and Papaji. Without my twenty years sitting at their feet this book could not exist. Sri Ramana Maharshi came into my life quietly and invisibly, gradually becoming my main inspiration and guide. I particularly thank him as this book is offered in homage to his exemplary life and for making the ancient teachings available to us in contemporary language.

I am particularly indebted to David Godman for sharing his wealth of knowledge, gathered over thirty years, about all aspects of Sri Ramana. I am also indebted to James Swartz for his wonderful introduction to *Vedanta* and the many hours we spent together in fascinating conversation. These dialogues and interviews were made in 2002 during a retreat year I spent in Tiruvannamalai. In addition I would thank David and James for their patience as the years passed.

An interview or dialogue is a spontaneous and unique conversation. My thanks to Kali Devi for her sensitive editing of the interview transcripts, accurately produced by Dev Gogoi and Sathya from the original recordings. Also to Kali Devi for patiently proof reading the manuscript over and over again and for the invaluable day-to-day support she gave to the whole team, and particularly to me. To Mahima and Darshana who, while translating this book into German, added some final proofing touches.

I should like to thank Sri V. S. Ramanan, president of Sri Ramana Ashram, for permission to use photographs of Sri Ramana and the Ashram available from the Ashram shop. To Kali Devi and Darshana who have taken the majority of the recent photos of Ramana Ashram and around Arunachala. To Dev Gogoi and to Graham Boyd for their fine photographs of Arunachala. To Cartier-Bresson for his timing to be there as Sri Ramana left his body and to Welling for his classic photograph that graces the cover.

To Parvati and Darshana for the graphic design of the numerous art pages and to Parvati for her graphic advice with the cover design. Thank you Parvati for the wonderful map offered with the Preview DVD in the back of the book. Also to Darshana for the fine editing of the Preview DVD and the amazingly beautiful DVD Film *Arunachala Shiva,* available separately.

My heart-felt thanks to all the residents of the Open Sky House Community for giving such loving, energetic support, creating a space for all those working actively on the book. Finally my deep thanks and appreciation to Parvati, the director of Open Sky Press, for her painstakingly careful work formatting the book and supervising our printer in a style that has produced such a fine quality.

Premananda 2009

Contents

Self-enquiry

As each thought arises one must
be watchful and ask to whom is
this thought occurring. The answer
will be 'to me'. If you enquire
'Who am I?' the mind will return
to the source from whence it
issued. The thought which arose
will also submerge.

Sri Ramana Maharshi

Original sketch from Sri Ramana Maharshi

Introduction

Arunachala Shiva is my homage to the spiritual greatness of Bhagavan Sri Ramana Maharshi who awakened to his true nature in 1896 at the age of sixteen. A few weeks after this event he left home and made his way to Arunachala, a holy mountain in Tiruvannamalai, South India, which is reputed to be *Shiva* himself. Sri Ramana spent his whole life living on the mountain, which he took to be his Master. He is considered by most spiritual adepts to be one of the greatest Indian Sages of our times.

Sri Ramana's small booklet *Who Am I? (Nan Yar)* contains the core of his teachings with a focus on Self-enquiry. This booklet grew out of a meeting between Sri Ramana and a spiritual seeker who had a burning desire to find the answer to his question, 'Who am I?' Although Sri Ramana had not studied the scriptures when he first answered the questions, it is a spiritual classic that is in line with both the *Vedanta* and *Yoga* traditions. He answered the questions posed to him that day from the Self, reflecting the ancient wisdom of India and the contemporary wisdom of his time.

There is no doubt that the importance Sri Ramana gave to Self-enquiry as the most direct route to Self-realisation has attracted enormous attention from serious Western seekers of Truth in the last years. It is not only his teachings which have attracted attention but also his exemplary lifestyle and the *sattvic* (quiet and peaceful) nature of his mind, which is reflected in the architecture of his ashram, which he designed. Thousands of Western seekers visit the ashram every year to stay for some days in the simple but glorious peace of that place. It is always a delight to sit on the red clay floor, eating, with one's own hand, the delicious vegetarian food which is served from buckets onto a banana leaf plate.

This silent atmosphere of the ashram can be felt in the one hundred photographs on the thirty-six colour art pages. They span Sri Ramana's life from the earliest photo of him, aged twenty-one or two, to his death in 1950. Several relatively unknown photographs have been obtained, including the two photographs taken by the famous French photographer, Cartier-Bresson, on the days before and just after Sri Ramana's passing. The photographic pages also chart the development of Ramana Ashram from its beginnings right through to today, and they introduce us to some of the people who were fortunate to spend time with Sri Ramana. The beauty of Sri Ramana's guru, Arunachala, *Shiva* incarnate, graces every page.

The first steps of this book were taken in 1992 while I stayed in the room next to David Godman at Ramana Ashram. He was kind enough to explain Self-enquiry to me and to introduce me to Sri Lakshmana Swamy, one of the last living direct disciples of Sri Ramana. Later David was also part of the large community of Westerners living around Papaji in Lucknow. On Papaji's birthday in September 2000, he was happy to give the interview about his life and his relating with Papaji. His story is a classic example of how a Master does his real work. Later, in 2002, we recorded the interviews about Sri Ramana's Life, Teaching and Devotees. At that time he also offered me his commentary on *Who Am I?* and supported this project by having the interviews on his website. As the material was so compelling I decided to continue with its publication even though it has taken me several years.

In the same period in 2002 I stayed in Tiruvannamalai on a personal retreat and it was then that I met James Swartz. Most evenings he could be found in a local restaurant holding forth to a rapt audience his views on *Vedanta*. We became friends and we spent many hours together in dialogue. From our talks I gained a greater inner clarity and I was particularly happy during the many hours in which he patiently explained the finer points of *Vedanta* to me. This led directly to me asking him to dialogue with me on the teachings of Sri Ramana, which are presented in this book, with James bringing his knowledge of *Vedanta* to bear on the interpretation of these teachings. It is a valuable piece of work and by deciding to publish this with David's interviews it creates the ingredients for a lively debate on the correct interpretation of the important essence of Sri Ramana's teachings.

Arunachala Shiva offers four sections. In the first section, David Godman introduces us to Sri Ramana's life and to the lives of many of his closest disciples. He goes into the teachings in detail, particularly Self-enquiry. The complete original text of *Who Am I? (Nan Yar)*, edited by Sri Ramana in the 1920s, is included in the second section. In section three, commentaries from David, James and myself on *Who Am I? (Nan Yar)* set out the important key questions and answers. One of the contentious issues is the question about 'destroyed mind'. David advocates this strongly in Chapter 2 as an essential part of Sri Ramana's teaching and James offers an opposing interpretation in his commentaries. In the fourth section the life story of each commentator provides a unique and interesting glimpse into the adventures of serious spiritual seekers.

The interviews and dialogues with David, James and myself have been edited into an amazing ninety minute DVD Film, *Arunachala Shiva*. It contains archive material of Sri Ramana, film of the current ashram and of course, beautiful footage of Arunachala. This film visually expresses the important highlights of Sri Ramana's life and teachings. In the back of this book you will find a Preview DVD giving a taste of the full length film. High quality photographs taken from the Open Sky House archive of Arunachala and Ramana Ashram are available for printing on this Preview DVD. In addition, there is a loose map of Arunachala with the main pilgrimage temples, ashrams and hotels printed on fine quality paper.

H. W. L. Poonja, known affectionately as Papaji, the Lion of Lucknow, was a direct disciple of Sri Ramana. During the years from 1990 to Papaji's death in 1997, many Western seekers flocked to Lucknow to sit in his presence. I was one of them. He always said he was a channel for the teachings of Sri Ramana, but of course these teachings belong to the ancient spiritual tradition rather than to any one Master. Papaji was my guru and later Sri Ramana became my main inspiration and guide.

In the last fifteen years there has been an explosion of Western spiritual teachers, mainly devotees of Papaji, travelling throughout the world offering *Satsang* (meeting in Truth). As a result, their message has touched a growing number of Western seekers and it seems increasingly important to open up the ancient teachings so that this wider audience can understand their meaning. I would like this book to contribute to making the teachings of Sri Ramana more accessible and in this way also the ancient wisdom. I would like it to challenge entrenched spiritual ideas and encourage healthy debate. Finally, this is my homage to Sri Ramana who has guided me over the last years on my own journey as a spiritual teacher.

Premananda 2009

Foreword
Alan Jacobs

What a glorious title for such a fine book! *Arunachala Shiva*. The holy mountain reputed to be Lord *Shiva* himself has been a renowned pilgrimage centre for millennia and perhaps above all the home for fifty years of that celebrated world teacher, the revered *jnani* (one who has realised the Self), Sri Bhagavan Ramana Maharshi.

Premananda, the respected Western master of *Advaita Vedanta*, once again uses his powerful interview skills to fully explore the inspired teachings of Sri Bhagavan, in considerable depth. Premananda's work as a spiritual master has taken him to Australia, New Zealand, India and Europe, including Russia. Over the past six years he interviewed many Indian saints and sages, resulting in his successful and masterly publication, *Blueprints for Awakening – Rare Dialogues with 16 Indian Masters on the Teachings of Sri Ramana Maharshi*. A further volume of Western masters will be published shortly.

For his dialogues in *Arunachala Shiva* Premananda has chosen David Godman, a well known author on Sri Ramana Maharshi, and James Swartz, *Vedanta* teacher and author. He fully questions and cross examines them both, probing Sri Bhagavan's teachings in depth, so as to elucidate their full meaning, with clarity. These interviews will prove a great help for the very many spiritual aspirants, Western and Eastern, who wish to learn more about Sri Ramana and his message for contemporary humanity – a teaching that promises to bring them to Self-realisation if they will only follow his suggestions with determination and persistence.

With his book *Be As You Are*, David Godman has compiled perhaps the best introduction to Sri Bhagavan's teachings, and it is now established as a standard work of reference. David is generally regarded as one of the most knowledgeable people in the world on Sri Bhagavan's life, teaching and disciples. He has written or edited fourteen books on topics related to Sri Bhagavan.

James Swartz studied under the great *Vedanta* master Swami Chinmayananda and now uses his excellent writing skills to explain this most ancient of truths in terms fully understandable to the Western seeker. His commentaries on Sri Ramana's teachings from a *Vedanta* point of view create the possibility of a lively debate. Premananda has chosen his dialogue partners most wisely.

The book rightly opens with Premananda interviewing David Godman whose exhaustive research reveals many intimate details of Sri Bhagavan's life for the first time. Premananda and David then move on, in two enthralling chapters, to discuss more about Sri Ramana's subtle teachings and the lives of those devotees who were close to him.

The next section contains the key text of Sri Bhagavan's own *Who Am I? (Nan Yar)*. This is the foundation, seminal essay on the highly important teaching of *atma vichara*, or Self-enquiry, which Sri Bhagavan always spoke of as the direct path and sure route to Self-realisation, providing this teaching was conscientiously practised. Then Grace would flow.

Premananda then engages James Swartz in a dialogue on Sri Bhagavan's unique enlightenment experience, which occurred while he was still a teenage schoolboy. James fully explores Sri Bhagavan's own description of this event and makes some very illuminating comments which are most helpful to all those who wish to understand the implications of this event.

James also comments on *Who Am I? (Nan Yar)* in a most helpful fashion. His analysis of this important text from a *Vedanta* viewpoint is quite brilliant and is strongly recommended for those seriously interested in the practice of Self-enquiry and the meaning of the Self and realisation in Sri Bhagavan's teaching. Premananda and James go on to discuss Self-enquiry as described by Sri Ramana in his book *Self-Enquiry*.

If this was not enough, in a further chapter David Godman analyses, explains and comments on *Who Am I? (Nan Yar)* in his own lucid and scholarly fashion.

To complete the commentary section, Premananda gives us his own appreciation of the practice of Self-enquiry and explains how it is done, in a most practical form. For devotees who find Self-enquiry difficult to commence, Premananda's commentary will prove clear and compelling.

These chapters on Self-enquiry will greatly assist the many aspirants struggling to come to grips with this essential *sadhana* (spiritual practice), which, along with devotional surrender, forms the backbone of Sri Bhagavan's great gift to humanity.

This is perhaps an appropriate time to discuss Self-enquiry in more depth and detail. Sri Bhagavan describes it as the direct path to Self-realisation and it can be found recorded in the classic *Advaita* scripture, the *Yoga Vasistha*. In this profound philosophic work, punctuated by enlightening stories and fables, the sage Vasistha instructs his pupil, Prince Rama, in Self-enquiry, repeating several important instructions as the book develops. From then on, in the *Advaitic* literature, we see little or nothing concerning this practice. This is because it became essentially reserved for the initiated mature students. So, it became a concealed or hidden teaching. It was Sri Bhagavan's great innovative gift to our weary humanity to bring this practice right to the forefront of his teaching, from the very beginning, when he gave written answers to questions after his Self-realisation.

Who Am I? (Nan Yar) has almost become a *mantra* (sacred sound) of Sri Bhagavan's teaching. So Self-enquiry became an open secret available to anyone, without changing their life style. Devotees can practise and hasten the day of their liberation through this magnificently effective *sadhana*. I advise all those who are in earnest about Self-realisation to study well Sri Bhagavan's essays in his *Collected Works, Who Am I?* and *Self-Enquiry*. During his lifetime, a copy of *Who Am I?* was given to each newcomer who visited his ashram for *darshan* (being in the presence of a saint).

Self-enquiry as a practice is only found amongst *Advaita* teachers following Sri Bhagavan's teaching. It is not given in other traditions where *bhakti* (devotion) or *karma Yoga* (work given to the divine) are largely the chosen paths for liberation. Of course meditation is taught in all traditions, but not necessarily with any reference to Self-enquiry.

There is no doubt that Self-enquiry has become very popular in the West largely through the burgeoning of a great many *Advaita* teachers who have sprung up since Sri Bhagavan's *maha samadhi* (consciously leaving the body at the time of death) in 1950. It is however, often sidelined because of the subtle difficulty which can be found in its commencement, and the need for supervision to become well established in the practice. Often it is taught in an inadequate, over-simplistic form which fails to be really effective in destroying the latent tendencies which veil and occlude the full potency of the real Self. Sri Bhagavan gave many different approaches to Self-enquiry, which he referred to as the direct path to Self-realisation, to suit the needs of the different maturity and temperaments of his devotees.

There is the questioning method applied when thought and emotions arise, to ask who is having these thoughts or emotions. This pulls the mind to a sudden halt, into silence. Alternatively, it could be putting attention on the real Self, or the central feeling of 'I amness', or just becoming aware of one's own awareness. It could be the radical practice of diving into the heart, with or without breath control, as taught by Sri Bhagavan in the *Ramana Gita*. Or one can use the real I, which is the name of God, repeating it as I-I-I, using it as a *mantra*. One needs to read his *Collected Works* and answers to question in his *Talks*, reading the indexed references to Self-enquiry zealously, to fully ground oneself in the practice, and then exercise it persistently and diligently. Then the veil and occlusion to the real Self is lifted, the *vasanas* (tendencies of the mind) emerge, and the ego or false sense of 'me' topples. Self-realisation inevitably follows for the assiduous practitioner of Self-enquiry in due course, so says Bhagavan Sri Ramana!

Following these important chapters, Premananda turns to questioning both James and David about their own life stories, enthralling spiritual quests which reveal their own spiritual findings. Premananda also subjects himself to an in-depth interview.

David Godman's own pilgrimage and spiritual search had led him to Ramana Ashram, then on to see H.W.L. Poonja or Papaji, Nisargadatta Maharaj, Annamalai Swami, Lakshmana Swamy and many other of

Bhagavan's principal, close devotees. David tells us about his colourful experiences with many of the sages he has met, interviewed and worked with, when writing their biographies.

David settled down in India and has lived in Tiruvannamalai for thirty years where he assiduously continues to edit and translate major works on Sri Bhagavan's teachings by sages such as the famed Tamil poet, Sri Muruganar. The many devotees of Sri Bhagavan owe this fine writer and biographer a great debt for his dedicated work over some thirty years.

James Swartz' colourful life makes exciting reading. After being a successful businessman he turned to the psychedelic movement of the 60s. His journeys into conciousness eventually led him to his master, Swami Chinmayananda. James studied *Vedanta* under this great master. His unique gift to his readers and those who go to him for guidance is his ability to communicate the wisdom of *Vedanta* in modern language. He maintains a fascinating website where he debunks many spiritual myths and is currently publishing his new book, *How to Attain Enlightenment*.

Premananda's life journey chronicles his years living in Japan, India, USA, Australia and now Europe. He tells how his time with Osho prepared him for the meeting with his *sadguru* (guru who liberates) Papaji, and how identification with 'Premananda' fell away. His work as a spiritual master has taken him to many countries and has also resulted in a residential Satsang community near Cologne in Germany.

Premananda's deep love for Sri Ramana has been the catalyst for this and other books, and the result is a platform for valuable discussion and debate about the interpretation of Sri Ramana's teachings.

What does this excellent book achieve? In my opinion it tells us why the teachings of this supreme guru, Sri Ramana Maharshi, have become so widely influential in the twentieth and twenty-first centuries and have led to a spiritual renaissance and interest in *Advaita Vedanta* in both India and the West, spreading like a prairie bush fire. The book also adds to the understanding of Sri Ramana's teachings in a positive way and succeeds in presenting a novel understanding of his work.

This is undoubtedly an important seminal work on the teachings of Sri Bhagavan Ramana Maharshi. It will prove to be a most useful introduction for those encountering *Advaita* for the first time as well as a valuable handbook and guide for all those currently engaged in following his teachings, both in the East and the West. The book is handsomely graced with forty pages of beautiful colour photos, and is exceptionally well designed. It includes a Preview DVD with extracts from the DVD Film, *Arunachala Shiva*, which will be offered separately from the book.

It has been a privilege to be invited to write the foreword to this important book which I am sure will assist the very many thousands who are intensely interested in this most treasured teaching, both now and in the future. Premanada is once again to be congratulated and thanked for his diligent work in adding an important and significant contribution to the renowned Sri Ramana Maharshi literature.

Alan Jacobs
President, Sri Ramana Maharshi Foundation U.K.
London, July 2009

The greatest error of a man is to think that he is weak by nature, evil by nature. Every man is divine and strong in his real nature. What are weak and evil are his habits, his desires and thoughts, but not himself.

Sri Ramana Maharshi

INTRODUCTION

Above: Views of Virupaksha
Cave after 1903

Left: Skanda Ashram

Right top: Skanda Ashram
view from summit path

Right centre: Sri Ramana
and the Mother around
1920
Group with the Mother
and Kunju Swami (sitting
far right) at Skanda Ashram
1916-18

Bottom: Classic Arunachala
south face

CHAPTER 1

Sri Ramana's Life at Arunachala

*David Godman in dialogue
with Premananda*

[Sri Ramana's direct words are in bold]

*David takes us through the various stages of Sri
Ramana's life. The chapter begins with Sri Ramana
born into a family in South India in Tamil Nadu in
1879. This family life came to an end after his sudden
spiritual realisation at age sixteen. The call to his beloved
Arunachala, the holy mountain in Tiruvannamalai,
was too strong to resist. David tells us the details of Sri
Ramana's life at Arunachala from his period of deep
samadhi in Arunachaleswara Temple to his time living
up on the mountain in Virupaksha Cave and then at
Skanda Ashram; later as a world-renowned Master in
the ashram he constructed at the foot of the mountain.*

Bhagavan Sri Ramana Maharshi was given this title in 1907 by Sri Ganapati Sastri, a Vedic scholar. David, can you begin by telling us something about his early life and how he awakened as a young boy in Madurai?

Bhagavan's given name was Venkataraman and he was born in 1879 into a family of South Indian Brahmins in Tiruchuzhi, a small town in Tamil Nadu. He came from a pious, middle-class family. His father, Sundaram Iyer, was, by profession, an 'uncertified pleader'. He represented people in legal matters, but he had no acknowledged qualifications to practise as a lawyer. Despite this handicap, he seemed to have a good DA, and he was well respected in his community.

Venkataraman had a normal childhood that showed no signs of future greatness. He was good at sports, lazy at school, indulged in an average amount of mischief, and exhibited little interest in religious matters. He did, though, have a few unusual traits. When he slept, he went into such a deep state of unconsciousness that his friends could physically assault him without waking him up. He also had an extraordinary amount of luck. In team games, whichever side he played for always won. This earned him the nickname Tangakai, which means 'golden hand'. It is a title given to people who exhibit a far-above-average amount of good fortune. Venkataraman also had a natural talent for the intricacies of literary Tamil. In his early teens he knew enough to correct his Tamil school teacher if he made any mistakes.

His father died when he was twelve and the family moved to Madurai, a city in southern Tamil Nadu. Sometime in 1896, when he was sixteen years of age, he had a remarkable spiritual awakening. He was sitting in his uncle's house when the thought occurred to him that he was about to die. He became afraid, but instead of panicking he lay down on the ground and began to analyse what was happening. He began to investigate what constituted death: what would die and what would survive that death. He spontaneously initiated a process of Self-enquiry that culminated, within a few minutes, in his own permanent awakening. In one of his rare written comments on this process he wrote: **'Enquiring within "Who is the seer?" I saw the seer disappear leaving**

That alone which stands forever. No thought arose to say "I saw". How then could the thought arise to say "I did not see"?' In those few moments his individual identity disappeared and was replaced by a full awareness of the Self. That experience, that awareness, remained with him for the rest of his life. He had no need to do any more practice or meditation because this death experience left him in a state of complete and final liberation. It is something very rare in the spiritual world: that someone who had no interest in the spiritual life should, within the space of a few minutes, and without any effort or prior practice, reach a state that other seekers spend lifetimes trying to attain.

I say 'without any effort' because this re-enactment of death and the subsequent Self-enquiry seemed to be something that happened to him, rather than something he did. When he described this event for his Telugu biographer, the pronoun 'I' never appeared. He said, 'The body lay on the ground, the limbs stretched themselves out' and so on. That particular description really leaves the reader with the feeling that this event was utterly impersonal. Some power took over the boy Venkataraman, made him lie on the floor and finally made him understand that death is for the body and for the sense of individuality, and that it cannot touch the underlying reality in which they both appear.

When Venkataraman got up he was a fully enlightened sage, but he had no cultural or spiritual context to evaluate properly what had happened to him. He had read some biographies of ancient Tamil saints and he had attended many temple rituals, but none of this seemed to relate to the new state that he found himself in.

What was his first reaction? What did he think had happened to him?

Years later, when he was recollecting this experience, he said that he thought at the time that he had caught some strange disease. However, he thought that it was such a nice disease he hoped he wouldn't recover from it. At one time, soon after the experience, he also speculated that he might have been possessed. When he discussed the events with Narasimhaswami, his first English biographer, he repeatedly used the

Tamil word *avesam*, which means possession by a spirit, to describe his initial reactions to the event.

Did he discuss it with anyone? Did he try to find out what had happened to him?

Venkataraman told no one in his family what had happened to him. He tried to carry on as if nothing unusual had occurred. He continued to attend school and kept up a veneer of normality for his family, but as the weeks went by he found it harder and harder to keep up this facade because he was pulled inside more and more. At the end of August 1896 he fell into a deep state of absorption in the Self when he should have been writing out a text he had been given as a punishment for not doing his schoolwork properly.

His brother scornfully said, 'What is the use of all this for one like this?' meaning, 'What use is family life for someone who spends all his time behaving like a *Yogi*?'

The justice of the remark struck Venkataraman, making him decide to leave home forever. The following day he left, without telling anyone where he was going or what had happened to him. He merely left a note saying that he was off on a '**virtuous enterprise**' and that no money should be spent searching for him. His destination was Arunachala, a major pilgrimage centre a few hundred miles to the north. In his note to his family he wrote '**I have, in search of my father and in obedience to his command, started from here.**' His father was Arunachala, and in abandoning his home and family he was following an internal summons from the mountain of Arunachala.

He had an adventurous trip to Tiruvannamalai, taking three days for a journey that, with better information, he could have completed in less than a day. He arrived on September 1st 1896 and spent the rest of his life here at Arunachala.

Could you paint a picture of what Arunachala is like, and what it signifies? Perhaps also say what it would have been like when Sri Ramana first arrived.

The town of Tiruvannamalai, with its associated mountain, Arunachala, has always been a major pilgrimage centre. The town's heart and soul haven't changed that much in recent times despite the presence of auto-rickshaws, TV aerials and a vast expanse of suburbs. The basic culture and way of life of people in Tiruvannamalai have probably been the same for centuries. Marco Polo came to Tamil Nadu in the 1200s on his way home from China. His descriptions of what people were doing and how they were living are very recognisable to people who live here today.

Tiruvannamalai has one of the principal *Shiva-lingam* (phallic symbol of the divine) temples in South India. There are five temples, each corresponding to one of the elements: earth, water, fire, air and space. Tiruvannamalai is the fire temple.

The earliest records of this place go back to about AD 500, at which point it's already famous. Saints were touring around Tamil Nadu in those days, praising Arunachala as the place where *Shiva* resides, and recommending everyone to go there. There's a much older tradition that suddenly appears in the historical record about 1,500 years ago, simply because a major cultural change resulted in people making proper monuments and writing things down. I would say that Bhagavan was, in this historical context, the most recent and probably the most famous representative of a whole stream of extraordinary saints who have been drawn by the power of this place for at least, I would guess, 2000 years.

When was the big Shiva *temple built?*

It grew in layers, in squares, from the inside out. Once upon a time there was probably a shrine about the size of a small room. You can date all these things because the walls of temples here are public record offices. Whenever a king wins a war with his neighbour he gets someone to chisel the fact on the side of a temple wall. Or, if he gives 500 acres to someone he likes that fact also is chiselled on the temple wall. That's where you go to see who's winning the battles and what the king is giving away, and to whom.

The earliest inscriptions, they're called epigraphs, on the inner shrine date from the ninth century, so that's probably the time it was built. Progressively, up to about the 1600s, the temple got bigger and bigger and bigger. It reached its current dimensions in the seventeenth century. For people who have never seen this building, I should say that it's huge. I would guess that each of the four sides is about two hundred yards long, and the main tower is over two hundred feet high.

And that's where Bhagavan came to when he arrived?

When Bhagavan was very young he intuitively knew that Arunachala signified God in some way. In one of his verses he wrote, '**From my unthinking childhood the immensity of Arunachala had shone in my awareness.**' He felt, '**This is the holiest place, this is the holiest state, this is God Himsef.**' He was in awe of Arunachala and what it represented without ever really understanding that it was a pilgrimage place that he could actually go to. It wasn't until he was a teenager that one of his relatives actually came back from here and said, 'I've been to Arunachala.'

Bhagavan said it was an anticlimax. Before, he had imagined it to be some great heavenly realm that holy, enlightened people went to when they died. To find out that he could pay five rupees and go there on the train was a bit of a let down.

His first reaction to the word 'Arunachala' was absolute awe. Later there was a brief period of anticlimax when he realised it was just a place on the map. Later still, after his enlightenment experience, he understood that it was the power of Arunachala that had precipitated the experience and pulled him physically to this place.

Look, there [Arunachala] stands as if insentient. Mysterious is the way it works, beyond all human understanding. From my unthinking childhood, the immensity of Arunachala had shone in my awareness, but even when I learned from

someone that it was only Tiruvannamalai, I did not realise its meaning. When it stilled myself and drew me to itself and I came near, I saw that it was stillness absolute.

The verse I just quoted from chronicles the early stages of his relationship with the mountain.

The last line contains a very nice pun. '*Achala*' is Sanskrit for 'mountain' and it also means 'absolute stillness'. On one level this poem is describing Bhagavan's physical pilgrimage to Tiruvannamalai, but in another sense he is talking about his mind going back into the Heart and becoming totally silent and still.

When he arrived, and this is something you won't find in any of the standard biographies, he said he stood in front of the temple. It was closed at the time, but all the doors, right through to the innermost shrine, spontaneously opened for him. He walked straight in, went up to the *lingam* and hugged it.

He didn't really want this version of events publicised for two reasons. First, he didn't like letting people know that miracles were happening around him. When such events happened, he tried to play them down. Second, he knew that the temple priests would get very upset if they found out that he had touched their *lingam*. Even though he was a Brahmin, the temple priests would take his act to be a contaminating one, and they would have had to order a special elaborate *puja* (prayer ceremony) to reconsecrate the *lingam*. Not wanting to upset them, he kept quiet.

Yes, we've come from the temple just now and there's a huge lock on the door.

Yes. Ordinarily, no outsider can get anywhere near the *lingam*. Looking after it is a hereditary profession. No one outside this lineage is allowed over the metal bar that is about ten feet in front of the *lingam*.

There is another interesting aspect to this story. From the moment of his enlightenment in Madurai there was a strong burning sensation in Bhagavan's body that only went away when he hugged the *lingam*. Touching the *lingam* grounded or dissipated the energy. The *lingam* in the temple is not just a representation of Arunachala. It is held to be Arunachala itself. The hugging of the *lingam* was the final act of physical union between Bhagavan and his guru, Arunachala.

I have not read of any other visit by Bhagavan to the inner shrine. This may have been the only time he went. One visit was enough to transact this particular piece of business. Bhagavan always loved the physical form of the mountain, Arunachala, and spent as much time as he could on its slopes, but his business with the temple *lingam* was completed within a few minutes of his arrival in 1896.

Am I right in thinking that from then on he pretty much stayed within the confines of the temple?

After this dramatic arrival he stayed in various parts of the temple for several months. The day he arrived he threw away all his money into a local tank; he shaved his head, which is a sign of physical renunciation; he threw away all his clothes and he just sat quietly, often in a deep *samadhi* (immersed in the Self) in which he was completely unaware of his body or his surroundings. It was his destiny to stay alive and become a great teacher, so people force-fed him and looked after him in other ways. Without that particular destiny to fulfil, he would have probably given up his body or died from physical neglect. For the first three or four years he was here, he was mostly unaware of anything around him. He rarely ate, and at one time his body started to rot. Portions of his legs became open, festering sores, but he didn't even notice.

This is when he was sitting down in that kind of basement?

Yes. Have you been there? It's called Patala *Lingam*. He was in that place for about six weeks. At the end of that period he had to be physically carried out and cleaned up.

In his early years here he said that he would open his eyes without knowing how long he had been oblivious to the world. He would stand up and try to take a few steps. If his legs were reasonably strong, he would infer that he had been unaware of his body for a relatively short period – perhaps a day or two. If his legs buckled when he stood to walk, he would realise that he had probably been in a deep *samadhi* for many days, possibly weeks. Sometimes he would open his eyes and discover that he was not in the place where he had sat when he closed his eyes. He had no recollection of his body moving from one place to another within one of the temple *mantapams* (porches).

Did anyone recognise him as a great saint, or at least as someone special?

There were a few. Seshadri Swami, who was also a local saint, spotted him while he was sitting in the Patala *Lingam*. He tried to look after him and protect him, but without much success. Bhagavan has spoken of one or two other people who intuitively knew that he was in a very elevated state, but in those days, they were very few in number.

Were they people from the temple?

Seshadri Swami lived all over the place. There were probably two or three other people who even then recognised him as being something special. Some people revered him simply because he was living such an ascetic life, but there were other people who seemed to know that he was in a high state. The grandfather of a man who later became the ashram's lawyer was one whom Bhagavan said had a full appreciation of who he really was.

In those days you could easily take his behaviour as a sign of being a bit crazy, couldn't you?

People get the benefit of the doubt here, especially if they are sitting all day, absolutely still, and not eating. That's hard to fake. You don't sit in full lotus, absolutely motionless for a few days just to get a free meal. But at the same time, it doesn't prove you are enlightened. There was a man here in Bhagavan's time who sat eighteen hours a day in full lotus with his eyes closed. His name was Govind Bhat and he lived in Palakottu, a *sadhu* (ascetic) colony adjacent to Ramana Ashram. He tried to attract devotees even while Bhagavan was alive, but he didn't do very well. In the end it is the enlightenment not the physical antics that attracts the real devotees.

So how did it happen that he moved from the temple up onto the hill?

Have you been to a place called Gurumurtham? It's a temple a mile out of town. A man who was looking after Bhagavan invited him to go and stay in a mango orchard that was next to this temple. He moved out there for about a year and a half. That was the furthest away from the mountain he ever went in all his fifty years here. Even there he was mostly unaware of his body and the world. He said his fingernails grew to be several inches long. He didn't comb or wash his hair for a couple of years. Many years later he commented that if one doesn't comb one's hair it becomes very matted and it grows very quickly. By the end of his time at Gurumurtham, he had long matted hair and long fingernails.

He has said that he could hear people whisper outside, saying 'This man's been in there for hundreds of years.' Because of the extent of his asceticism, he looked old even when he was eighteen.

From the way you're telling the story, it has always been clear that he was a saint.

Clear to whom? It is easy to say this in hindsight, but at the time there were many local people who had no opinion of him at all. The population of Tiruvannamalai around 1900 was probably in the region of 20,000. If twenty people came to see him regularly, and the rest didn't bother, that means ninty-nine percent of the local people either didn't know anything about him, or didn't care enough to pay him a visit.

His uncle, who came in the 1890s to try and bring him home, asked people in town, 'What's he doing? Why is he behaving like this?' The replies he received were not positive. His uncle was led to believe that he was just a truant who should be taken home. Even in later years there were many people in Tiruvannamalai who didn't have a high opinion of him. The people who became his devotees are the ones who left some records, so the published opinions of him are a bit one-sided.

So by the time he was twenty were there devotees already coming to spend time with him?

He arrived when he was sixteen and for the next two or three years he sometimes had one full-time attendant, plus a few people who occasionally came to see him.

It wasn't really until the early years of the last century that people started coming regularly. By the beginning of the first decade of the twentieth century he had a small group of followers. A few people brought him food regularly and a few others were frequent visitors. A large number of curiosity seekers would come to have a look at him and go away. Apart from these tourists, he seems to have had perhaps four or five regular devotees.

Were those local people?

They were mostly locals. One woman called Akhilandamma, who lived about forty miles away, used to come from her village and bring him food once in a while. Another, Sivaprakasam Pillai, lived in another town, but he came for *darshan* (being in the presence of a saint) regularly. Just about everyone else lived here in Tiruvannamalai.

And he went from the mango orchard up onto the hill?

Around 1901 he moved up to Virupaksha Cave and stayed there for about fifteen years, but it was not a good place to live all year round. In summer it was too hot. He stayed there for about eight months a year and then moved to other nearby caves and shrines such as Guhai Nama Shivaya Temple, Sadguru Swami Cave and a place called Mango Tree Cave.

They are all less than a five-minute walk from Virupaksha Cave. There's a big tank up there, Mulaipal Tirtham, a little lower down the hill from Virupaksha Cave. This was the *sadhus'* water supply. Everybody up there was dependent on that tank, so all their caves and their huts were in walking distance of it.

Now it has become a small farm up there, a lot of cows and what have you.

Things move on.

But in fact there's a stream that runs right past Virupaksha Cave.

It doesn't run all year, and when Bhagavan moved into the cave it wasn't there at all. There was a big thunderstorm one summer that produced an avalanche that carried away many of the rocks that were near the cave. After the debris had been cleared away, it was discovered that a new spring was coming out of nearby rocks. The devotees said that it was a gift from Arunachala, and Bhagavan seemed to agree with them.

It seems a nice little water supply.

It's very seasonal. We have just had a week and a half of good rain. If it doesn't rain, within a week it will dry up, so it's not that good a source.

Is that the same spring that goes through Skanda Ashram?

No, Virupaksha Cave has an independent spring. Skanda Ashram probably has the best spring on that side of the hill. That spring also didn't exist when Bhagavan first moved onto the hill. He went on a walk there – it's a few hundred feet higher up the mountain from Virupaksha Cave – noticed a damp patch and recommended that it be dug out to see if there was a good water source there. There was, and the stream that now flows through Skanda Ashram is the highest source of permanent water on the hill. It's about 600 feet above the town.

Does that mean Skanda Ashram didn't exist in those days?

That's right. It's named after a man called Kandaswami who started building it in the early years of the last century. Kandiswami did a massive amount of work on the site. When he started, it was a forty-five degree scree slope. He dug back into the side of the hill and used the excavated soil and rocks to make a flat terrace on the side of the hill. He planted many coconut and mango trees, which are still there. It's a beautiful place now, a shady oasis on the side of the hill.

So when Bhagavan moved up there, it was pretty well set. There were some buildings and a terrace?

The terrace was there and the young trees had been planted, but there was only one small hut that was not big enough for everyone. The devotees of the time did some fundraising and erected the structure that can be seen there today.

Do you know how many people were there with Bhagavan? Half a dozen?

In Virupaksha Cave about four or five would be a good average. By the time Bhagavan moved to Skanda Ashram, the average numbers were probably up to ten or twelve. I am talking about people who lived with Bhagavan full-time, and who slept with him at night. There were many other people who just visited and left.

So even in the cave there were in fact people living there with him?

Yes, they ate with him and slept there at night. Many of them left during the day to do things elsewhere. They were not sitting there all the time. They were all men, by the way. Until Bhagavan's mother arrived in 1916, only men were allowed to sleep in Virupaksha Cave. Even though there was no formal structure, the people who lived with Bhagavan tended to regard themselves as celibate *sadhus*. They regarded the cave as a men-only ashram.

Initially these *sadhus* didn't want Bhagavan's mother to move in with them. However, when Bhagavan declared, 'If you make her leave, I will also leave along with her,' they had to back down and allow her to stay.

So, when he lived in the cave he wasn't in retreat or in solitary silence. The image of Bhagavan is always of this totally silent, totally alone person.

He behaved differently in different phases of his life. In the late 1890s, when he was in his late teens, he almost never interacted with anyone. Most of the time he just sat with his eyes closed, either in the temple or in nearby temples and shrines. He knew what was going on because in later years he would often talk about incidents from this era, but he hardly ever spoke. The period of rarely speaking lasted for about ten years, up to about 1906. He hadn't taken a vow of silence, he had just temporarily lost the ability to articulate sounds. When he tried to speak, a kind of guttural noise would initially come out of his throat. Sometimes he would have to make three or four attempts to get the words out. Because it was so hard to speak, he preferred silence.

Around 1906-07, when he recovered his ability to speak normally, he began to interact verbally with the people around him. By this time he was also spending a lot of time wandering around by himself on Arunachala. He loved being out on the mountain. It was his main passion, his only attachment.

And that would be alone? He would go around alone?

Occasionally he would take people out for brief walks but mostly he was alone.

Is it on record who was his first disciple? Perhaps we shouldn't say 'first disciple'.

There were people who looked after him in his early years here who could be regarded as his earliest devotees. The most prominent was

Palaniswami who looked after him from the 1890s until passing away in 1915. The two of them were inseparable for almost twenty years.

So this man would have lived at the cave with Bhagavan?

Yes, he was the full-time attendant at Virupaksha Cave. He also lived with Bhagavan at Gurumurtham.

And gradually other people were attracted and would become fairly permanent. Presumably, there was no formal initiation.

I really don't know who decided 'Okay, you can sleep here tonight.' There was no management, no check-in department. Everyone was welcome to come and sit with Bhagavan – all day if they wanted to. And if they were still there at night, they could also sleep there. If food was available, everyone who was present would share.

Bhagavan never had much to do with who was there and who wasn't, who was allowed to stay and who wasn't. If people wanted to stay they stayed, and if they wanted to leave they left.

And presumably that continued. I mean, he was never actively involved in managing the ashram, was he?

In the Virupaksha period there wasn't a lot of work going on. It was a community of begging *sadhus* who just stayed with Bhagavan whenever they felt like it. People would go to town, beg on the streets, collect the food, and bring it back to Virupaksha Cave. Bhagavan would mix it all up together, distribute it, and that was the food for the day. If not enough food was begged, people went hungry. Nobody was cooking, so there was no work to do except for occasional cleaning. After his mother came in 1916, the kitchen work started. Slowly, slowly, it got to the situation where if you wanted to live full-time with him, you had to work. Even today the people who eat and sleep full-time in the ashram have to work there. It's not a place for people who want to sit and meditate all day. If you want to do that, you live somewhere else.

So that would have started when they moved to Skanda Ashram?

It got a bit more organised when Bhagavan moved to Skanda Ashram, but it was still a community of begging *sadhus* right up to the early 1920s. Bhagavan himself went begging in the 1890s. I wouldn't say he encouraged begging, but he thought it was a good tradition. Go out and beg your food, eat what people give you, sleep under a tree and wake up the next day with nothing. He heartily approved of a lifestyle like this, but it wasn't one he could follow himself once he settled down and an ashram grew up around him.

And he wore just a loincloth?

In the beginning, for the first few months, he was naked. A couple of months after he arrived there was a big festival in the temple. Some devotees lifted him up and dressed him in a loincloth because they knew that he might be arrested if he sat in a prominent place with no clothes on. For most of his life he only wore a loincloth, occasionally supplemented by a *dhoti* (length of cotton cloth) that he would tie under his armpits, rather than round his waist. It gets quite cold here on winter mornings, but he never seemed to want or need more clothes.

When did the ashram begin to get big?

Coming down the hill was the big move in Bhagavan's life. When his mother died in 1922, she was buried where the ashram is now located. The spot was chosen because it was the Hindu graveyard in those days. After her death Bhagavan continued to live at Skanda Ashram, but about six months later he came down the hill and didn't go back up. He never gave any reason for staying at the foot of the hill. He just said he didn't feel any impulse to go back to Skanda Ashram. That's how the current Ramana Ashram started.

So the ashram's actually built on a Hindu burial ground?

Yes. In those days the graveyard was well outside the town. Now the town has expanded to include Ramana Ashram and the present Hindu graveyard is now a mile further out of town.

How did the ashram come to take over the land round here?

The place where Bhagavan's mother was buried was actually owned by a math, a religious institution, in town. When she died, the devotees had to get permission from the head of this math to bury her on this land, but there was no problem since he was also a devotee. He had a high opinion of Bhagavan, so he handed over the land to the emerging Ramana Ashram.

And the first building, was it the shrine over the Mother's grave?

Well, shrine is a bit of a fancy word. A really wonderful photo was taken here in 1922, shortly after Bhagavan settled here. The only building is a coconut-leaf hut. It looks as if one good gust of wind would blow it over. People who came to see him that year have reported that there wasn't even room for two people in the room where Bhagavan lived. That was the first ashram building here: a coconut-leaf hut that probably leaked when it rained.

It's very beautiful now: water, trees, peacocks. It must have been very primitive eighty years ago.

I talked to the man who cleared the land here. He told me there were large boulders and many cacti and thorn bushes. It wasn't really forest. It's not the right climate for a luxuriant forest, and there isn't much soil. The granite bedrock is often close to the surface, and there are many rocky outcrops. This man, Ramaswami Pillai, said that he spent the first six months prising out boulders with a crowbar, cutting down cacti and levelling the ground.

When the building started, was Bhagavan himself involved in that?

I don't think he built the first coconut-leaf hut himself, but once he moved here he was very much a hands-on manager. The first proper building over the Mother's *samadhi* (burial shrine) was organised and built by him.

Have you seen how bricks are made around here? It's like making mud pies. You start with a brick-shaped mould. You make a pile of mud and then use the mould to make thousands of mud bricks that you put out in the sun to dry. After they have been properly dried, you stack them in a structure the size of a house that has big holes in the base for logs to be put in. The outside of the stack is sealed with wet mud and fires are lit at the base. Once the fire has taken, the bottom is sealed as well. The bricks are baked in a hot, oxygen-free environment, in the same way that charcoal is made. After two or three days the fires die down, and, if nothing has gone wrong, the bricks are properly baked. However, if the fires go out too soon, or if it rains heavily during the baking, the bricks don't get cooked properly. When that happens the whole production is often wasted because the bricks are soft and crumbly – more like biscuits than bricks.

In the 1920s someone tried to make bricks near the ashram, but the baking was unsuccessful and all the half-baked bricks were abandoned. Bhagavan, who abhorred waste of any kind, decided to use all these commercially useless bricks to build a shrine over his mother's grave. One night he had everyone in the ashram line up between the kiln and the ashram. Bricks were passed from hand to hand until there were enough in the ashram to make a building. The next day he did bricklaying himself as he and his devotees raised a wall around the *samadhi*. Bhagavan did a lot of work on the inside of the wall because people felt that, since it was going to be a temple, the interior work should be done by Brahmins.

This was the only building that he constructed himself, but years later, when the large granite buildings that make up much of the present ashram were erected, he was the architect, the engineer and building supervisor. He was there every day, giving orders and checking up on progress.

You say he abhorred waste. Can you expand on that a little?

He had the attitude that anything that came to the ashram was a gift from God, and that it should be properly utilised. He would pick up stray mustard seeds that he found on the kitchen floor with his fingernails and insist that they be stored and used; he used to cut the white margins off proof copies of ashram books, stitch them together and make little notebooks out of them; he would attempt to cook parts of vegetables, such as the spiky ends of aubergines, that are normally thrown away. He admitted that he was a bit of a fanatic on this subject. He once remarked, 'It's a good thing I never got married. No woman would have been able to put up with my habits.'

Going back to his building activities, how involved in day-to-day decisions was he? Did he, for example, decide where the doors and windows went?

Yes. Either he would explain what he wanted verbally, or he would make little sketches on the backs of envelopes or on scrap pieces of paper.

What you're describing now is a totally different Bhagavan from the one who sat in samadhi *all day. Most people think that he spent his whole life sitting quietly in the hall, doing nothing.*

He didn't like sitting in the hall all day. He often said that it was his prison. If he was off doing some work when visitors came, someone would come and tell him that he was needed in the hall. That's where he usually met with new people. He would sigh and remark, 'People have come. I have to go back to jail.'

'Got to go sit on the couch.'

Yes. 'Got to go and sit on the couch and tell people how to get enlightened.'

Bhagavan enjoyed all kinds of physical work, but he particularly enjoyed cooking. He was the ashram's head cook for at least fifteen years. He got up at two or three o'clock every morning, cut vegetables and supervised the cooking. When the new ashram buildings were going up in the 1920s and 30s, he was also the supervising engineer and architect.

I think what you've just been speaking about is very important. People tend to have an image of him as a man who sat on a couch, looking blissful and doing nothing. You are describing a completely different man.

His state didn't change from the age of sixteen onwards, but his outer activities did. In the beginning of his life here at Arunachala he was quiet and rarely did anything. Thirty years later he had a hectic and busy schedule, but his experience of who he was never wavered during this later phase of busy-ness.

I like the way you're speaking because in a way you're debunking a lot of spiritual myths.

Bhagavan never felt comfortable with a situation in which he sat on a couch in the role of a 'guru', with everyone on the floor around him. He liked to work and live with people, interacting with them in a normal, natural way, but as the years went by the possibilities for this kind of life became less and less.

One of the problems was that people were often completely overawed by him. Most people couldn't act normally around him. Many of the visitors wanted to put him on a pedestal and treat him like a god, but he didn't seem to appreciate that kind of treatment.

There are some nice stories of new people behaving naturally and getting a natural response from Bhagavan. Major Chadwick wrote that Bhagavan would come to his room after lunch, go through his things like an inquisitive child, sit on the bed and chat with him. However, when

Chadwick once put out a chair in the expectation of Bhagavan's arrival, the visits stopped. Chadwick had made the transition from having a friend who dropped by to having a guru who needed respect and a special chair. When this formality was introduced, the visits ended.

So he saw himself as a friend not as the master?

Bhagavan didn't have a perspective of his own, he simply reacted to the way people around him thought about him and treated him. He could be a friend, a father, a brother, a god, depending on the devotee's way of approaching him. One woman was convinced that Bhagavan was her baby son. She had a little doll that looked like Bhagavan, and she would cradle it like a baby when she was in his presence. Her belief in this relationship was so strong, she actually started lactating when she held her Bhagavan doll.

Bhagavan seemed to approve of any guru-disciple relationship that kept the devotee's attention on the Self or the form of the guru, but at the same time he still liked and enjoyed people who could treat him as a normal being.

Bhagavan sometimes said that it didn't matter how you regarded the guru, so long as you could think about him all the time. As an extreme example he cited two people from ancient times who got enlightened by hating God so much that they couldn't stop thinking about Him.

There is a Tamil phrase that translates as 'mother-father-guru-God'. A lot of people felt that way about him. Bhagavan himself said he never felt that he was a guru in a guru-disciple relationship with anyone. His public position was that he didn't have any disciples at all because, he said, from the perspective of the Self there was no one who was different or separate from him. Being the Self and knowing that the Self alone exists, he knew that there were no unenlightened people who needed to be enlightened. He said he only ever saw enlightened people around him.

Having said that, Bhagavan clearly did function as a guru to the thousands of people who had faith in him and who tried to carry out his teachings.

During which period was Bhagavan actively involved in the building work?

The ashram started to change from coconut-leaf structures to stone buildings around 1930. The big building phase was from 1930 to 1942. The Mother's Temple was built after that, but Bhagavan wasn't supervising the design and construction of that so much. That work was subcontracted  to expert temple builders. Bhagavan visited the site regularly, but he wasn't so involved in design or engineering decisions.

If anybody had visited during those twelve years they would have found a Bhagavan who was not sitting on the couch. They would have found him out working, supervising workers?

It would have depended on when they came. Bhagavan had a routine that he kept to. He was always in the hall for the morning and evening chanting – two periods of about forty-five minutes each. He would be there in the evening, chatting to all the ashram's workers who could not see him during the day because of their various duties in different parts of the ashram. He would be there if visitors arrived who wanted to speak to him. He walked regularly on the hill, or to Palakottu, an area adjacent to the ashram. These walks generally took place after meals. He would fit in his other jobs around these events. If nothing or no one needed his attention in the hall, he might go and see how the cooks were getting on, or he might go to the cowshed to check up on the ashram's cows. If there was a big building project going on he would often go out to check up on the progress of the work. Mostly though, he did his tours of the building sites after lunch when everyone else was having a siesta.

He supervised many workers, not just the ones who put up the buildings. Devotees in the hall would bind and rebind books under his supervision, the cooks would work according to his instructions, and so on. The only area he didn't seem inclined to get involved in was the ashram office. He let his brother, Chinnaswami, have a fairly free rein there, although once in a while he would intervene if he felt that something that had been neglected ought to be done.

In earlier years, up to 1926, he would also walk round the base of Arunachala quite regularly.

Would a few people follow him?

Yes, large crowds would go with him in the later years, and when he passed through town there would be even more people waiting for him, trying to feed him, or attempting to get him into their houses. He turned down all these invitations. After the 1890s he never entered a private house in town.

He stopped going round the hill in 1926 because people started fighting over who should stay behind in the ashram. No one wanted to be left behind, but someone always had to remain to guard the property.

Finally he said, 'If I stop going there won't be any more fights about who is going to stay behind.' He never did the walk again.

You were saying he was a very natural person who liked very natural people. I presume he also liked animals.

Almost all of them. I have read that he didn't particularly like cats, but I don't know what the evidence is for that. As far as I can make out, he loved all the animals in the ashram. He showed a particular fondness for the dogs, the monkeys and the squirrels.

And they, presumably, lived in the ashram as well?

Bhagavan used to say that people in the ashram were squatting on land that belonged to the animals, and that the local wild animals had prior tenancy rights. He never approved of animals being driven away either to make more room for people or because some people didn't like having animals around. He always took the side of the animals whenever there was any attempt to throw them out or inconvenience them in any way.

He had squirrels on his sofa. They moved in and made nests in the grass roof over his head, they ran all over his body, and had babies in his cushions. Once in a while he'd sit on one and accidentally suffocate it. They were all over the place.

So he obviously enjoyed having the animals close by. Was this shared by others in the ashram?

It was natural and normal for him, but it was not natural and normal for many of the people who congregated around him. Bhagavan always had to fight in the animals' corner to make sure they got proper treatment, or were not unnecessarily inconvenienced.

By the 1940s the Old Hall that Bhagavan had lived in since the late 1920s was too small for the crowds of people that wanted to see him. So the big New Hall, the stone building in front of the Mother's Temple, was built for him in the 1940s. It was a large, grandiose, granite space that resembled a temple *mantapam*, but it was an intimidating place for some people and for all of the animals.

When Bhagavan was shown where he was going to sit, he asked, 'What about the squirrels? Where are they going to live?' There were no niches for them to sit in, or grassy materials to raid for their nests.

Bhagavan also complained that the building would intimidate some of the poor people who wanted to come and see him. He always saw things like this from the side of the underdog, whether animal or human.

That large stone couch seems to be for the wrong person.

Yes, that wasn't his style at all. There was a sculptor making a stone statue of him at the same time that the finishing touches were being made to this New Hall. When Bhagavan was told that this new carved, granite sofa was for him, he remarked, 'Let the stone swami sit on the stone sofa.'

He eventually did move into this hall because there was nowhere else where he could meet with large numbers of people, but he didn't stay there long.

And that was about a year before he gave up his body?

The temple over his mother's *samadhi* was inaugurated in March 1949, and Bhagavan moved into the New Hall shortly afterwards. He developed a cancer, a sarcoma, on his arm that year. It physically debilitated him to the extent that he couldn't walk to his bathroom and back. At that point his bathroom was converted into a room for him. That's where he spent the last few months of his life.

That's the place they call the Samadhi *Room?*

Yes. An energetic Tamil woman, Janaki Amma, came to the ashram in the 1940s. When she asked to be shown to the women's bathroom, she was told that there wasn't one. She arranged for one to be built, and this was the room that Bhagavan spent his final days in. It was the nearest bathroom to the New Hall that he moved into in 1949. It became his bathroom at that time because no one wanted to inconvenience him by making him walk any further. He refused to let anyone help him when he walked to this bathroom, even when he was extremely weak. Have you seen the video of him in his last year?

Yes.

It's excruciating to watch. His knees have massive swellings on them, and they seem to shake from side to side. It is clear from this footage that he was extremely debilitated, but he would never let anyone help him to move around. There is an elaborate stone step in the doorway of the New Hall. Devotees would have to stand by, completely helpless, as Bhagavan would attempt to climb over this obstruction. No one was allowed to offer assistance. Eventually, when this step proved to be too much of an obstacle, he moved into the bathroom and stayed there until he passed away in April 1950.

Is it right that during that time he was still available?

He was very insistent that anyone who wanted to see him could have *darshan* at least once a day. When people realised he wasn't going to be here much longer, the  crowds increased. For the last few weeks there was a walking *darshan*. People would file past his room and *pranam* (bow down) to him one by one.

And that went on until his last day?

Yes, he gave his final public *darshan* on the afternoon of the day he died.

I actually met someone who walked past him the day before he died.

He insisted that the public should have as much access as possible. Up until the 1940s, the doors of his room were open twenty-four hours a day. If you wanted to see him at 3 a.m. no one would stop you from walking in and seeing him. If you had some problem, you could go and tell him in the middle of the night.

So even though he was doing a lot of work – cutting vegetables, working on the buildings and so on – he was always available?

In that era of his life there weren't too many people around him. You are talking about the years when he was actively involved in cooking and building work. In those days, if a group of people came to see him, he would go to the hall to see what they wanted.

Everybody who lived in the ashram had a job. You were either working in the cowshed or the kitchen, the garden, the office, and so on. These ashram residents were not allowed to sit with Bhagavan during the day because they had work to do. In the evening all the ashram workers would gather around Bhagavan, and for a few hours they would generally have him to themselves. The visitors would usually go home in the evening. The people whom he saw during the day in the hall would be visitors to the ashram, along with a few devotees who had houses nearby.

Was everyone free to question him?

In theory, yes, but many people were far too intimidated to approach him. He would sometimes talk without prompting, without being questioned. He liked to tell stories about famous saints, and he often told stories about what had happened to him in various stages of his life. He was a great storyteller, and whenever he had a good story to tell he would act out the parts of the various protagonists. He would get so involved in the narratives he would often start crying when he came to a particularly moving part of the story.

So the impression of him being silent is not really true?

He was silent for much of the day. He told people that he preferred to remain in silence, but he did speak, often for hours at a time, when he was in the mood.

I'm not saying that everyone who came to see him got a prompt verbal answer to his or her question. You could come and ask an apparently earnest question and Bhagavan might ignore you. He might stare out of the window and show no sign that he had even heard what you had said. Someone else might come in and ask a question and get an immediate reply. It sometimes looked like a bit of a lottery, but everyone in the end got what they needed or deserved. Bhagavan responded to what was going on in the minds of the people who were in front of him, not just to their questions, and since he was the only person who could see what was going on in that sphere, his responses at times seemed to outsiders to be occasionally random or arbitrary.

Many people would ask something and not get a spoken answer, but they would find later that merely sitting in his presence had given them the peace or the answer they required. This was the kind of response that Bhagavan preferred to make: a silent, healing stream of grace that gave people peace, not just a satisfactory spoken answer.

God is an unknown entity.
Moreover, He is external.
Whereas the Self is always with
you and it is you. Why do you
leave out what is intimate and
go in for what is external?

Sri Ramana Maharshi

INTRODUCTION

Above: *Arunachala from Skanda Maha Puranam*

Left: *Sri Ramana with devotees, around 1940*

Below: *Beginning of Ramana Ashram with bamboo hut over the Mother's Shrine 1922*
Sri Ramana with cow Lakshmi

Right centre: *Ramana Ashram from Arunachala*
Samadhi for cow Lakshmi

Right bottom: *Ramana Ashram cowshed, first permanent building*

CHAPTER 2

Sri Ramana's Teachings

*David Godman in dialogue
with Premananda*

[Sri Ramana's direct words are in bold]

*David sets out Sri Ramana's teachings in a brilliantly clear
and simple manner. He unfolds the details of* Who am I?
(Nan Yar), *in particular focusing on explaining Self-
enquiry. He uses Sri Ramana's analogy of the mind as
a bull who is tempted back to its stable with tasty hay
to explain the steps to Self-realisation offered by Self-
enquiry. He compares this with the dualistic premise of
spiritual practices such as meditation. David stresses the
advantages gained by having a living Master, sharing
some stories about how Sri Ramana related to his disciples.
We may be surprised to hear this sometimes manifest as
anger, not only the peace-filled silence and benevolent
gaze for which he is more commonly known.*

David, when did Sri Ramana begin to give out teachings, and what were they? I have been told that when he was living in Virupaksha Cave on the hill someone came to him and asked what his teachings were. He apparently wrote them out in a small booklet. Can you say something about this?

This was 1901. He didn't even have a notebook. A man called Sivaprakasam Pillai came and asked questions. I suppose his basic question was 'What is reality? How is it discovered?' The dialogue developed from there, but no words were spoken. Bhagavan wrote his answers with his finger in the sand because this was the period in which he found it difficult to articulate sounds. This primitive writing medium produced short, pithy answers.

Sivaprakasam Pillai didn't write down these answers. After each new question was asked, Bhagavan would wipe out his previous reply and pen a new one with his finger. When he went home, Sivaprakasam Pillai wrote down what he could remember of this silent conversation.

About twenty years later he published these questions and answers as an appendix to a brief biography of Bhagavan that he had written and published. I think there were thirteen questions and answers in this first published version. Bhagavan's devotees appreciated this particular presentation. Ramana Ashram published it as a separate booklet, and with each edition more and more questions and answers were added. The longest version has about thirty.

At some point in the 1920s Bhagavan himself rewrote this series of questions and answers as a prose essay, elaborating on some answers and deleting others. This is now published under the title *Who Am I?* in Bhagavan's *Collected Works* and separately as a small pamphlet. It is simply Bhagavan's summary of answers written with his finger more than twenty years before.

It sounds fairly brief.

Yes, it is probably about six pages in most books.

The key is this question 'Who am I?' Is that right?

The essay is called *Who Am I?* but it covers all kinds of things: the nature of happiness, what the world is, how it apparently comes into existence, how it disappears. There is also a detailed portion that explains how to do Self-enquiry.

Is it something you do in the morning as a practice? Is it something you do once or regularly? Is it like a breathing technique or a type of meditation?

Papaji [a direct disciple of Sri Ramana and Premananda's guru] always used to say, 'Do it once and do it properly.' That's the ideal way, but I only know of two or three people who have done it once and got the right answer: a direct experience of the Self. These people were ready for a direct experience, so when they asked the question, the Self responded with the right answer, the right experience.

Like Papaji himself?

Papaji never did Self-enquiry, although he did advocate it vigorously once he started teaching.

I'm thinking of two remarkable people who both came to Bhagavan in the late 1940s. One was a woman who had had many visions of Murugan, her chosen deity. She was a devotee who had never heard of Self-enquiry. She didn't even know much about Bhagavan when she stood in front of him in April, 1950. She was one of the people who had walking *darshan* (being in the presence of a saint) in Bhagavan's final days. As she stood in front of Bhagavan, the question 'Who am I?' spontaneously appeared inside her, and as an answer she immediately had a direct experience of the Self. She said later that this was the first time in her life that she had experienced *Brahman* (the absolute reality).

The second person I am thinking of is Lakshmana Swamy. He, too, had not done any Self-enquiry before. He had been a devotee for only a few months and during that time he had been repeating Bhagavan's name as a spiritual practice. In October 1949 he sat in Bhagavan's presence and closed his eyes. The question 'Who am I?' spontaneously appeared inside him, and as an answer his mind went back to its source, the Heart, and never appeared again. In his case it was a permanent experience, a true Self-realisation.

In both cases there had been no prior practice of Self-enquiry, and in both cases the question 'Who am I?' appeared spontaneously within them. It wasn't asked with volition. These people were ready for an experience of the Self. In Bhagavan's presence the question appeared within them, and in his presence their sense of individuality vanished. In my opinion, being in the physical presence was just as important as the asking of the question. Many other people have asked the question endlessly without getting the result that these people got from having the question appear in them once.

I should also like to point out that both these people had their experiences in the last few months of Bhagavan's life. Though his body was disintegrating, physically enfeebling him, his spiritual power, his physical presence, remained just as strong as ever.

Are you saying that Self-enquiry is not a practice, that it is not something that we should do laboriously, hour after hour, day after day?

It is a practice for the vast majority of people, and Bhagavan did encourage people to do it as often as they could. He said that the practice should be persisted with, right up to the moment of realisation.

It wasn't his only teaching, and he didn't tell everyone who came to him to do it. Generally, when people approached him and asked for spiritual advice, he would ask them what practice they were doing. They would tell him, and his usual response would be, 'Very good, carry on with that.'

He didn't have a strong missionary zeal for Self-enquiry, but he did say that sooner or later everyone has to come to Self-enquiry because this is the only effective way of eliminating the individual 'I'. He knew that most people who approached him preferred to repeat the name of God or worship a particular form of God. So, he let them carry on with whatever practice they felt an affinity with. However, if you came to him and asked, 'I'm not doing any practice at the moment, but I want to get enlightened. What is the quickest and most direct way to accomplish this?' he would almost invariably reply, 'Do Self-enquiry.'

Is he on record as saying that it is the quickest and most direct way?

Yes. He mentioned this on many occasions, but it was not his style to force it on people. He wanted devotees to come to it when they were ready for it.

So even though he accepted whatever practices people were involved in, he was quite clear the quickest and most direct tool would be Self-enquiry?

Yes, and he also said that you had to stick with it right up to the moment of realisation. For Bhagavan, it wasn't a technique that you practised for an hour a day, sitting cross-legged on the floor. It is something you should do every waking moment, in combination with whatever actions the body is doing. He said that beginners could start by doing it sitting, with closed eyes, but for everyone else he expected it to be done during ordinary daily activities.

With regard to the actual technique, would you say that it is to be aware, from moment-to-moment, of what is going on in the mind?

No, it's nothing to do with being aware of the contents of the mind. It's a very specific method that aims to find out where the individual sense of 'I' arises. Self-enquiry is an active investigation, not a passive witnessing.

For example, you may be thinking about what you had for breakfast, or you may be looking at a tree in the garden. In Self-enquiry you don't simply maintain an awareness of these thoughts, you put your attention on the thinker who has the thought, the perceiver who has the perception. There is an 'I' who thinks, an 'I' who perceives, and this 'I' is also a thought. Bhagavan's advice was to focus on this inner sense of 'I' in order to find out what it really is. In Self-enquiry you are trying to find out where this 'I' feeling arises, to go back to that place and stay there. It is not simply watching, it's a kind of active scrutiny in which one is trying to find out how the sense of being an individual person comes into being.

You can investigate the nature of this 'I' by formally asking yourself, 'Who am I?' or 'Where does this "I" come from?' Alternatively, you can try to maintain a continuous awareness of this inner feeling of 'I'. Either approach would count as Self-enquiry. You should not suggest answers to the question, such as 'I am consciousness' because any answer you give yourself is conceptual rather than experiential. The only correct answer is a direct experience of the Self.

It's very clear, what you just said, but almost impossible to accomplish. It sounds simple, but I know from my own experience that it's very hard.

It needs commitment, it needs to be practised. You have to keep at it and not give up. The practice slowly changes the habits of the mind. By doing this practice regularly and continuously, you remove your focus from superficial streams of thoughts and relocate it at the place where thought itself begins to manifest. In that latter place you begin to experience the peace and stillness of the Self, and that gives you the incentive to continue.

Bhagavan had a very appropriate analogy for this process. Imagine that you have a bull, and that you keep it in a stable. If you leave the door open, the bull will wander out, looking for food. It may find food, but a lot of the time it will get into trouble by grazing in cultivated fields. The owners of these fields will beat it with sticks and throw stones at it to chase it away, but it will come back again and again, and suffer repeatedly, because it doesn't understand the notion of field boundaries. It is just programmed to look for food and to eat it wherever it finds something edible.

The bull is the mind, the stable is the Heart where it arises and to where it returns, and the grazing in the fields represents the mind's painful addiction to seeking pleasure in outside objects. Bhagavan said that most mind-control techniques forcibly restrain the bull to stop it moving around, but they don't do anything about the bull's fundamental desire to wander and get itself into trouble.

You can tie up the mind temporarily with *japa* (repetition of God's names) or breath control, but when these restraints are loosened, the mind just wanders off again, gets involved in more mischief and suffers again. You can tie up a bull, but it won't like it. You will just end up with an angry, cantankerous bull that will probably be looking for a chance to commit some act of violence on you.

Bhagavan likened Self-enquiry to holding a bunch of fresh grass under the bull's nose. As the bull approaches, you move away in the direction of the stable door and the bull follows you. You lead it back into the stable, and it voluntarily follows you because it wants the pleasure of eating the grass that you are holding in front of it. Once it is inside the stable, you allow it to eat the abundant grass that is always stored there. The door of the stable is always left open, and the bull is free to leave and roam about at any time. There is no punishment or restraint. The bull will go out repeatedly, because it is the nature of such animals to wander in search of food. And each time it goes out, it will be punished for straying into forbidden areas.

Every time you notice that your bull has wandered out, tempt it back into its stable with the same technique. Don't try to beat it into submission, or you may be attacked yourself, and don't try to solve the problem forcibly by locking it up.

Sooner or later even the dimmest of bulls will understand that since there is a perpetual supply of tasty food in the stable there is no point wandering around outside, because that always leads to suffering and punishment. Even though the stable door is always open, the bull will eventually stay inside and enjoy the food that is always there.

This is Self-enquiry. Whenever you find the mind wandering around in external objects and sense perceptions, take it back to its stable, which is the Heart, the source from which it rises and to which it returns. In that place it can enjoy the peace and bliss of the Self. When it wanders around outside, looking for pleasure and happiness, it just gets into trouble, but when it stays at home in the Heart, it enjoys peace and silence. Eventually, even though the stable door is always open, the mind will choose to stay at home and not to wander about.

Bhagavan said that the way of restraint was the way of the *Yogi* (practitioner of *Yoga*). *Yogis* try to achieve restraint by forcing the mind to be still. Self-enquiry gives the mind the option of wandering wherever it wants to, and it achieves its success by gently persuading the mind that it will always be happier staying at home.

In that very moment when you realise there's plenty of grass at home and therefore no need to go out, would you call that awakening?

No, I would just call it understanding.

That's only understanding? Surely once you've perceived that there are piles of grass at home, why would you want to go out again?

The notion of being better off at home belongs to the 'I', and that 'I' has to go before realisation can happen.

Let's pursue this analogy a little more. What I will say now is not part of Bhagavan's original analogy, but it does incorporate other parts of his teaching. For realisation, for a true and permanent awakening, the bull has to die. While it is alive, and while the door is still open, there is always the possibility that it will stray. If it dies, though, it can never be tempted outside again. In realisation, the mind is dead.* It is not a state in which the mind is simply experiencing the peace of the Self. When the mind goes voluntarily into the Heart and stays there, feeling no urge at all to jump out again, the Self destroys it, and Self alone remains.

This is a key part of Bhagavan's teachings: the Self can only destroy the mind when the mind no longer has any tendency to move outwards. While those outward-moving tendencies are still present, even in a latent form, the mind will always be too strong for the Self to dissolve it completely.

This is why Bhagavan's way works and the forcible-restraint way doesn't. You can keep the mind restrained for decades, but such a mind

---

* This is a contentious issue. See the Introduction to *Blueprints for Awakening*, Premananda, Open Sky Press, 2008, London.

will never be consumed by the Self because the desires, the tendencies, the *vasanas*, are still there. They may not be manifesting, but they are still there.

Ultimately, it is the grace or power of the Self that eliminates the final vestiges of the desire-free mind. The mind cannot eliminate itself, but it can offer itself up as a sacrifice to the Self. Through effort, through enquiry, one can take the mind back to the Self and keep it there in a desire-free state. However, mind can't do anything more than that. In that final moment it is the power of the Self within that pulls the last remains of the mind back into itself and eliminates it completely.

You say that in realisation the mind is dead. People who are enlightened seem to think, remember, and so on, in just the same way that ordinary people do. They must have a mind to do this. Perhaps they are not attached to it, but it must still be there otherwise they couldn't function in the world. Someone who had a dead mind would be a zombie.

This is a misconception that many people have because they can't imagine how anyone can function, take decisions, speak, and so on without a mind. You do all these things with your mind, or at least you think you do, so when you see a sage behaving normally in the world, you automatically assume that he too is coordinating all his activities through an entity called 'mind'.

You think you are a person inhabiting a body, so when you look at a sage you automatically assume that he too is a person functioning through a body. The sage doesn't see himself that way at all. He knows that the Self alone exists, that a body appears in that Self and performs certain actions. He knows that all the actions and words that arise in this body come from the Self alone. He doesn't make the mistake of attributing them to an imaginary intermediary entity called 'mind'. In this mindless state, no one is organising mental information, no one is deciding what to do next. The Self merely prompts the body to do or say whatever needs to be done or said in that moment.

When the mind has gone, leaving only the Self, the one who decides future courses of action has gone, the performer of actions has gone, the thinker of thoughts has gone, the perceiver of perceptions has gone. Self alone remains, and that Self takes care of all the things that the body needs to say or do. Someone who is in that state always does the most appropriate thing, always says the most appropriate thing, because all the words and all the actions come directly from the Self.

Bhagavan once compared himself to a radio. A voice is coming out of it, saying sensible things that seem to be a product of rational, considered thought, but if you open the radio, there is no one in there thinking and deciding.

When you listen to a sage such as Bhagavan, you are not listening to words that come from a mind, you are listening to words that come directly from the Self. In his written works Bhagavan uses the term *manonasha* to describe the state of liberation. It means, quite unequivocally, 'destroyed mind'.

The mind, according to Bhagavan, is just a wrong idea, a mistaken belief. It comes into existence when the 'I' thought, the sense of individuality, claims ownership of all the thoughts and perceptions that the brain processes. When this happens, you end up with a mind that says, 'I am happy' or 'I have a problem' or 'I see that tree over there'.

When, through Self-enquiry, the mind is dissolved in its source, there is an understanding that the mind never really existed, that it was just an erroneous idea that was believed in simply because its true nature and origin were never properly investigated.

Bhagavan sometimes compared the mind to a gatecrasher at a wedding who causes trouble and gets away with it because the bride's party thinks he is with the bridegroom and vice versa. The mind doesn't belong to either the Self or the body. It's just an interloper that causes trouble because we never take the trouble to find out where it has come from. When we make that investigation, mind, like the troublesome wedding guest, just melts away and disappears.

Let me give you a beautiful description of how Bhagavan spoke. It comes from part three of *The Power of the Presence*. It was written by G.V. Subbaramayya, a devotee who had intimate contact with Bhagavan. It illustrates very well my thesis that the words of a sage come from the Self, not from a mind:

Sri Bhagavan's manner of speaking was itself unique. His normal state was silence. He spoke so little, casual visitors who only saw him for a short while wondered whether he ever spoke. To put questions to him and to elicit his replies was an art in itself that required an unusual exercise in self-control. A sincere doubt, an earnest question submitted to him never went without an answer, though sometimes his silence itself was the best answer to particular questions. A questioner needed to be able to wait patiently. To have the maximum chance of receiving a good answer, you had to put your question simply and briefly. Then you had to remain quiet and attentive. Sri Bhagavan would take his time and then begin slowly and haltingly to speak. As his speech continued, it would gather momentum. It would be like a drizzle gradually strengthening into a shower. Sometimes it might go on for hours together, holding the audience spellbound. But throughout the talk you had to keep completely still and not butt in with counter remarks. Any interruption from you would break the thread of his discourse and he would at once resume silence. He would never enter into a discussion, nor would he argue with anyone. The fact was, what he spoke was not a view or an opinion but the direct emanation of light from within that manifested as words in order to dispel the darkness of ignorance. The whole purpose of his reply was to make you turn inward, to make you see the light of truth within yourself.

Can we go back to the analogy of the bull that has to be enticed back into its stable? It seems the bull, which represents the mind, has to die. When the mind dies, can this be considered a full awakening? Is there a difference between awakening and enlightenment? Obviously, we're just using words, but are there two different states?

The Self is always the same. Self being aware of the Self is always the same. Different levels of experience belong to the mind, not the Self.

Mind can be temporarily suspended, having been replaced by what appears to be a direct experience of the Self. Nevertheless, this is not the *sahaja* state, the permanent natural state in which the mind can never rise again. These temporary states are very subtle experiences of the mind. The bliss and peace of the Self are being experienced, being mediated through an 'I' that has not yet been fully eliminated.

For example, I experience being in this room. I mediate it through my senses, through my knowledge, my memory. When the 'I' goes back into the Heart and remains still without rising, there, in that state, it experiences the emanations of the Self; the quietness, the peace, the bliss.

This is still an experience, and as such it is not enlightenment. It's not the full awareness of the Self. That full awareness is only there when there is no 'I' that mediates it. The experiences of the Self that happen when the 'I' is still existing may be regarded as a 'preview of forthcoming attractions', like the trailers for next week's movie, but they are not the final, irreversible state. They come and they go, and when they go, mind returns with all its usual, annoying vigour.

How does one progress from these temporary experiences to a permanent one? Is keeping still enough, or is grace required?

I would like to bring in Lakshmana Swamy again at this point. I mentioned him earlier as being an example of someone who realised the Self in Bhagavan's presence through the practice of Self-enquiry. So we are dealing with an expert here, someone who knows what he is talking about.

Lakshmana Swamy is quite clear on this point. He says that devotees can, by their own effort, reach what he calls 'the effortless thought-free state'. That's as far as you can go by yourself. In that state there are no more thoughts, desires or memories rising up. They are not being suppressed; they simply don't rise up anymore to grab your attention.

Lakshmana Swamy says that if you reach that state through your own intense efforts and then go and sit in the presence of a realised being, the power of the Self will make the residual 'I' go back to its source where it will die and never rise again. This is the complete and full realisation. This is the role of the guru, who is identical with the Self within: to pull the desire-free mind into the Heart and destroy it completely.

As I mentioned before, this won't happen if the desires and tendencies of the mind are still latent. They all have to go before this final act of execution can be achieved. The disciple himself has to remove all the unwanted lumber from his mental attic, and he also needs to be in a state in which there is no desire to put anything more into it. The guru cannot do this work for him; he has to do it himself. When this has been accomplished, the power of the Self within, the inner guru, will complete the work.

We've both had this experience of living around Papaji, and we have both heard him say, 'You've got it!' Was he referring to that first temporary state or the second, final, irrevocable state?

I would say almost invariably the first. His particular knack, his talent, his skill, was to completely pull the mental chair out from underneath you. He would somehow, instantaneously, disentangle you from the superstructure, the infrastructure, of the mind, and you would fall – plop! – right into the Self. You would then immediately think, 'This is great! This is wonderful! I'm enlightened!'

He had this astonishing talent, this power of being able to rub your nose in the reality of the Self. It was completely spontaneous because most of the time he wasn't even aware that he was doing it. Somehow, in his presence people lost this sense of functioning through the individual 'I'. When this happened you would be completely immersed in the feeling, the knowledge of being the Self. However, it wouldn't stick for the reasons I have already given. If you haven't cleared out all the lumber from your mental attic, these experiences will be temporary. Sooner or later the mind will reassert itself and this apparent experience of the Self will fade away. It might last ten days, ten weeks, ten months or even years, but then it goes away and just leaves a memory.

Does that mean that this second, final state is very, very rare?

In the *Bhagavad Gita, Krishna* says, 'Out of every thousand people one is really serious, and out of every thousand serious people only one knows me as I really am.' That's one in a million, and I think that's a very generous estimate. Personally, I think it's far fewer than that.

There are many people nowadays who travel around the world giving Satsang (meeting in Truth). Many of them place themselves in Bhagavan's lineage. Would you like to say anything about this?

First of all, Bhagavan never authorised anybody to teach. So anyone who claims they've got Bhagavan's permission to teach isn't telling the truth. People might claim they are in the Sri Ramana Maharshi lineage, which means that Bhagavan is their guru or their guru's guru. I don't necessarily think that this gives people authority to teach. Authority to teach can come from someone who has realised the Self, and it can also come from the Self within. It was the power of the Self that gave Bhagavan himself the authority to speak and teach. No human teacher gave him that authority.

Papaji used to say, 'If you are destined to be a guru, the Self within will give you the power to do the work. That authority doesn't come from anywhere else, or anyone else.' Papaji told me once that Arunachala gave Bhagavan the power and authority to be a *sadguru* (guru who liberates). I think most people would agree with that.

Bhagavan was never authorised to teach by a human guru because he didn't have one. In fact, I don't think Bhagavan particularly wanted to be a teacher. In his early years on the hill he tried to run away from his devotees on three occasions, but he never got very far because he was severely limited by his love of Arunachala. There's a limit to how well you can hide yourself on Arunachala. If you are willing to run away to the Himalayas you can get away with it, but if you are just dodging from rock to rock in Tiruvannamalai, people will catch up with you sooner or later. After the third unsuccessful attempt, Bhagavan realised that it was his destiny to have people around and to teach them.

Can we go back to the story of Bhagavan's life? I have been struck by the stories about his final days. He had a skin cancer on his arm, but never seemed to give it much interest. Could it have been treated by Western medicine?

He did receive the best Western medical treatment. He had four operations, which were all done by very competent surgeons, but it was a malignant growth that kept coming back. The only thing that might have cured him was amputation. He drew the line at that and refused to have his arm amputated. You shouldn't get the impression, though, that he wanted all this treatment. Whenever he was asked what should be done, his reply was 'Let nature take its course.'

The doctors were brought by the ashram authorities and by devotees who didn't want to see him suffering. Bhagavan accepted all their treatments, not because he felt that he needed to be cured, but because the various treatments were offered as acts of devotion. Allopaths, homeopaths, ayurvedic doctors, nature-cure experts and herbalists all came, and he accepted all their treatments. He didn't really have much interest in whether they succeeded or not because there was nothing left in him that could say 'I want this to happen' or 'I don't want this'. He let everyone, one by one, play with his body. He let the surgeons cut him open; he let the herbalists put poultices on.

That is how he lived his whole life. He basically let his whole life happen.

Yes. He probably knew better than the doctors what would work for him and what would not, but he didn't interfere. He let them do whatever they wanted to do. There's one story from his final days that I really like. Some village herbalist came along and made a concoction of leaves and put it on his arm. The high-powered allopaths were horrified. They thought they were losing valuable time as this bundle of leaves was sitting on Bhagavan's arm. Finally, they ganged up on this man and compelled the ashram manager to take the poultice off so they could get back to work with their scalpels. Even though Bhagavan had agreed to have this poultice on, he accepted the decision to take it off.

I have already said that Bhagavan didn't like to waste anything. He took the poultice off himself and put it on the neck of somebody who had a cancerous growth there and said, 'Well, let's see if it does you any good.' That man got better and Bhagavan died.

His whole life was a living example of total surrender to 'life taking its course'. It seems to me that this is a message that doesn't always come through because it's the Self-enquiry that is connected to his name.

I think the key word to understanding Bhagavan's behaviour is a Sanskrit term, *sankalpa*, which means 'will' or 'intention'. It means the resolve to follow a particular course of action or a decision to do something. That is a *sankalpa*. Bhagavan has said that this is what separates the enlightened being from the unenlightened.

He said unenlightened people are always full of *sankalpas*, full of decisions about what they're going to do next: how they are going to plan their lives; how they are going to change their current circumstances to benefit themselves the most in the long or the short term future. Bhagavan maintained that the true *jnani* (one who has realised the Self) has no desire whatsoever to accomplish anything in this world. Nothing arises in him that says, 'I must do this, I must be like this.'

The title of my book, *The Power of the Presence*, actually came from an answer on this topic. I will read you what I wrote:

Narayana Iyer once had a most illuminating exchange with Bhagavan on this topic, an exchange that gave a rare insight into the way that a *jnani's* power functions:
'One day when I was sitting by the side of Bhagavan I felt so miserable that I put the following question to him: "Is the *sankalpa* of the *jnani* not capable of warding off the destinies of the devotees?"

'Bhagavan smiled and said: **"Does the *jnani* have a *sankalpa* at all? The *jivanmukta* (liberated being) can have no *sankalpas* whatsoever. It is just impossible."**

'I continued: "Then what is the fate of all us who pray to you to have grace on us and save us? Will we not be benefited or saved by sitting in front of you, or by coming to you?"

'Bhagavan turned graciously to me and said: "**A person's bad *karma* (result of all actions) will be considerably reduced while he is in the presence of a *jnani*. A *jnani* has no *sankalpas* but his *sannidhi* (presence) is the most powerful force. He need not have *sankalpa*, but his presiding presence, the most powerful force, can do wonders: save souls, give peace of mind, even give liberation to ripe souls. Your prayers are not answered by him but absorbed by his presence. His presence saves you, wards off the *karma* and gives you the boons as the case may be, [but] involuntarily. The *jnani* does save the devotees, but not by *sankalpa*, which is non-existent in him, only through his presiding presence, his *sannidhi*."'**

Is that what the Dalai Lama and the Buddhists call compassion?

I don't know enough about Buddhism to comment on that.

'No *sankalpas*' means that in an enlightened being there are no feelings or thoughts such as, 'I must help this person', 'this person needs to be helped', or 'this situation needs to be changed'. Everything is totally okay as it is. By abiding in that state, somehow an energy, a presence, is created that takes care of all the incoming problems.

It's like a desk in the outer office. All the incoming requests are processed, and processed very efficiently, in the outer office. The door to the inner office is closed, and behind it the *jnani* sits at his desk all day doing absolutely nothing. However, by abiding in his natural state the energy is created that somehow deals with all the requests that come in. The *jnani* needs to be there in the inner office, just being himself, because if he wasn't there, the outer office wouldn't be able to function at all.

That would reinforce the time-honoured idea that you have to go and sit with an enlightened one.

I agree, but such people are hard to find. In my opinion there are very few of them.

Well, I think your opinion has some authority because you have been living here for about thirty years. During this time you have met many people who were with Bhagavan. You have an unusual, analytical way of looking at things; you have had your own practice here, and you have served several teachers in this lineage. That should be enough to give you some authority to talk about these things.

I have opinions, but I am not an authority. Don't try to make me into one. You can find many people who have been here twenty-five years or more, and none of them agrees with me. You are quite free to go and listen to them and believe anything they have to say.

Is there anything else you'd like to say that summarises what we've been talking about?

Find a teacher whose mind is dead and spend as much times as possible in his or her presence. That's my advice to everyone who is serious about enlightenment.

That's interesting. We met a teacher in Rishikesh who said the same thing, 'You have to find a guru.'

There is a limit to what you can accomplish by yourself. Sitting in the presence of a true guru will always do you more good than meditating by yourself. I am not saying that meditation is not useful. Intense meditation will purify the mind and it may lead you to a competent guru, but being with a guru is like freewheeling downhill on a bike instead of pedalling uphill.

Papaji had an interesting notion. He said that if you meditate intensively enough, you will accumulate the *punyas*, which are spiritual brownie points, that somehow earn you the right to sit in the presence of a realised being. However, he said that once you had entered the presence of a realised being, it was more productive to sit quietly and not make any effort at all. When you sit in the presence of such a being, it is the power of the Self coming off and through that person that makes you progress further, not anything you do there.

Slightly changing the subject. You could say in the last ten to fifteen years there's more and more interest in Sri Ramana and his teaching.

I think he's very much an iconic figure; somehow he is the yardstick by which other people measure their status in the spiritual world. But beyond that, there doesn't seem to be a lot of interest in finding out about him and what his teachings were. He's just a symbol in a way, of everything that's best in Indian spirituality, but most people don't pursue that very far and find out much about him.

I think there's some truth in that. The symbol is this man lying on a couch, silent, with beautiful eyes. The way you describe him and the work you're doing seem to be very important because you're actually adding the flesh to the bones. Probably when a more rounded picture of him emerges, then that image of him as a silent icon onto which you can project what you like is going to change. He obviously said a lot of things which actually might be things that people don't want to hear. A silent guru is very handy – the beautiful eyes – everybody can love him. But as soon as the guru starts talking and putting you in touch with things about your ego that you might not want to know, then of course it gets a bit uncomfortable!

There is a very biased record available of what Bhagavan was like. Everyone I have spoken to who knew Bhagavan personally has told me the books give a misleading picture. They just don't tell you how strict, how severe, how randomly angry he got. It was hell, being with him. People sit down and write: I walked into the hall, he looked at me and I was in peace and bliss.

That's right. What about anger, for example?

The twenty-five occasions he screamed at them don't get reported. (Laughter) Lakshmana Swamy told me this, for example. He said, 'You never knew who he was going to turn on, for what reason!' You see, at each particular moment he's reacting to what's going on in somebody's mind. If I start screaming at you, people will think, 'What did he say, what did he do?' For Bhagavan, it's what is in that person's head in that moment. So what was going on externally was often nothing to do with how Sri Ramana was reacting. He's seen or felt something going on inside you, some attitude ... something, and quite randomly he'd look at someone and really abuse them for nothing they'd done, just something he could see in that man that needed to be abused in that moment.

Lakshmana Swamy said he was watching Bhagavan walk across the courtyard by the dining room, seeing a man from Chennai feed puffed rice to a peacock. Now that should have scored some points with Bhagavan. He liked people taking care of the animals. He just looked at this man and screamed at him and said, 'Go back to your court in Chennai; you don't even know how to feed peacocks properly!' What's going on? Who knows. Something was going on in that man's mind as he was feeding the peacocks and Bhagavan screamed at him. People tell me this happened all the time.

The thing that is interesting for me is that the picture you are painting now is much more like the picture I have of Papaji ...

Right.

... and the picture one gets of Zen masters with their disciples. Suddenly you know this idealistic picture of the silent man on a couch, with beautiful eyes, is only a rather faint kind of impression of him.

I think probably he was that very rare conjunction of saint and *jnani*. He was a very saintly man, relative to someone like Papaji who actually was a worldly man. Papaji had diabetes, high blood pressure, he could be cranky all day because of his body chemistry. Bhagavan wasn't cranky in that way but he really could, for no visible reason, turn on people and get very angry. Everybody was a little bit afraid of him. That's not something that comes out. He comes across as a very benign Santa Claus figure, whom everybody goes to with their problems. But most people were just too terrified even to speak to him.

If we look at his influence in the world, it seems to me that there is growing interest in Sri Ramana and his teachings. This is partly due to a tree of Western people who visited and wrote about him. There was Paul Brunton, then Major Chadwick, Arthur Osborne wrote several books, S.S. Cohen and then later Robert Adams. Robert Adams probably did more direct teaching than the others, whereas, say Osborne was more a writer.

If we are talking about people who made the West aware of Sri Ramana's existence and his teaching then the number one, or earliest, would be Paul Brunton. Probably for about twenty years his writings were the principal reason why people came to Bhagavan.

Did he become a teacher?

He became a very reclusive, publicity-shy teacher himself in the 1950s. But basically teaching his own stuff – not in any way a messenger for Bhagavan or his teachings. From the 1950s onwards for, I would say about twenty-five years, it was Arthur Osborne, because for at least twenty years the three books that he wrote or edited were the only books any Westerner was likely to find in a Western bookstall. This is the pre-video age, the pre-'messengers touring around the world giving *Satsang'*. In the sixties, seventies, early eighties, if you wanted spiritual information you got it from your friendly neighbourhood book stall. Those were the only three widely distributed books on Bhagavan.

After those, in fact, came your book, the Penguin Be As You Are.

It came out in 1985 and it's been by far the largest selling book on Bhagavan in the West over the last twenty years. Most people who came from the West during those years because they had read a book, that was the one they had read. I am not saying that because it's good, it's just outstandingly well distributed by Penguin. They have shifted a massive number of copies.

Well, I think that may be your humility speaking. Anybody listening to these stories that you're telling would understand you have an incredibly thorough knowledge of Sri Ramana and his teachings. Part of the current interest in Sri Ramana is of course the build up of the books, but in fact Papaji has acted as a huge recent influence as well.

Right, Papaji was the next big influence. Let's call him the 'run away' teacher – somebody who ran away from any kind of permanent base of following until about 1990, when his health deteriorated to the point where his legs wouldn't let him run anymore. Then he had to sit still and let people find him. Robert Adams became prominent in the early 1990s. He paralleled Papaji in so far as he had spent thirty or forty years hiding in India and America, moving on whenever people started to gather around him, not telling people where he was going next. Then he also got sick in the 1990s, settled down, and people found him. I think he was a lesser influence in terms of numbers than Papaji.

But of all the people I've come across who have publicly been teaching Bhagavan's teachings, I find Robert the most orthodox. If you read *The Silence of the Heart*, you can't find a single word that Bhagavan himself wouldn't have said. All the other people, whether it is Annamalai Swami, Lakshmana Swamy, Papaji, they focus on one aspect of the teachings and develop that. There is something very orthodox about Robert Adams, but at the same time very engagingly communicative. I really like the way he puts Bhagavan's message out.

Yes, for me he's a very nice mixture of Self-enquiry and the bhakti *approach, the way of the heart.*

Papaji was shown his book, I think it was in 1993 or 94. He took it along to *Satsang* and read it from cover to cover. He never did that for any other living teacher. There was something about the quality of the way this man was communicating Bhagavan's teachings. You just knew this man knew what he was talking about and that he was articulating in a very clear, persuasive way.

One of Osho's most well-known Dynamic Meditation techniques uses 'Who am I?' in one segment and it later becomes 'who, who, who'. When Osho talked about that meditation in his early days he actually gave tremendous credit to Sri Ramana. In those days, basically his technique was to malign everybody he cold think of maligning. The only people who didn't get maligned were Krishnamurthi and Sri Ramana Maharshi, and in fact the worst thing he could find to say about him was that he was a great mystic but not a great teacher.

Bhagavan said people who came to him expecting a teaching from his mouth had the wrong idea of what was going on there. The famous story of Natanananda was that he came every month on full moon, desperate to get some verbal initiation from Bhagavan. He wanted to be told how to get enlightened. Being a very rules-conscious Brahmin, he didn't think it was his prerogative to open the conversation. So he would just sit there, quietly hoping Bhagavan would tell him how to get enlightened. Every month for a year this happened. Finally he gave up waiting and said, 'Please tell me. I've been coming here every month for a year and you haven't communicated anything to me.' Bhagavan said, 'If you can't understand what I am communicating, that's not my problem. That's yours.' The whole point is that he was constantly communicating himself – not merely to the people in front of him, but to all his devotees wherever they were, and to anybody else who wanted to get in touch with him – on a nonverbal level. He didn't need to give out verbal teachings. He only needed to be himself and that was enough.

His influence in the spiritual world seems to be enormous now and that has happened from a sense of non-teaching, or nonverbal teaching anyway. So the image we have of this silent man isn't totally false because inherent at the core of his teaching, even when it is all translated, is this 'be quiet'.

He said it's like the continuous flow of electricity in a wire and that verbal communication is like plugging something in. You make a fan whirl around by plugging it in. It is not a perfect analogy because he was saying that when you plug something into this flow, somehow it stops flowing in its normal nonverbal channels and has to be externalised into this kind of whirring fan or conversation. And he said that left to himself, being quiet, the maximum radiation was going on and that somehow the conversations interrupted it. So, in a sense, every time somebody made him speak the illumination or the radiation was a bit less. So the full-on communication happened when he was sitting quietly by himself.

It seems to me that nicely concludes things because it brings us back to this image of this man on a couch, being silent.

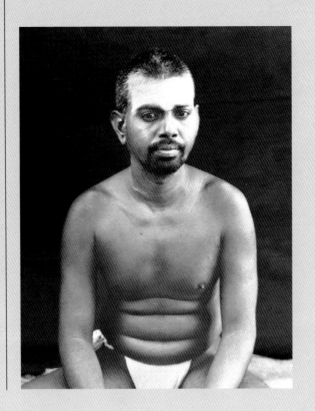

Happiness lies deep within us,
in the core of our own being.
Happiness does not exist in any
external object, but only in us,
who are the consciousness that
experiences happiness.

Sri Ramana Maharshi

INTRODUCTION

Above: Ramana Ashram Dining Hall (left) and Old Hall (right)

Left: Ramana Ashram, view from main path to Arunachala

Below: Ramana Ashram well

Right top: Sri Ramana in 1930s Group in 1935

Right centre: Sri Ramana with Muruganar sitting far right

Right bottom: Arunachala south face

CHAPTER 3

Sri Ramana's Devotees

*David Godman in dialogue
with Premananda*

[Sri Ramana's direct words are in bold]

*David walks us through the main characters who were
close to Sri Ramana. We see how he responded to different
people depending on their state of mind, and how his
way of teaching and interacting with devotees changed
over the years. There were the early Western visitors
such as Paul Brunton and Arthur Osborne whose books
introduced Sri Ramana to the West. Papaji was also a
major influence in making Sri Ramana known outside of
India. Muruganar, Sadhu Om and Viswanatha Swami
wrote, translated, edited or compiled many volumes in
praise of Sri Ramana. Sri Bhagavan's mother and his
brother, Chinnaswami, also became devotees. David
tells delightful stories of the animals who shared Sri
Ramana's life, most notably Lakshmi the cow.*

David, I'd like to ask you to make an introduction to the men whose lives brought them to Sri Ramana. Many of them spent most of their lives in close orbit around him. Some of them acted as assistants and helpers and others were there simply for the teaching, living nearby. When you look at the photographs in the dining hall at Ramana Ashram, it's clear that there was a small group which gradually expanded in the 30s and 40s, mostly men and all looking powerful and serious.

Some of these men never lived at Ramana Ashram. There was a man who lived in Madurai and came occasionally to see Bhagavan. He was an old school friend, but whenever there was a big family problem he'd come and beg Bhagavan for protection, promotion, funds or whatever. That was a common way of relating to Bhagavan.

What was his name?

This was Rangan. He was actually in the same class as Bhagavan in Madurai. So he had a very intimate relationship that started at school. Although he revered him as a great guru, he had a kind of easy familiarity that comes from knowing someone when you are doing your homework together and sitting at the back of the class together. They had a very friendly one-on-one relationship.

Bhagavan responded to people's states of mind. People who were natural and spontaneous with him got a very good natural and spontaneous response. The longer people stayed and the more in awe of him they became, the more formal the relationship seemed to get. Major Chadwick, who didn't know the traditions and the rules of the ashram, arrived and treated Bhagavan as, well, not an ordinary person, but he didn't have this kind of veneration that most of the other people seemed to have. Bhagavan really liked this. I think he was tired of being put on a pedestal. So after lunch Bhagavan would wander along to Chadwick's room, walk in, sit down and go through his books, open his bags and chat about this and that. People were really annoyed with Chadwick for treating Bhagavan as a friend. But that was his mental state at the time, he was just a man who dropped in after lunch and had a chat with him.

Then slowly, slowly, Chadwick somehow rediscovered him as god and guru and started making special preparations for the after-lunch visit. Then the visits stopped. He could drop in spontaneously, but as soon as you started getting things ready for him, even a drink of water, he wouldn't come any more.

It seems one of his characteristics was that he liked to be very involved in the food preparation, and also he wanted to be available all the time.

Let's distinguish between his characteristics and responding to people's states of mind. So because Rangan related to Bhagavan as an old school friend, Bhagavan responded in the same way. He told him very, very revealing things sometimes that no one else got from him. But there were certain fixed personality and character traits that didn't vary from person to person. There was an intense frugality that bordered on parsimoniousness; he hated wasting anything. He'd pick up single grains of rice off the floor and order them to be taken to the kitchen and stored.

He was very, very particular about not being given better treatment than anybody else. This was a big issue for many people in the ashram because they wanted to show their devotion by giving him better quality objects, more food in the dining room, better quality food. I think for several decades there was just a running battle between Bhagavan, who was saying, 'Serve my devotees better than you serve me and I'll be happy,' and devotees who could never accept this and were always trying to give him more and better than anybody else was getting.

You tell a lovely story about orange juice, that the devotees wanted him to have orange juice for his health and his reply was that the ashram couldn't afford to give everybody orange juice.

This is true, but if two hundred glasses of orange juice had come out of nowhere then he would have happily taken his and everybody else would have had theirs. What he refused to do was drink a glass in front of everybody else when nobody else had that option.

And this seemed to be totally natural. This was just his way.

Natural in a sense. He joked on several occasions, 'It's a good job I never got married, no woman would ever put up with me.' He really was fanatical when it came to economy, frugality, the way he cooked. The people who worked in the kitchen would say his word was absolute law. There was absolutely no possibility for ever varying any routine that he told them to do. What he was trying to teach them wasn't cooking or preparing a meal on time, it was absolute obedience to the guru.

He would bring in some completely inedible, hard, spiky plant and say 'Boil this, we are having this for breakfast.' You couldn't say, 'But it's inedible, not even the goats would eat it.' You said 'Yes Bhagavan,' and you had to stand there and stir this pot for four hours in total faith this would turn into something tasty because Bhagavan had told you to do it. And more often than not, five minutes before breakfast when you were still stirring spiky, thorny branches, he'd come in and stick his finger in or stir it and suddenly it would turn into something tasty. The whole point wasn't to be rational or efficient, it was to have absolute obedience and surrender to Bhagavan.

You have another story which illustrates this about spinach. Bhagavan insisted spinach should be prepared in a particular way.

Now a spinach root is short, incredibly thin – we are talking about one millimeter diameter all the way down. When you eat spinach you just take the leaves off and you do something with them. But Bhagavan wanted all the roots to be pounded by hand and the juice taken out of them and put in the rason. They are kind of nobbly roots. They had to scrub them with a brush by hand, one by one, then they had to pound all these things and maybe get one drop of juice for every root and it might have taken ten minutes to get it. The notion that you would throw away the roots, unused, was totally alien to his way of doing things. There was one drop of useful juice in each root that had to be got out before the leftovers were composted. He insisted that each and every root be scrubbed, pounded, and the juice added to some part of the meal.

One day when he wasn't there no one could be bothered, so they found a place, somewhere they decided he never went, and took all the roots and buried them. On that particular morning, of course, he varied his routine, took a walk to the spot where all these roots were buried, poked it with his stick and dug them up.

What I like about this is that he never said a word; he never complained, he never said, 'You didn't obey my instructions.' He took them all back to the kitchen, he personally scrubbed every single root, he personally hand-pounded every single root, spent the whole morning getting those ten drops of useless juice to throw in the rason, added the juice and went to the hall and sat down. The actual doing of it was the lesson. He never told anybody off for disobeying him, but that lesson was to show that you couldn't get away with cheating and if you tried then Bhagavan would waste the whole morning cleaning up after you.

Very strong stuff, and in a way at variance with his image as a saintly old man with a white beard, sitting on a couch, who never said anything and in a sense never did anything.

He didn't have a lot to do with the cooking when his mother was alive. In the early 20s various people, including his brother, were the cooks and then around 1927 a whole group of devotees came who ended up in the kitchen and he ended up working with them every day. Although he did have a passion for food, I think one of the reasons he started doing this was that he wanted to work on this particular group of devotees. Teaching them devotion and surrender in the context of kitchen work was really what it was all about rather than just an extra pair of hands to make the meal.

This is at odds with some image we might have of Sri Ramana.

The books available in the West tended to be written by the lawyers, the doctors, the people who had writing talents who could find a publisher. So they tended to describe their visits to the Old Hall where Bhagavan sat and answered philosophical questions, told people to do Self-enquiry or told stories. The people who worked in the kitchen were for the most part illiterate, so they didn't ever get around to writing books or telling their side of the story. So in a sense, it's a one-sided image of Bhagavan because the people who wrote the books were the intellectuals who asked the intellectual questions and that's the type of books they mostly wrote.

I guess most of us have read Paul Brunton's books. He was the main early influence on the West.

He wasn't the first foreigner to come but I think his book, *A Search in Secret India*, from 1935 when it came out, through to the late 50s when Arthur Osborne wrote his books, was the book that inspired most of the foreigners to come to India. It was a best seller for decade after decade and he gave a highly complementary picture of Bhagavan. Many of the more famous foreigners came after reading this book.

The image of Brunton is of a middle-class gentleman in a white suit and gold-rimmed glasses. Presumably he would have met Bhagavan in the hall. He wouldn't have been particularly interested in what was going on behind the scenes.

Interestingly enough, foreigners were such a rarity at the time he came to Ramana Ashram that it was published in the newspapers the day before. Headline: 'Foreigner Goes to Ramana Ashram'. It was a major news story that some foreign journalist was interested enough to go Tiruvannamalai to see Bhagavan. What I find a little bit strange is that prior to his visit he'd spent probably at least a year touring around India, trying to find saints and sages to include in his book. Bhagavan's name had never come up. I find this quite remarkable. Even at that time, 1930, he had a very good national reputation and I'm surprised no one mentioned him to Brunton before.

Do you have any sense of why that would be?

Maybe he was destined to go and see all these other people first. If he'd come straight here there wouldn't have been such a good book! The Kanchi Shankaracharya sent him here just as he was to leave India by ship for Europe.

So going back more to the sequence of these disciples, would you like to talk about the ones closest during the 20s and then go through to the 30s?

There was a group of say ten or twelve people who seem to be standard fixtures from the late Skanda Ashram period onwards. Not many of them have left accounts. Kanchi Swami has written about them, very entertainingly. There are people like Dhandapani Swami. If you look at any old photo of Ramana Ashram, he's about three times the size of anybody else and he has a big stick! He was a temporary manager here in the 1920s. He was also the cook and he had a massive family, which he brought to Ramana Ashram. There were all sorts of odd characters in those days. There was a man called Soldier Swami who somehow took it on himself to be Bhagavan's bodyguard. Nobody thought he needed a bodyguard, he was just ex-military and he used to stand at the gate and salute everybody who came in, with a stick. One day he got upset over some complaint somebody had made against him, so he climbed to the top of a coconut tree and refused to come down and went on a hunger strike, at the top of the coconut tree!

Normal devotee behaviour! (Laughter)

This is not an image of everybody sitting in *padmasanam* (lotus position) doing Self-enquiry. These were a highly eccentric bunch of people, each with their own idea of who Bhagavan was, who they where and what their relationship was to him.

Now, there is a man I really like. He's relatively unknown and his name is Mastan. What is extraordinary about him is that I think he got enlightened on his first visit to Bhagavan, very early in the Virupaksha Cave period. Bhagavan himself says he came before 1903 and one account I've read of Mastan's life says he was one of the people who went begging with Bhagavan in 1896, on the streets of Tiruvannamalai.

He really is about as early as you can get. He was a Muslim, which was strange in itself. His family were weavers and he used to go into *samadhi* sitting at his family loom when he was a child. His parents just thought that he was being lazy and would clip him across the ear to wake up and get on with his work. He was definitely ready for someone like Bhagavan. A woman from his village, Akilandamma, took him to Bhagavan, probably around 1903, I'm not sure. According to Mastan's own account Bhagavan just looked at him once and absolutely paralysed him. Mastan said, 'He put me in his own state.' That was his only comment. He was rooted to the spot for eight hours, he wasn't even sitting down, he hadn't even got as far as being close enough to *pranam* (bow down) to Bhagavan. He just stood, Bhagavan looking at him. He didn't move for eight hours.

On many of his subsequent visits, Bhagavan himself said he never got further than the gate. Bhagavan would be inside the cave, not even aware that he was there. Mastan would climb up the steps to Virupaksha Cave, he would get hold of the gate railings to push, and it was like they were electrified, he would be stuck there, totally paralysed in *samadhi* (immersed in the Self) for six to seven hours. This was before he had even seen Bhagavan.

I got a story from Viswanatha Swami. He was one of Bhagavan's relatives and he came around 1922. He said that Bhagavan had told him, walking in the forest once, that Mastan was in a completely different category from any other devotee who came. Which is an amazing endorsement, because Bhagavan very rarely praised people like that.

MASTAN SWAMI

1878 - 1931
Born in the village of Desur, Tamil Nadu, to a Muslim family of weavers. He was one of Bhagavan's earliest disciples and came to him already conversant with Advaitic texts and imbued with intense dispassion.

Although he didn't publicly proclaim his enlightenment, the key proof if you like, for me, is that when he died he immediately sent Kunju Swami to his village and ordered him to build a very special kind of tomb which is only reserved for enlightened people. The only other times he did that were for the cow Lakshmi and his mother. So I think that would indicate that Mastan was also in that state.

So he would be the first.

Yes, somewhere in the early years of the twentieth century.

THE MOTHER

†1922

Azhagammal was born at Pasalai in Tamil Nadu. An exceptionally loving and generous person, her husband died at the age of forty-seven leaving her with four children. In 1916 she came to Arunachala with Sri Ramana's younger brother, Nagasundaram, and took up the life of a sannyasin (renunciate). Sri Ramana gave her intense, personal instruction, while she took charge of the ashram kitchen.

Next would be Bhagavan's mother at Skanda Ashram.

Mother in 1922 and Lakshmi the cow in 1948. I think a key element in these enlightenments is Bhagavan putting his hand on their heart centre. This is something very unique to Bhagavan. I hadn't heard of any other guru who even mentioned the right-hand side of the chest as being the heart centre where the 'I' finally has to subside and die. Bhagavan himself said this was his own experience, and that he could find occasional references to this centre in various non-spiritual books, such as medical encyclopedia, but he couldn't produce any scriptural proof that would corroborate his own theory: that the 'I' thought had to descend into this right-hand heart centre and die for liberation to happen.

What was crucial in the case of both his mother and then Lakshmi the cow, in 1948, is that he said that as he was putting his hand in this particular place, images of all their future lives were running fast-forward in his head, and somehow by doing this he was cutting off all their future rebirths. His particular notion was that the 'I' goes into the heart at the moment of death but the *vasanas* (tendencies of the mind) that make subsequent births have not been eliminated, so those *vasanas* will take a new form and whatever desires are pending from previous births you will act out in that new form.

What is meant by vasanas?

Vasanas are the habits and tendencies of the mind that make you do or want to do all the things that you do.

Is it a psychological imprint which psychologists might say happens in the first four years of your life?

Why does Mozart pick up the violin at four and find he can play it? This could be a *vasana* from a past life. A *vasana* can be a talent, it can be an ability or inclination; something that's in there that makes you live your life the way you do, do the things that you do, inspires you, turns you into the kind of person you are. It's all part of a preconditioned script, if you like. The intensity of each desire for each particular object would vary from person to person, but they are all there from the moment of birth.

Is it ever discussed in terms of genetics?

It's absolutely nothing to do with your parents. It's a continuation of whatever was going on in your previous lives. The body you have might be brought into existence because you have a particular set of desires that can best be fulfilled in certain circumstances. If you have artistic inclinations you might have been born in an artist family, but you are not getting your artist genes from your parents. According to this theory, you are put into those circumstances because you have those tendencies and that is the best place to manifest them.

Bhagavan was actually cutting off all these tendencies, which he said produce future births. In each of their cases he saw several lifetimes that we have to assume would have happened if he hadn't intervened. These were very decisive interventions. Had he not been there or had he not done this, the implication would be that they wouldn't have been enlightened. They didn't do it through their own efforts, their practice, or even through their readiness, because Bhagavan seems to be saying that in each case there were future lifetimes for these people which he cut off by this final act of power.

In the Zen tradition you surrender to the master and then at a certain moment, maybe after you've been given a koan to answer for years, suddenly the master bangs you on the head. Because his timing is perfect, it acts as a catalyst to an awakening. Is that something similar do you think?

ANNAMALAI SWAMI

1906 - 1995
Born Sella Perumal in a small village in Tamil Nadu. From an early age he showed a keen interest in spirituality. He first met Bhagavan in 1928 and became his personal attendant. He went on to oversee all phases of the ongoing construction of Ramana Ashram.

His mother was sick and unconscious when he did this, there was no question of doing something which would awaken her into a new state. She had been sick for several days; he knew she was dying that day, and somehow he cut off all her future rebirths by this final act of removing all her *vasanas* before she died.

In the case of Annamalai Swami, after many years of working as a foreman in the building of the ashram, one day he and Bhagavan are together in the bathroom and suddenly Bhagavan hugs him then says something like, 'It would be good if you could just go and sit and be quiet. No more building work for you.'

Not exactly. This wasn't Bhagavan's way. Annamalai Swami was the attendant in the bathroom that day and he asked a question: 'The *ananda* (bliss) that *sadhus* (ascetics) get from smoking dope, is this the same *ananda* enlightened people have?' Bhagavan imitated a stoned *sadhu*, he kind of staggered around the bathroom, saying 'Oh, *ananda, ananda, ananda,*' pretending to be an enebriated *sadhu*, and just at the right moment he lurched on to Annamalai Swami and gave him a big hug. In that moment Annamalai Swami said he lost all consciousness of the world.

I couldn't really get him to elaborate on exactly what happened in this moment. It wasn't an enlightenment experience, because he said he had to work hard for many years afterwards. He just said he was aware of the Self in that moment and the world disappeared. Bhagavan left him in the bathroom and went back to the hall. When he came to, he was just standing by himself in the bathroom and he said he knew in that moment his career at Ramana Ashram was over. It wasn't a question of Bhagavan telling him anything.

He went back to his room, cleared out his stuff, took his keys and gave them to Chinnaswami. Everyone was absolutely amazed. This was a man who had worked twelve to fifteen hours a day, non-stop for twelve years and had no quarrels and no fight, so there was no reason for him to leave. He just handed in his keys and said, 'I am off to meditate in Palakottu.' Of course he went to Bhagavan and announced his decision. This is something interesting: it was very hard to get Bhagavan to give you a decision about something you wanted to do. What he wanted you to do was make the right decision and tell him, and then he showed some sign he approved. He really didn't like imposing solutions on people.

So Annamalai Swami knew this particular side of him. He went up to him and told Bhagavan he'd decided to leave the ashram and go to Palakottu to meditate. He said Bhagavan was so obviously approving of this that he knew he had made the right decision and he said within an hour his whole twelve-year building career was over. He walked to Palakottu with absolutely nothing – no money, no means to support himself – found a hut which somebody was leaving that day and moved in.

Am I right in thinking Sri Ramana would come on his walk sometimes and continue some relationship, although Annamalai himself never set foot in the ashram again?

Bhagavan generally would go to Palakottu after lunch and meet many of the *sadhus* who lived there. The tradition at Ramana Ashram was, and still is, that if you want to live in the ashram you have to do some work. So the people who decided they wanted to meditate all day generally had huts in Palakottu and they came and sat in the hall. They were free to come anytime they wanted. It was a very precarious existence in so far as most of them had no money. They'd go out begging or they'd depend on donations, but the great freedom was you could come and sit with Bhagavan anytime you wanted. The ashram workers had the security of a room and food, but they weren't allowed in the hall until after six o'clock at night.

I think the Palakottu colony started around 1930. Bhagavan would go for a walk after lunch, as a kind of 'digest the lunch' stroll, and he would generally go once around the Palakottu tank. Anybody who needed any problem solved or wanted to speak to him could talk to him then. Sometimes he would walk into your house unannounced and sit down. It wasn't that he knocked on everybody's door everyday – he'd go for his walk, if you bumped into him he would say hello and ask you what was happening. Sometimes he'd just walk in to someone's house because he knew he was needed in some way.

When exactly did the ashram start operating?

They came down the hill from Skanda Ashram in 1922. Bhagavan's mother died in May and Bhagavan came down in December that year. He said it wasn't a decision to come, it was that once he arrived he never had any desire to go home again, to Skanda Ashram. He simply came, sat at the *samadhi* (burial shrine) and at four o'clock in the afternoon when he would've usually got up and gone home, he said there was no urge to get up and go home, so he didn't. That was the end of Skanda Ashram. He stayed.

So then the ashram was gradually built through the 20s?

Right. Nobody really knew if this was to be a permanent arrangement or if he was just going to be down there for a week. For a while there was a split in the community. Then when it became clear Bhagavan wasn't going back, everybody moved down. Skanda Ashram was abandoned, more or less.

So by the 30s the ashram would have been fairly well established; there would have been some solid buildings, and presumably an expanded community of devotees.

From 1922, right through the 20s, Ramana Ashram was a collection of coconut leaf huts and mud buildings, the sort of thing that could've been flattened in half an hour by a very average cyclone. It wasn't a very substantial place. The first major construction was probably the cow shed in 1933. That's when it started looking like the place it is today – granite buildings built on a large scale. Prior to that everything was very simple and primitive.

So when Paul Brunton came in about 1935 it still would have been very simple.

Well, in the 1930s he describes it as a jungle hermitage which is probably what it was. There's a lovely little book which I found in the ashram archives by a retired major general who came here in the beginning of the Second World War. He had been sent by the British government to practise jungle warfare in Sri Ramana Nagar. I mean, that kind of tells you what the place looked like; it wasn't suburbs, it was pretty solidly forested in those days with a few huts which were in the ashram.

So what we see when we're up on the hill looking around, which is mainly rice fields and so on, that would have been forests in those days?

I've looked at old pictures of the mountain and I have to admit none of them have as many trees on the mountain as today. I often wondered where these mythical forests were. Annamalai Swami said when he came in 1928 there was a ring of forest all around

PAUL
BRUNTON

1898 - 1981
Paul Brunton was born in London. He was a writer, mystic, and philosopher. He studied a wide variety of Eastern and Western esoteric teachings and his works had a major influence on the spread of Eastern mysticism to the West. He visited Sri Ramana in 1931 and his book A Search in Secret India, *published in 1934, is considered to be the starting point for Sri Ramana's fame beyond India.*

the foot of the hill that extended about as far as the tarmac *pradakshina* (circumambulation) road. It went about one or two hundred feet up the hill and that was about it.

So where we see the rice-field plains, they were there already in those days?

There were far fewer people and I suspect they weren't growing rice. The massive availability of water from electric pumps is a recent innovation. It was always a semi-arid area growing peanuts, raggi – that kind of crop mostly.

MURUGANAR

1895 - 1973
Sri C. K. Subrahmanyam grew up in an atmosphere of Tamil learning. He first met Bhagavan in 1923. He composed thousands of poems praising Bhagavan, recording his teachings and expressing gratitude to Bhagavan for having established him in the Self. He was one of Bhagavan's foremost disciples.

In the 30s the devotee population would have expanded. Were there some other interesting characters?

Oh, absolutely. Muruganar was a major one, we have to talk about him. Before he came to see Bhagavan, Muruganar was a very well respected Tamil scholar and a devotee of Mahatma Gandhi. Dhandapani Swami, his father-in-law, gave him a copy of *Aksharamanamalai*, Bhagavan's 108 verses to Arunachala, and initially he just read it as a poet, checking out its literary merits. But there was definitely some strong attraction to come to Bhagavan. He came in 1923 when the ashram at the foot of the hill was very small and primitive. On the day he arrived he said there was one coconut leaf hut and Bhagavan was the only person present in it. That was a common experience of people who came during 1922 and 1923. They would arrive and find Bhagavan sitting in this small hut. That was it, no attendant, no structure, no hierarchy, just you and him.

Muruganar had composed eleven verses in the main temple in town, one of which was mildly complaining – why are you sitting there doing nothing when the British are winning our country; why aren't you doing something useful like Gandhi? But the predominant theme of all these verses was: I am coming to you because I think that you're *Shiva* incarnate. I want your grace, please help me.

Bhagavan came out of his hut and Muruganar tried to sing these verses. He said he couldn't even speak in Bhagavan's presence. He was completely paralysed. Bhagavan got tired of waiting and he said, 'Give me the paper, I will sing them for you.' He went through the whole eleven verses and chanted them out loud and gave the paper back. Murugana stayed on that occasion.

It is a common tradition among the *sadhus*, not so much in the south as the north, but still there were several people at that time getting stoned. Bhagavan didn't approve. He told them he didn't approve, but he never forbade them doing it, that wasn't his style. He just let it be known it wasn't a good idea and then people could do what they liked. So at some point on his first visit Muruganar was given some drink which had *ganja* in it. He started having massive, wild hallucinations and racing around the ashram. Bhagavan sent Kanchi Swami to look after him. He was having visions of all the gods. It was a very traumatic first visit.

Muruganar came back a few months later and had similar visions without the *ganja* and became a very addicted devotee. I can't think of a better word; he had this absolute compulsion to stick to Bhagavan and not leave him. There's a lovely story that when he had to go back to work after his weekend visits, he physically couldn't get on the train. Bhagavan would force him to leave the ashram, he'd get sent to the station and there he couldn't put his foot on the train. The train would come in to the station and leave. He would walk back to the ashram and say: 'I couldn't get on the train.' Finally, Bhagavan had to send somebody with him to the station to physically load him in the train, to make sure he didn't get off and come back.

This situation persisted for a couple of years until his mother died in 1926. Then he completely gave up his householder life. He abandoned his wife and came to Bhagavan and never left. He lived as a wandering *sadhu*, begged his food, and spent the rest of his life with Bhagavan. Now at some point, probably in the first year or so, he said he was picking leaves for leaf plates with Bhagavan in Palakottu at night. He said Sri Ramana just looked at him and in that moment he got enlightened.

Now the thing about Muruganar is that you could never ever get him to talk about his personal history. He seemed to think that Muruganar the person had ceased to exist. So his life is all shrouded in a very ambiguous mystery. What did happen was from that moment on he started spontaneously composing verses in praise of Bhagavan. He was already a good poet before he came to Bhagavan, but somehow this experience turned him into a magnificent, spontaneous poet who could just churn out verses non-stop all day, every day. He took a vow that he wasn't going to write about anything except the greatness of Bhagavan for the rest of his life. He stuck to that and many, many of these verses never got recorded.

He operated with a slate and a chalk for a long time. Suddenly this verse would come into his head, he'd scribble down four Tamil lines. Five minutes later another would arrive from wherever these things came from, so he'd wipe out the previous one and write the next one. So only when people were around were these things recorded. His collected works in Tamil have been brought out in the last ten or fifteen years. There are twenty thousand poems in that. These are the ones that didn't get wiped out, that are absolutely magnificent. The vast majority are praising Bhagavan, thanking him, describing his greatness.

But there's a very small, select body of poems which are very important. He remembered what Bhagavan had said in the hall and then he would go home and convert Bhagavan's teachings into Tamil poetry. Now why these are important is that Bhagavan took Muruganar's poetry very seriously, and whenever Muruganar gave him verses he'd written he would go through them very carefully. He would edit them, he would rewrite them, he would put them in a good order. So these are in a way the most reliable sources of Bhagavan's teachings, because Bhagavan himself put in a massive amount of editing work on them. All through the 20s and 30s Muruganar was working on these verses. They were brought out under the title *Guru Vachaka Kovai* and each year, as new verses came along, the editions got bigger and bigger. The current edition is one thousand two hundred and forty verses.

Has this been translated into English?

There is an English version in the ashram book stall called *Garland of Guru's Sayings* by a Chennai professor, Swaminathan. You get a good feeling for the poetry, but not necessarily for the philosophy. Something has to go – when you have very good poetry and very good philosophy, and when you try to put it in English, you have to make a choice.

Swaminathan was a poet; he loved Tamil poetry. He was an English professor, his English was excellent. His inclination was to make them sound like good poems, whereas my inclination is to find out exactly what Bhagavan said because these are very precisely worded teaching statements and it doesn't matter whether the lines scan or rhyme. What we need to know is exactly what Sri Ramana said. So I would veer to the opposite extreme and get the most reliable, accurate translation because these are hardcore philosophy. You really need to sit down with a Tamil pandit, a good philosopher, and work out all the nuances of each particular verse or you lose things.

SADHU OM

1922 -1985
Sadhu Om was born in Punnai Nalloor, Tamil Nadu. His yearning for spiritual knowledge was so strong that by his fourteenth year, he was composing many verses and songs in Tamil. He first met Sri Ramana in 1946. Through poetry, a close bond was created between Muruganar and Sadhu Om. On Muruganar's death, Sadhu Om became his literary executor and spent the rest of his life editing and translating Murugana's works.

And this is what Sadhu Om and Michel James did?

Sadhu Om was Muruganar's literary executor. Just before Muruganar died he insisted that all his manuscripts, all these twenty thousand poems, everything he'd ever done, be given to Sadhu Om. He inherited this massive treasure of verses and spent the rest of his life editing them, bringing them out in Tamil. Michael came along in the late 70s and they cajoled him into making English translations of *Guru Vachaka Kovai*, but that particular work was never published because mostly they were working on Tamil books at that time.

So this is still unpublished?

It's unpublished. In the last volume he records teachings. I didn't know this existed. I got very excited when I found this out. There are approximately two thousand five hundred verses in the final volume in which Muruganar is putting down direct quotations from Bhagavan. Two lines, couplets, so what have suddenly appeared are five thousand new lines of Bhagavan's teachings that no one has ever seen before.

Wow, that's recently, like in the last year or two?

Right, that was totally unexpected, so I have got my Tamil pandit!

I hope this is a new book.

That's a new project. [Since published by David Godman as *Padamalai*, 2005, and *Guru Vachaka Kovai*, 2008] My pandit said, 'Oh my God, this would take years.' I said, 'I don't care; this is something that can't be ignored, to have five thousand lines of Bhagavan's direct teaching suddenly appear out of nowhere.'

You are probably aware of the story of Rumi the Sufi master, who was perhaps a favourite for Sufis. Through wonderful translations of his poetry he has suddenly become a world-wide figure. So it seems that this kind of poetry, although apparently praising and thanking Sri Ramana, can actually be seen as thanking the beloved, and can be inspiring.

I love this stuff. When I was making *Padamalai*, people would email and ask what I was doing. I just had a standard attachment of thirty of Muruganar's verses. I was emailing them out all over the world and saying this is what I am doing. Different people have tackled Muruganar in different ways. Swaminathan turns out a version that might be a Wordsworth talking *Advaita*. It's very kind of romantic-nineteenth-century. Sadhu Om turns out stuff that reads like a carburetor manual. It's very exact, very precise, but incredibly clunky. Is this poetry?

The whole essence of Tamil poetry is that it is endless sub-clauses one after the other, all qualifying each other or qualifying some parts of the verse. And to make that sound good in English is extraordinarily difficult. I will read you three or four. This is Muruganar praising Bhagavan in a work called *Sri Ramana Anubhuti* which means 'the experience of Sri Ramana'.

8. I have ended the confusion of my bewildered, suffering mind. A lowly cur, I have merged with the gracious feet of my Master. In the surging brilliance of his Divine Wisdom's splendour the broad ocean of deadly desires has disappeared completely.

9. The dark prison which bound my tortured soul crumbled and I became his servant finding joyous life in the open sky of his ambrosial grace. The knot which locked my spirit to my physical body was sundered by the bright sword of my Master's glance and was no more.

12. I was a learned fool. My flawed mind knew nothing until I came to dwell with him whose glance filled my heart with the light of awareness. Dwelling in that gracious state of peace whose nature is holy silence, so hard to gain and know, I entered into union with the deathless state of the knowledge of reality

13. As the deadly delusion of a body-bound ego faded, a flower of pure light unfolded at his holy feet. That radiance grew ever brighter with my love, until I realised the flawless knowledge of the Self, manifesting as the unbroken awareness I-I, within my heart.

15. He became one with my very soul, the supreme Lord, the flawless *Brahman*, the life of all that is, the jewel of the Self, turning my soul's night to day, with the fulsome rays of true wisdom's sun.

16. The confusion of the senses ended and the world's illusion was dispelled, as grace's bright sun rose, absorbing me in itself

and obliterating all distinctions. And as I entered the light of the life lived in the holy silence of the glorious non-dual state, the 'I' and all that arises from it subsided and dissolved away.

And so on for twenty thousand verses. What I like about this is that he doesn't repeat himself, or hardly ever. Can you imagine – you've got a format of four lines and your basic subject is 'thank you Sri Ramana' and you can just go on like this? Every single verse you think, 'Wow, this is great. Where's the next one?'

That strikes me as a very important work, to get that out into the world.

Well, this one is out. My friend Robert made an English translation for a Sri Ramana group in Bangalore, which published it. This is just an extract. *Guru Vachaka Kovai* is out with a flowery poetical rendering, published by the ashram. I am definitely planning to work on these new two thousand five hundred verses by Muruganar which were only recently published.

From what you've seen of those verses is there much that would change the image of Sri Ramana's teaching in any way?

I talked to the man who is going to translate. He just gave me samples and I looked at maybe forty to fifty verses and I said 'Great! Let's do it all.' He told me that there are whole areas included in this work which *Guru Vachaka Kovai* doesn't touch. That's why he wants to go ahead with it – it's not simply clarifying or expanding on previously given teachings; there are whole new areas of the teaching which haven't been brought out before which appear in this work.

Tell us about Viswanatha Swami.

His father was Bhagavan's first cousin, so that makes him a second cousin, anyway he's in the family. He ran away from home when he was, I think seventeen, and came to Bhagavan around 1920 when Bhagavan was still at Skanda Ashram. Bhagavan told him off for running away, even though he himself had run away at the same age, and sent a message to his father to come and collect him. Then two years later, just before Bhagavan left Skanda Ashram, he came back with his family's somewhat reluctant permission and stayed for the rest of his life. He was a very well educated Sanskrit scholar. He knew very good Tamil. He was the person everybody called up in the 30s and 40s when any book came in and Bhagavan said we need a Tamil translation, even from Sanskrit to English or Tamil to English. He did a lot of work. He translated many ashram books into Tamil. I think he did the edition of *Talks* and *Maharshi's Gospel*. He was also a major devotee of Ganapathi Muni, as were most of the Sanskrit knowing Brahmins of the era.

It's hard to pin down and give a particular story about him. The one story that really shows him in a good light is that in 1950, after Bhagavan passed away, there was a committee meeting in the ashram on 'what shall we do next?'. It was decided that Muruganar, who we have just talked about, and Viswanatha Swami should be allowed to stay free in the ashram for the rest of their lives, without any work being assigned to them, simply because they best exemplified the spirit of Bhagavan and they were the best people to have around who could keep that tradition going.

So they became honorary ashramites.

Right.

But in fact Viswanatha Swami was the editor of The Mountain Path *(the ashram's journal) for many years.*

Very reluctantly; he didn't want the job. He used to hide in Palakottu, to avoid the ashram sending work

VISWANATHA SWAMI

1904 - 1979
Viswanatha Swami, a relative of Sri Ramana, joined him in 1923. He gave up politics and became a brahmachari (celibate). He was learned in Tamil and Sanskrit and translated many of the ashram's books. He wrote the 108 Names of Sri Bhagavan, which is sung even today in the ashram. He also wrote a moving account of Bhagavan's last days. He spent some time as editor of the ashram's journal The Mountain Path.

to his room. I mean, he was kind of on the run from getting involved in editing.

You actually met him when he was how old?

In his seventies I suppose.

How did he strike you? What kind of impression do you have of him?

Everything about Viswanatha Swami was dignified. The way he walked, the way he spoke, the way he wrote, his excellent command of English, and he also seemed to be a natural linguist. He was compelled by circumstances to write his reminiscences just before he died as material was needed to put in *The Mountain Path*, to fill up the empty spaces. There are four wonderful serialised stories of him coming to Bhagavan and what happened. They are written very elegantly, giving a really nice intimate picture of what it was like to live with Bhagavan. There's a quiet, mellow, dignified beauty about his descriptions that really makes you wish you were there. There is something about that account that touched everybody and I think that came from his own inner state, his inner experience.

He was engaged by the ashram to write the official story of how Bhagavan died. There is a tiny little pamphlet called *The Last Days and Maha Nirvana of Bhagavan Sri Ramana*, it's about six or seven pages, in the ashram bookstore. It's the best description of how Bhagavan passed away. He was in the room when Bhagavan died and he said that was the spiritual climax of his life. He said there was no feeling of wanting him to be alive, of grief, he said that there was just absolute total silence. He said, in that moment, watching Bhagavan die, he experienced the Self. That was the climax of his years with Bhagavan, realising he wasn't the body, understanding that he was the Self, Bhagavan was the Self.

I think he uses the word ecstasy, he actually experienced the ecstasy of the Self at that moment. I don't know if it's in your book.

Yes. These are his words from *The Power of the Presence*:

'The climax of my own spiritual experiences in the proximity of Bhagavan took place during his last moments. As I stood in that small room everything became shadowy, enveloped by indivisible pure awareness, the one-and-only, ever-present reality. There was not the least feeling of separation from Bhagavan or even the least vestige of sorrow on his physical death. Instead, there was a positive ecstasy and an elation of spirit which is nothing but the natural state of the Self.'

I think that's actually quite important because certainly in the West, people have become very used to feeling very sad and distraught when somebody passes away, and here is a man who had dedicated his whole life to somebody, he absolutely loved this person, he was there at that moment and he describes ecstasy.

There is a big samadhi *next to the room where Bhagavan spent his last days. Who is buried there?*

CHINNASWAMI

1886 - 1953
Sri Ramana's younger brother, Nagasundaram, came to Virupaksha Cave with his mother in 1916. He stayed with Sri Bhagavan, eventually becoming a sannyasin and assuming the name Niranjanananda. He became known as Chinnaswami, meaning the younger swami. He was Ramana Ashram's first manager.

Chinnaswami (Bhagavan's brother and the ashram's first manager) was absolutely passionate about the Mother's Shrine – she was his mother as well as Bhagavan's – and he spent eleven years building it. He had wanted, ever since 1930, to have this big temple. Bhagavan didn't give the go ahead until 1939. He spent until 1950 putting it up, so when he passed away they built his *samadhi* in front of the main entrance. That way he could look in from his *samadhi* and have his mother's *darshan* (being in the presence of a saint).

Let's look at Lakshmana's story.

Lakshmana Swamy realised the Self in 1949. On the day Bhagavan died, Lakshmana saw him early that afternoon and had an absolutely blissful, ecstatic experience standing in front of Bhagavan. There was no feeling of grief. He said just to see him was an incredible moment of ecstasy. Even though he had realised the Self, there was something extra in that moment.

LAKSHMANA
SWAMY

*1925
Lakshmana Swamy was born at Gudur, Andhra Pradesh. In 1949 in his search for a guru, he spent time at Ramana Ashram. He practised Self-enquiry as suggested by Sri Ramana and became permanently established in the Self. To satisfy people, he gave public darshan once a year, eventually increasing to twice a year. He now lives in Tiruvannamalai and only gives darshan on special festival days.

He went back to his room. He had a photo of Bhagavan propped up on a stool and it fell off the stool for no apparent reason at all. So he put it back on again, making sure it was in a position that it wouldn't fall off. He sat down and it promptly fell off again. At that point he realised this was a message of some sort, that something was about to happen to Bhagavan. But he said at that moment he went into a kind of *samadhi* – it wasn't his choice or decision – that he completely lost the awareness of the world, his body, and didn't come back till eight forty-five that night when there was a great noise in the ashram, and he realised that Bhagavan had probably passed away. The sound of several thousand people grieving is unmistakable.

He rushed in, got there as quickly as he could. By the time he got there, they had already moved the body from the place he passed away to the front verandah of the New Hall. He said he stood there looking at that body and he said some part of him felt he should shed a tear for the passing away. I won't say it was a guilty conscience but he felt this was an appropriate thing to do at this moment. This is the man who has given him realisation, this is the most important person he has ever met, the person he loves the most. So he thinks: This person has now passed away, I should cry like everybody else. But he said in that moment there was an absolute certainty that nothing had happened.

He said he knew that Bhagavan was the Self, that half an hour before he had been the Self, that half an hour afterwards, when the body was gone, he was still the Self, and nothing of any importance whatsoever had happened. With that knowledge he just went back to his room and went back into *samadhi* again. For somebody who is in that state, the physical passing away is quite literally a non-event, nothing has happened. The people who thought Bhagavan was a body were the ones who were tearing their hair and their saris and screaming. The ones who had reached the state that Bhagavan was in were the ones who were in ecstasy and peace when he died.

This is an important thing for people in the West to hear. It confronts the way most of the world looks on death, which is probably the ultimate fear for most people. They have all kinds of strategies in their lives, certainly in middle age, to somehow avoid this moment of death. So to hear such a powerful account that 'nothing really happens', which is, as I understand it, the teaching of most great saints, is very important.

All through the 1940s Bhagavan's health was deteriorating. He was constantly telling people, 'Don't take me to be the body, because if you do, when this body dies you'll all be crying.' And he said, 'See who you are now, see who I am now. Take advantage of the chance you've got now, while it's available. Otherwise you are going to be grieving when I die.' That's what happened to the vast majority of the people, and the fortunate few, who were serious enough, lucky enough, dedicated enough, found themselves to be that same Self that Bhagavan was. When he passed away they realised there was nothing to grieve over.

You and I both sat at Papaji's feet for a number of years and I think we share a tremendous respect and devotion for him. In another interview (see Chapter 10) you described some of your feelings when he left his body, when the ashes were put in the Ganga at Haridwar. You also had a strong spiritual experience at that time, which wasn't in any way to do with grief – you felt ecstatic.
I wasn't present when Papaji left his body, but I was connected with him and I didn't experience any grief at all, although as you say he was the

most important person in my life and the person I loved the most. I was living close to Osho's ashram in Pune when Osho left his body. Again, I experienced no grief at all, in fact an enormous celebration. I can say that it was a very strong experience to see that the reality of death is so different from the kind of dramatic line that we get from Hollywood and stories in the West.

H.W.L. POONJA
(Papaji)

1910 - 1997
In 1944 he met his master, Sri Ramana. He cared for his extended family by working as a mining supervisor in the jungles of Kerala. After retirement, when health problems prevented him from travelling, he settled in Lucknow. Here thousands of Western devotees came to sit in his presence. Many of these devotees now travel in the West offering Satsang.

Would you like to say something about Papaji? You've talked and written a lot about him, but would you perhaps put him into the context of the structure of the disciples around Sri Ramana? He was coming and going to and from the ashram and his awakening happened on one of his visits. It was only later he stayed for a longer time, in the late 40s.

This is all very inconclusive. There are two parallel biographies of Papaji that don't meet at many points, and you can take your pick. One is that he got enlightened when he was eight, that nothing ever happened spiritually to him after the age of eight. And the other one is this very dramatic story of running around India looking for various gurus, finally coming to Ramana Ashram around 1944, having a climactic meeting with Bhagavan and becoming realised on that day. Now, the more I talked to him, the more he insisted that his final experience happened when he was eight, which makes it very hard to construct a meaningful explanation of what happened at Ramana Ashram. That was his story and he was sticking to it!

He stuck to both stories?

When you asked him, 'Okay, you were enlightened at eight, and so what did Bhagavan give you that you didn't have before? What happened in Ramana

Ashram?' he said, 'The experience of the Self needs to be confirmed and corroborated by a master, and that's what happened when I met Bhagavan.' His tendencies from a previous life as a *Krishna Yogi* had made him run around looking for visions of a physical *Krishna* to give him ecstasy when he should have been satisfied with the experience of the Self.

He said in a way that's what Bhagavan gave him. All the dialogues that took place when he encountered Bhagavan related to this problem Papaji had of seeking some kind of external vision of *Krishna* which would give him ecstasy, whereas Bhagavan told him, 'What comes and goes is not real. Only the Self is real and it never comes and goes. What use is a God who comes and goes? Stay as the Self.' So, in a sense, what he received was the destruction of his desire for an external form of God to give him ecstasy. He didn't receive anything new, he didn't become more enlightened. Somehow, he was shown the diamond he already had, and was told 'Stop looking for anything else – you are wasting your time, you've got it already.' That in a sense was what the meetings with Sri Ramana were about, Sri Ramana saying 'Look, you've got this already, why are you running around looking for external gods? Be happy with what you've got.'

But isn't this in fact what everybody has got already?

We all tend to think that Self-realisation would be self-evident, obvious, so overwhelming, real, peaceful, ecstatic, blissful, that we would know that we have got it. This doesn't seem to be the case. In Bhagavan's case, at the age of sixteen he gets this experience. Theory number one was that he had been possessed. He uses the Tamil word *avesam*, which can only mean that some strange spirit has possessed you. Number two, he thought he had caught some strange new disease. His attitude to that was 'Well, it's an improvement on all my previous diseases; I hope this one stays. There was absolutely no feeling in him that this is the meaning of life, this is the final goal of all human activities. He knew it was a good state to be in, but he had no cultural context in which to place it, no feeling that this was in any sense a conclusion. That was something that became firmly established in him when he came to Arunachala.

101

How would Sri Ramana ever really know that? In those early days as a young boy down in the temple and up in the cave, did he get the confirmation that he wasn't crazy and that in fact he was in a spiritual state because of the way respected spiritual entities treated him, had a certain reverence for him?

I don't think he had that measure of self-reflection on what had happened. He tried to live a normal life at home for six weeks, failed, ran away, came to Tiruvannamalai and dropped all his possessions, threw his money away, sat down and went into *samadhi*. There was no feeling of 'I must do this because of this or to accomplish that'.

It just happened.

It was a tidal wave that swept him here, washed him up in the Arunachala temple, deposited him there, and he promptly went into *samadhi* and that was it. I think at some point it must have come to him – this is *purna*, the fullness, the completion. He never said when it happened – the experience never varied from that first moment – but at some point he would have discarded all the erroneous interpretations of what it was all about. It wasn't a possession, it wasn't a disease.

He said around 1898, when one of his early attendants started bringing books to him to read and explain, he suddenly realised that for centuries and centuries large portions of India had been trying to attain this state which had come to him quite spontaneously, and it was only at that moment that he even discovered the vocabulary associated with this event.

He said. 'I read *Brahman* (the absolute reality) in a book years after I became *Brahman*. If that's what they call it, that's what I am.' He didn't really have the philosophical, cultural background to say, 'I am That, I am *Brahman*, I am realised.' Those terms were meaningless to him, he didn't know what they were. I think to some extent that happened with Papaji. He said the only cultural context in which to place his eight-year-old experience was his mother's fanatic desire to have a vision of *Krishna* which would make her happy. So she projected that onto him and, being an impressionable eight year old, he somehow identified it with *Krishna* without fully appreciating the enormity and the finality of what had happened to him.

So when did that understanding come to Papaji actually?

With Bhagavan. He said, 'This is what my master gave me. He gave me absolute certainty, not just of who and what I was but the unshakable conviction I would never ever need anything more again. He cut off this quest for an external source of ecstasy and made me satisfied with what I had.'

When I came to Papaji we had three meetings where I asked him three questions. In the first of those he said something like, 'If you have a diamond don't take it to a fishmonger, take it to a diamond merchant.' I didn't get what he meant in that moment, but later I understood. By Sri Ramana knowing that, he was able to be Papaji's diamond merchant and say, 'Actually, what you've got there is a diamond.'

We haven't really talked much about Lakshmana Swamy, but his chief disciple, Saradamma, has told me exactly the same thing. She said Lakshmana Swamy would talk about meditation, enlightenment, Self-realisation, and they were completely meaningless terms to her. She didn't want to meditate, she was just absolutely totally in love with his name, his form. She was doing *japa*, repetition of his name, eighteen hours a day, dreaming about him at night. She didn't care about listening to lectures on philosophy or him telling her that she should do Self-enqiry. In her case, that absorpion in the name and form of guru was enough and she realised the Self very young, when she was eighteen, without having the slightest idea what had happened.

She'd been listerning to this man say 'Self-realisation', 'enlightenment', for years. When the event happened to her, she didn't make the connection with those words. She said, 'I knew I was peace, I knew I was bliss, I knew I was finished, but there wasn't this need, desire, inclination to say, "What do I call this? Where am I? What's happened?" It's a non-verbal experience, it's complete, you don't think about it, you don't speculate about it.' She said it was only about a year later, when he casually remarked, 'Oh, now you are Self-realised' that she realised that was what he was talking about all those years – that's the word. That was also what happened with Bhagavan.

Sivaprakasam Pillai wrote a poem describing Bhagavan as the man who realised *Brahman* before he even knew what the word was. That is exactly what happened to Bhagavan, it's what happened to Saradamma. The experience comes and even though you might know the word *Brahman*, there's something inherent in that experience that you don't feel to label it or call it anything. It may be months or years later you think, 'That's *Brahman*, that's what they were talking about.' And in some cases such as Bhagavan or Papaji there seems to be an early lack of definitive authority. They don't know what's happened to them, it's a little bit bewildering. They speculate about it. In Bhagavan's case it's possession or it's a disease, and in Papaji's case somehow his mother convinces him it is not enough and pursuades him to spend a quarter of a century looking for *Krishna* visions. Papaji said, 'If I had had someone like Sri Ramana when I was eight, he would have stopped me in that moment. I wouldn't have wasted twenty-five years running around after teachers to show me God. It wouldn't have been necessary. He would've said "Right now you are God, accept it." That would have been that.'

In your recent series of books, The Power of the Presence, *you write about people who were close to Bhagavan. Presumably, you chose people who you feel had reached that final state.*

No, that wasn't the criterion at all. Initially, my aim was to bring into the public domain accounts by devotees of Bhagavan that hadn't been published before in English. I make no judgements about spiritual maturity or accomplishments. My prime consideration was, 'Has this been published before in English, and if it hasn't, is it interesting enough to print now?'

So you don't suggest in the book that they've reached this or that state?

I let people speak for themselves. The second chapter of part one of *The Power of the Presence* for example, is about a man, Sivaprakasam Pillai, who spent fifty years with Bhagavan. He was the person who recorded the answers that Bhagavan wrote in the sand in 1901. In many parts of this chapter he's lamenting, 'I've wasted my life, I'm worse than a dog, I've sat here for many years without making any progress.'

But this man might have got it in that period, even if he thinks he didn't.

In Bhagavan's day there was a daily chanting of Tamil devotional poetry. There was a fixed selection of material that took fifteen days to go through. Sivapraksam Pillai's poems were part of this cycle. Every fifteen days the devotees would sit in front of Bhagavan and chant 'I am worse than a dog', and so on.

Somebody asked Bhagavan, 'This man has been here fifty years and he is still in this state. What hope is there for us?' Bhagavan replied, 'That's his way of praising me.' When Sivaprakasam Pillai died Bhagavan commented, 'Sivaprakasam has become the light of *Shiva*.' *Prakasam* means 'light', so this was a pun on his name.

SIVAPRAKASAM PILLAI

1875 - 1948
Intellegent and pious, the young Sivaprakasam Pillai studied English, Tamil and philosophy. In 1902 he visited the saintly and ascetic young boy living on the hill and asked him the question which had been haunting his mind for so many years, 'Who am I?' He became a devotee and practised Self-enquiry his whole life.

This suggests that he had achieved this second, final state.

Bhagavan himself only gave public 'certificates of enlightenment' to his mother and the cow, Lakshmi. He did indirectly hint that other people had reached this state, but he would never name the names. He only named those two after they died.

In the collective consciousness of the ashram and the people who are associated with it, are there people that everyone accepts as enlightened, even though Bhagavan didn't publicly acknowledge their state?

Probably the most widely revered was Muruganar. He's an obvious candidate because right from the 1920s onwards he was writing Tamil poetry that spoke of his own realisation. He wrote more than 20,000 verses, and in a large number of them he was declaring his enlightenment. Many of these were published in Bhagavan's lifetime and Bhagavan made no attempt to discourage the notion that these were true accounts. Bhagavan often read out extracts from these books and this convinced many people that the contents must have been true.

KUNJU SWAMI

1897 - 1992
As a young boy, Kunju Swami was left in Bhagavan's care by a devotee. He came to Skanda Ashram in 1919 and became Sri Bhagavan's personal attendant. After twelve years in personal attendance on Bhagavan he felt an urge to devote himself entirely to sadhana. Kunju Swami spent his life with Bhagavan.

Are there some other candidates that Bhagavan himself seems to acknowledge?

There's the very interesting 'back door' we spoke about earlier of burial rites. Both his mother and Lakshmi the cow were given traditional burial rites that are reserved, according to an ancient Tamil scripture, for enlightened beings. Mastan was the only other devotee given these rites during Bhagavan's lifetime. I would take this to be a very strong but indirect endorsement of this man's state.

What can you tell me about Kunju Swami? Did many people regard him as being enlightened?

He was Bhagavan's attendant from 1920 to 1932. At the end of this period he left the ashram because he wanted to spend all his time meditating. With Bhagavan's permission he went to Palakottu, an area adjacent to the ashram, and lived there. He came to the ashram every day, mostly during the daily chanting, but he no longer worked there.

In the 1930s and 40s he became an unofficial ambassador for Ramana Ashram. Whenever someone was needed to attend a function in some other ashram or institution, Kunju Swami would be picked because he knew all the diplomatic rules of how to behave in every possible circumstance in spiritual institutions.

It's a very arcane body of knowledge. Kunju Swami knew what scriptures to chant in what place, what rules and regulations he had to obey, and so on. He also occasionally had to debate philosophy with the *sadhus* who lived in these places. It was not a job that just anyone could do. When they sent him out, the ashram management knew he wouldn't put his foot in it and give the ashram a bad name.

So he wasn't appointed to this job because he was particularly luminous?

I wouldn't say so. He was available and he enjoyed it. And, of course, Bhagavan always gave him permission to go. Many of the devotees who were around Bhagavan in the 1920s and 30s liked to live as wandering *sadhus*. They often took off on little trips and pilgrimages. A lot of them were free spirits who didn't like being tied down to one place for long.

Going back to my earlier question, is there a collective opinion that any other devotees realised the Self?

As I have already mentioned, the official line inside the ashram is that only Bhagavan's mother and Lakshmi the cow realised the Self because these are the only two beings whose enlightenment was publicly endorsed by Bhagavan. There are other contenders, but no full agreement on who they might be.

You spent five or six years living with Papaji. Would you put him in that category?

I would, yes, but a lot of people here would not agree with me.

You've already mentioned Lakshmana Swamy, so that's two. You also wrote a book about Annamalai Swamy. Is he on your list?

He didn't impress me the way the other two did. Annamalai Swamy had a nice quiet, humble presence. I admired his integrity, his unshakable devotion and commitment to Bhagavan, and I liked the way he answered questions put to him by visitors, but there's something about Lakshmana Swamy and Papaji that for me was completely different. There was an effortless radiant power that I felt coming off both of them. After a few minutes of sitting in their presence the mind would be completely silent. Bhagavan himself said that this was the best way to judge what state someone was in. Of course, this is still a subjective opinion because other people who sat with Papaji and Lakshmana Swamy didn't have the same experiences that I did.

Anybody else you would like to bring in?

There are the animals. Did we talk about the animals?

Not in great detail. Would you like to? That will be a nice little postscript, Lakshmi the cow.

Bhagavan was really different from just about every other teacher with his very strange notion that all kinds of enlightened beings – *rishis*, sages, gods – would pop in to see him in animal bodies. Bhagavan wasn't the sort to make jokes like this, but once in a while a bird would fly into the hall, sit on the window and cheep for a while and fly out. Then with a straight face he'd say, 'That was an enlightened *siddha* (one who has attained a paranormal ability) came to say hello.' But that's just one category of animal who used to show up. I really want to say something

COW LAKSHMI

1926-1948
Cow Lakshmi and her mother were presented to Sri Ramana by a devotee in 1926. The calf seemed irresistibly attracted to Sri Bhagavan and she would come to the hall along with the other devotees. Sri Bhagavan showed her exceptional grace and kindness. When she passed away Sri Ramana put his hand on her heart and announced publicly that she had realised the Self.

about Lakshmi the cow. She was an extraordinarily outstanding devotee of Bhagavan. (Laughter) She was born in a village about twenty miles from Tiruvannamalai and the owner had a dream in which he was asked to present a cow to Bhagavan. It sounds like a very major expedition. It involved rafting her down a river, transporting her in trucks. Even though it was close it was a major undertaking. So Lakshmi, then a calf, with her mother, was delivered to the ashram.

Bhagavan, who initially didn't want the headache of cows in the ashram, tried to make the owner take both cows away. But in the end one devotee agreed to look after them, so they stayed. They made a mess of the ashram, they trampled on the gardens. So they were sent off to town. But Lakshmi was then growing up and would come every day to the ashram and sit at Bhagavan's feet for the whole day, just the same way that every other devotee would. She would come in the morning, she might go out and munch some grass, but most of the day she'd be sitting in the hall the same as everybody else. Bhagavan showed enormous love for Lakshmi. He wouldn't let anyone maltreat her and on so many occasions said she was somebody special, very special. He would feed her the same food that was served in the dining room. One day, when he noticed Lakshmi wasn't getting enough grass, he refused to eat his meal in the dining room, said send it to Lakshmi instead.

She would prostrate to him and put her head on his lap, and on one occasion he stroked her head and said she was in *nirvikalpa samadhi* (highest state of conciousness). I mean this is not the sort of thing you expect to happen to a cow! For the first few years she was at Ramana Ashram there was no clock in the ashram at all. Somebody must have known what time it was because dinner, lunch, breakfast were served at regular times. Lakshmi would come two minutes before the appointed time to tell Bhagavan it was time to eat and take him to the dining room. This is a cow who knows the schedule of the ashram without a clock. She knows five minutes in advance of the dinner that dinner is coming and comes to tell Bhagavan it's time for him to go for dinner. Bhagavan himself said she understood every single word which he spoke. When it was time to build a cowshed – this is in 1933 – the ashram had coconut leaf huts, an occasional mud building with a tile roof and that was it. They didn't have any money and even if they did Bhagavan was so thrifty that nobody dared contemplate anything better than a tiled hut with mud walls. Suddenly he announced in 1933 that they were going to build this palatial mansion for Lakshmi.

He planned dressed granite walls with teak beams for the roof, which the ashram couldn't afford, had no money for. He overruled Chinnaswami (his brother and the ashram manager) and announced that this cowshed had to be built. He appointed Annamalai Swami to build it. When it was built it was, by a factor of ten, the biggest building in the ashram. It was far, far bigger than the hall he received his visitors in. And he said that if they served Lakshmi in this way they would get enough *punniyam* (merit) to have money for all the other buildings that they needed. The implication was that this was some kind of Lakshmi goddess. By serving Lakshmi, the ashram would prosper and if they didn't do this, it wouldn't. And this is what happened. The cowshed went up.

The day of the inauguration ceremony, at the exact moment fixed by the astrologers, Lakshmi came to the hall, took Bhagavan out. She knew this was her cowshed going up. Nobody had told her and it wasn't the meal time. It was whatever, say ten thirty-three in the morning, the right conjunction to do this, and at ten thirty-three she came and got Bhagavan and took him to the site. When the cowshed was finished she wouldn't go into it. She went to the hall and collected Bhagavan and made him come in first, and she went in behind him. But there are so many extraordinary stories about this cow. When she passed away in 1948 he put his hand on her heart and announced publicly that she realised the Self. He built the same *jnani samadhi* he had built for Mastan and for his mother and composed the verse in praise of her, celebrating her liberation. Even he marveled at this. He said, 'Not even for my own mother did I sing a song like this.' There was something about her devotion that absolutely captured him for fifteen or twenty years. When she died he said it was because of her that the ashram had grown. There was some power inherent in Lakshmi that Bhagavan sensed. By appreciating Lakshmi, by building her this monstrous cowshed, by looking after her, serving her, Bhagavan said the ashram grew the way it did.

Yes, I guess this story is quite hard for Western people to accept. In the Western world there is a certain attitude towards animals which, for example, puts cows in pens and fattens them up for slaughter. There is not much communication between human beings and animals in general, except maybe with dogs and cats.

In India, one of the things that hits you when you start travelling is that animals are included in the daily life. Animals are everywhere, like human beings are everywhere, and particularly cows. You can be in a busy street even in Delhi, and there will be four cows lying in the middle of an intersection. Nobody will try to move them. Traffic flow goes around. Something like that in New York or Sydney would be fairly scandalous.

I don't think you will find another example of cows being treated as human beings in a guru's *Satsang* (meeting in Truth) hall. She was a human being in a cow's body. Bhagavan not quite fully conceded, but wouldn't argue the case, that she was an incarnation of a woman called Girapati who served him on the hill from 1900 to 1920. She used to beg fruits and serve him every day.

I think that's a great story to finish with. I am speechless after that, only a moo would do! What I most love about this story is that the Western mind can't possibly get it and in a sense you must come to India to see the way that the animals are treated.

But she wasn't treated well by Indians. Bhagavan, for twenty years, had to defend against people who were trying to stop her coming in. He was absolutely insistent – she had priority. If the ashram vegetables had been eaten it wasn't Lakshmi's fault. He wouldn't let anyone treat her badly. Oh, she had calves on his birthday – that was really strange. For three successive years she delivered a calf as a birthday present for him.

That's pretty amazing. Beautiful. Thank you.

The Self is known to everyone but
not clearly. The Being is the Self.
Of all the definitions of God, none is
so well put as the Biblical statement
'I am that I am'. Knowing the Self,
God is known. In fact, God is none
other than the Self.

Sri Ramana Maharshi

Above: Sri Ramana with temple elephant

Left: The Mother's Shrine

Below: Ramana Ashram Old Hall

Right top: Sri Ramana's couch in the Old Hall

Right centre: Group 1948-49 in front of the gate to mountain path Painting in Old Hall of Sri Ramana on his couch

Right bottom: Arunachala north face from Girivalam Road between Adiannamalai village and Tiruvannamalai

CHAPTER 4

Who Am I? (Nan Yar)

Sri Ramana Maharshi's
original text

[Sri Ramana's direct words are in bold]

This is the standard introduction to the teachings of Bhagavan Sri Ramana Maharshi. Originally, the basis for the essay was the answers written by Sri Ramana in the sand of Arunachala in 1901, when he would have been twenty-two years old. The answers were given in response to questions asked by Sivaprakasam Pillai. The original work was rewritten in the 1920s by Sri Ramana and is one of the few texts edited and approved by him. The main focus is on Self-enquiry and the nature of the Self, the mind and the world.

All living beings desire to be happy always, without any misery. In everyone there is observed supreme love for oneself. And happiness alone is the cause of love. In order therefore, to gain that happiness which is one's nature and which is experienced in the state of deep sleep, where there is no mind, one should know oneself. To achieve this, the Path of Knowledge, the enquiry in the form of 'Who am I?' is the principal means.

1. Who am I?
The gross body which is composed of the seven humours (*dhatus*), I am not; the five cognitive sense organs, viz., the senses of hearing, touch, sight, taste and smell, which apprehend their respective objects, viz. sound, touch, colour, taste and odour, I am not; the five cognitive sense organs, viz., the organs of speech, locomotion, grasping, excreting and enjoying, I am not; the five vital airs, *prana*, etc., which perform respectively the five functions of in-breathing, etc., I am not; even the mind which thinks, I am not; the nescience too, which is endowed only with the residual impressions of objects and in which there are no objects and no functions, I am not.

2. If I am none of these, then who am I?
After negating all of the above mentioned as 'not this', 'not this', this Awareness which alone remains – that I am.

3. What is the nature of Awareness?
The nature of Awareness is Existence-Consciousness-Bliss.

4. When will the realisation of the Self be gained?
When the world which is what-is-seen has been removed, there will be realisation of the Self which is the Seer.

5. Will there not be realisation of the Self even while the world is there (taken as real)?
There will not be.

117

6. Why?
The seer and the object seen are like the rope and the snake. Just as the knowledge of the rope which is the substratum will not arise unless the false knowledge of the illusory serpent goes, so the realisation of the Self which is the substratum will not be gained unless the belief that the world is real is removed.

7. When will the world which is the object seen be removed?
When the mind, which is the cause of all cognition and of all actions, becomes quiescent, the world will disappear.

8. What is the nature of the mind?
What is called 'mind' is a wondrous power residing in the Self. It causes all thoughts to arise. Apart from thoughts, there is no such thing as mind. Therefore, thought is the nature of mind. Apart from thoughts, there is no independent entity called the world. In deep sleep there are no thoughts, and there is no world. In the states of waking and dream, there are thoughts, and there is a world also. Just as the spider emits the thread (of the web) out of itself and again withdraws it into itself, likewise the mind projects the world out of itself and again resolves it into itself. When the mind comes out of the Self, the world appears. Therefore, when the world appears (to be real), the Self does not appear; and when the Self appears (shines) the world does not appear. When one persistently inquires into the nature of the mind, the mind will end leaving the Self (as the residue). What is referred to as the Self is the *Atman*. The mind always exists only in dependence on something gross; it cannot stay alone. It is the mind that is called the subtle body or the soul (*jiva*).

9. What is the path of inquiry for understanding the nature of the mind?
That which rises as 'I' in this body is the mind. If one inquires as to where in the body the thought 'I' rises first, one would discover that it rises in the heart. That is the place of the mind's origin. Even if one thinks constantly 'I-I', one will be led to that place. Of all the thoughts that arise in the mind, the 'I'-thought is the first. It is only after the

rise of this that the other thoughts arise. It is after the appearance of the first personal pronoun that the second and the third personal pronouns appear; without the first personal pronoun there will not be the second and the third.

10. How will the mind become quiescent?
By the inquiry 'Who am I?' The thought 'Who am I?' will destroy all other thoughts, and like the stick used for stirring the burning pyre, it will itself in the end get destroyed. Then, there will arise Self-realisation.

11. What is the means for constantly holding on to the thought 'Who am I?'
When other thoughts arise, one should not pursue them, but should inquire: 'To whom do they arise?' It does not matter how many thoughts arise. As each thought arises, one should inquire with diligence, 'To whom has this thought arisen?' The answer that would emerge would be 'to me'. Thereupon if one inquires 'Who am I?', the mind will go back to its source; and the thought that arose will become quiescent. With repeated practice in this manner, the mind will develop the skill to stay in its source. When the mind that is subtle goes out through the brain and the sense-organs, the gross names and forms appear; when it stays in the heart, the names and forms disappear. Not letting the mind go out, but retaining it in the Heart is what is called 'inwardness' *(antarmukha)*. Letting the mind go out of the Heart is known as 'externalisation' *(bahirmukha)*. Thus, when the mind stays in the Heart, the 'I', which is the source of all thoughts will go, and the Self which ever exists will shine. Whatever one does, one should do without the egoity 'I'. If one acts in that way, all will appear as of the nature of *Shiva* (God).

12. Are there no other means for making the mind quiescent?
Other than inquiry, there are no adequate means. If through other means it is sought to control the mind, the mind will appear to be controlled, but will again go forth. Through the control of breath also, the mind will become quiescent; but it will be quiescent only so

long as the breath remains controlled, and when the breath resumes the mind also will again start moving and will wander as impelled by residual impressions. The source is the same for both mind and breath. Thought, indeed, is the nature of the mind. The thought 'I' is the first thought of the mind; and that is egoity. It is from that whence egoity originates that breath also originates. Therefore, when the mind becomes quiescent, the breath is controlled, and when the breath is controlled the mind becomes quiescent. But in deep sleep, although the mind becomes quiescent, the breath does not stop. This is because of the will of God, so that the body may be preserved and other people may not be under the impression that it is dead. In the state of waking and in *samadhi*, when the mind becomes quiescent the breath is controlled. Breath is the gross form of the mind. Till the time of death, the mind keeps breath in the body; and when the body dies, the mind takes the breath along with it. Therefore, the exercise of breath control is only an aid for rendering the mind quiescent *(manonigra)*; it will not destroy the mind *(manonasha)*.Like the practice of breath control, meditation on the forms of God, repetition of *mantras*, restriction on food, etc., are but aids for rendering the mind quiescent.

Through meditation on the forms of God and through repetition of mantras, the mind becomes one-pointed. The mind will always be wandering. Just as when a chain is given to an elephant to hold in its trunk it will go along grasping the chain and nothing else, so also when the mind is occupied with a name or form it will grasp that alone. When the mind expands in the form of countless thoughts, each thought becomes weak; but as thoughts get resolved the mind becomes one-pointed and strong; for such a mind Self-inquiry will become easy. Of all the restrictive rules, that relating to the taking of *sattvic* food in moderate quantities is the best; by observing this rule, the *sattvic* quality of mind will increase, and that will be helpful to Self-inquiry.

13. The residual impressions (thoughts) of objects appear unending like the waves of an ocean. When will all of them get destroyed?
As the meditation on the Self rises higher and higher, the thoughts will get destroyed.

14. Is it possible for the residual impressions of objects that come from beginningless time, as it were, to be resolved, and for one to remain as the pure Self?

Without yielding to the doubt 'Is it possible, or not?' one should persistently hold on to the meditation on the Self. Even if one be a great sinner, one should not worry and weep 'O! I am a sinner, how can I be saved?' One should completely renounce the thought 'I am a sinner' and concentrate keenly on mediation on the Self alone; then, one would surely succeed. There are not two minds – one good and the other evil; the mind is only one. It is the residual impressions that are of two kinds – auspicious and inauspicious. When the mind is under the influence of auspicious impressions it is called good; and when it is under the influence of inauspicious impressions it is regarded as evil.

The mind should not be allowed to wander towards worldly objects and what concerns other people. However bad other people may be, one should bear no hatred for them. Both desire and hatred should be eschewed. All that one gives to others one gives to one's self. If this truth is understood who will not give to others? When one's self arises all arises; when one's self becomes quiescent all becomes quiescent. To the extent we behave with humility, to that extent there will result good. If the mind is rendered quiescent, one may live anywhere.

15. How long should inquiry be practised?

As long as there are impressions of objects in the mind, so long the inquiry 'Who am I?' is required. As thoughts arise they should be destroyed then and there in the very place of their origin, through inquiry. If one resorts to contemplation of the Self unintermittently, until the Self is gained, that alone would do. As long as there are enemies within the fortress, they will continue to sally forth; if they are destroyed as they emerge, the fortress will fall into our hands.

16. What is the nature of the Self?

What exists is the Self alone. The world, the individual soul and God are appearances in it, like silver in mother-of-pearl; these three appear at the same time and disappear at the same time.

The Self is that where there is absolutely no 'I'-thought. That is called 'Silence'. The Self itself is the world; the Self itself is 'I'; the Self itself is God; all is *Shiva*, the Self.

17. Is not everything the work of God?

Without desire, resolve, or effort, the sun rises; and in its mere presence, the sun-stone emits fire, the lotus blooms, water evaporates, people perform their various functions and then rest. Just as in the presence of the magnet the needle moves, it is by virtue of the mere presence of God that the souls governed by the three (cosmic) functions or the fivefold divine activity perform their actions and then rest, in accordance with their respective *karmas*. God has no resolve; no *karma* attaches itself to Him. That is like worldly actions not affecting the sun, or like the merits and demerits of the other four elements not affecting all-pervading space.

18. Of the devotees, who is the greatest?

He who gives himself up to the Self that is God is the most excellent devotee. Giving one's self up to God means remaining constantly in the Self without giving room for the rise of any thoughts other than that of the Self.

Whatever burdens are thrown on God, He bears them. Since the supreme power of God makes all things move, why should we, without submitting ourselves to it, constantly worry ourselves with thoughts as to what should be done and how, and what should not be done and how not? We know that the train carries all loads, so after getting on it why should we carry our small luggage on our head to our discomfort, instead of putting it down in the train and feeling at ease?

19. What is non-attachment?

As thoughts arise, destroying them utterly without any residue in the very place of their origin is non-attachment. Just as the pearl-diver ties a stone to his waist, sinks to the bottom of the sea and there takes the pearls, so each one of us should be endowed with non-attachment, dive within oneself and obtain the Self-Pearl.

20. Is it possible for God and the Guru to effect the liberation of a soul?
God and the Guru will only show the way to liberation; they will not
by themselves take the soul to the state of liberation.

In truth, God and the Guru are not different. Just as the prey
which has fallen into the jaws of a tiger has no escape, so those who
have come within the ambit of the Guru's gracious look will be saved
by the Guru and will not get lost; yet, each one should, by his own
effort pursue the path shown by God or Guru and gain liberation.
One can know oneself only with one's own eye of knowledge, and
not with somebody else's. Does he who is Rama require the help of a
mirror to know that he is Rama?

*21. Is it necessary for one who longs for liberation to inquire into the
nature of categories* (tattvas)?
Just as one who wants to throw away garbage has no need to analyse
it and see what it is, so one who wants to know the Self has no need
to count the number of categories or inquire into their characteristics;
what he has to do is to reject altogether the categories that hide the
Self. The world should be considered like a dream.

22. Is there no difference between waking and dream?
Waking is long and dream short; other than this there is no difference.
Just as waking happenings seem real while awake, so do those in a
dream while dreaming. In dream the mind takes on another body.
In both waking and dream states thoughts, names and forms occur
simultaneously.

23. Is it any use reading books for those who long for liberation?
All the texts say that in order to gain liberation one should render the
mind quiescent; therefore their conclusive teaching is that the mind
should be rendered quiescent; once this has been understood there
is no need for endless reading. In order to quieten the mind one has
only to inquire within oneself what one's Self is; how could this search
be done in books? One should know one's Self with one's own eye
of wisdom. The Self is within the five sheaths; but books are outside

them. Since the Self has to be inquired into by discarding the five sheaths, it is futile to search for it in books. There will come a time when one will have to forget all that one has learned.

24. What is happiness?

Happiness is the very nature of the Self; happiness and the Self are not different. There is no happiness in any object of the world. We imagine through our ignorance that we derive happiness from objects. When the mind goes out, it experiences misery. In truth, when its desires are fulfilled, it returns to its own place and enjoys the happiness that is the Self. Similarly, in the states of sleep, *samadhi* and fainting, and when the object desired is obtained or the object disliked is removed, the mind becomes inward-turned, and enjoys pure Self-Happiness. Thus the mind moves without rest alternately going out of the Self and returning to it. Under the tree the shade is pleasant; out in the open the heat is scorching. A person who has been going about in the sun feels cool when he reaches the shade. Someone who keeps on going from the shade into the sun and then back into the shade is a fool. A wise man stays permanently in the shade. Similarly, the mind of the one who knows the truth does not leave *Brahman*. The mind of the ignorant, on the contrary, revolves in the world, feeling miserable, and for a little time returns to *Brahman* to experience happiness. In fact, what is called the world is only thought. When the world disappears, i.e., when there is no thought, the mind experiences happiness; and when the world appears, it goes through misery.

25. What is wisdom-insight (jnana drishti)?

Remaining quiet is what is called wisdom-insight. To remain quiet is to resolve the mind in the Self. Telepathy, knowing past, present and future happenings and clairvoyance do not constitute wisdom-insight.

26. What is the relation between desirelessness and wisdom?

Desirelessness is wisdom. The two are not different; they are the same. Desirelessness is refraining from turning the mind towards any objects. Wisdom means the appearance of no object. In other words, not seeking what is other than the Self is detachment or desirelessness; not leaving the Self is wisdom.

27. What is the difference between inquiry and meditation?
Inquiry consists in retaining the mind in the Self. Meditation consists in thinking that one's self is *Brahman*, Existence-Consciousness-Bliss.

28. What is liberation?
Inquiring into the nature of one's self that is in bondage, and realising one's true nature is liberation.

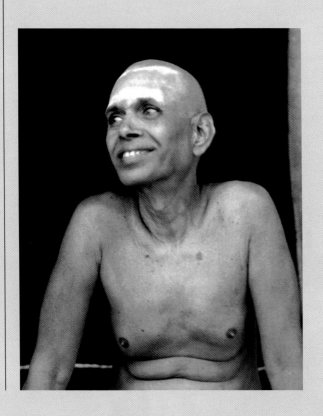

The question about the Heart
arises because you are interested in
seeking the source of Consciousness.
To all deep thinking minds, the
inquiry about the 'I' and its nature
has an irresistible fascination.

Sri Ramana Maharshi

COMMENTARY

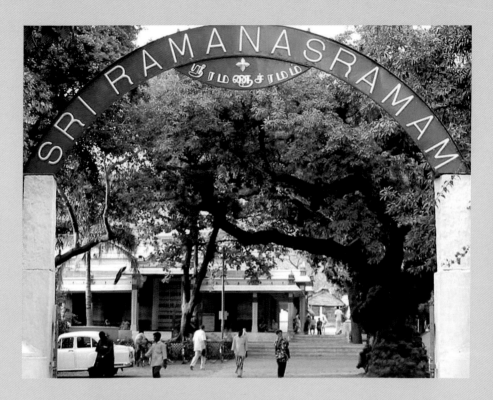

Above: *Ashram entrance 2002*

Left: *Mountain path to Skanda Ashram*

Below: *Classic Arunachala south face*

Right: *Sri Ramana in front of the Ashram post office in 1930s*

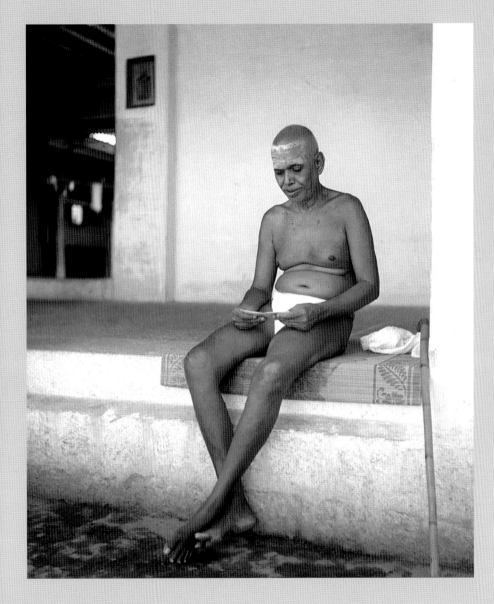

CHAPTER 5

Analysis of Sri Ramana's Enlightenment Experience from a Vedanta point of view

James Swartz in dialogue
with Premananda

[Sri Ramana's direct words are in bold]

A short chapter but a gem. James takes the whole text of Sri Ramana's Enlightenment, presented on a notice board in Ramana Ashram's New Hall, and makes a careful analysis. He unfolds Sri Ramana's words to give us many insights, from the Vedantic *point of view, into the subject of enlightenment and what knowing the Self actually is. This chapter will be an enormous help to anyone nearing the end of their journey.*

James, I would like to ask you about Sri Ramana's 'enlightenment experience'. I think it can bring important understanding to the subject of enlightenment and what knowing the Self actually is.
I copied Sri Ramana's text of what happened to him from the board in the New Hall next to the Mother's Shrine.

I felt I was going to die and that I had to solve the problem myself, there and then. The shock of the fear of death drove my mind inwards and I said to myself mentally without forming the words: Now death has come, what does it mean? What is it that is dying? This body dies. And I at once dramatised the occurrence of death. I lay with my limbs stretched out still as though rigor mortis had set in and imitated a corpse so as to give greater reality to the enquiry. I held my breath and kept my lips tightly closed so that no sound could escape so that neither the word 'I' nor any other word could be uttered. 'Well then,' I said to myself, 'the body is dead. It will be carried stiff to the burning ground and there reduced to ashes. But with the death of the body am I dead? Is the body "I"? It is silent and inert but I could feel the full force of my personality and even the voice of the "I" within me, apart from it. So I am spirit transcending the body. The body dies but the spirit that transcends it cannot be touched by death. That means that I am the deathless spirit.' All this was not a dull thought. It flashed through me vividly as living truth which I perceived directly, almost without thought process. 'I' was something very real, the only real thing about my present state, and all the conscious activity connected with my body was centered on that 'I'. From that moment onwards the 'I' or 'Self' focused attention on itself by a powerful fascination. Fear of death had vanished once and for all. Absorption in the Self continued unbroken from that time on. Other thoughts might come and go like the various notes of music but the 'I' continued like the fundamental *sruti* note that underlies and blends with all other states. Whether the body was engaged

in talking, reading, or anything else I was still centered on the 'I'. Previous to that crisis I had felt no perceptible or direct interest in it, much less any inclination to dwell permanently in it.

First, this is a typical Self-experience. Let's not pretend that it is very rare. It happens somewhere to someone every day. There is now a vast literature of these kinds of experiences.

The first thing one notices is the statement, '**The shock of the fear of death drove my mind inwards.**' The mind previously was facing the world. Now it is looking inwards. Spiritual literature is forever reminding us that the Truth dwells within.

Next we have Sri Ramana's reaction to the experience. This to me is an important aspect because it reveals the nature of Sri Ramana's mind very clearly. Ordinarily when we have intense experiences involving great pleasure or great pain our emotions take over and cloud our appreciation of the experience. We either get so frightened we can't report what happened accurately or we get so ecstatic we can't report what happen accurately. But Sri Ramana stayed cool as a cucumber. He says, '**Now death has come, what does it mean? What is it that is dying? This body dies.**'

Vedanta (*Vedic* philosophy) is concerned with meaning. Here you have it. Here you have an inquiring mind, one not fascinated by the experience, one seeking to understand the experience. Although perhaps the majority of the people coming through Tiruvannamalai are experience-happy, there are quite a few who have this kind of mind to some degree. They want to know. But very few have it to the degree that Sri Ramana did. This shows that he was a *jnani* (one who has realised the Self), a lover of knowledge. And using logic he draws the right conclusion, '**This body dies.**' Already we can see by implication that he knows he is other than the body. He has completely objectified it. Then he does quite an interesting thing, he dramatises it '**to give greater reality to the enquiry**'. The rest of his musings up to '**it is silent and inert**' are just further confirmation of his understanding that he is not the body.

Then we come to the realisation of the Self. This is the positive side, what happens when the world is negated. He says, '**… but I could feel the full force of my personality and even the voice of the "I" within me, apart from it.**' The word 'personality' is quite interesting. I don't know if this was an accurate translation of Sri Ramana's words. But what he probably meant was the *jivatman*, the Self embodied as an individual. I'm sorry to use these fancy Sanskrit terms but there is simply no English equivalent. The Self is unembodied, but it is capable of embodiment. It is called *jivatman*. Okay, we can call it the soul or the person but it's not quite right because it throws up too many imprecise associations.

So now he is aware of the dead body and the subtle body – what is called the personality – and '**… even the voice of the "I" within me, apart from it.**' You see the whole structure of the inner world. Then he concludes correctly, '**So I am spirit transcending the body.**' He has answered the 'Who am I?' question, which, up to this point, he had never even considered.

And then the icing on the cake; he describes *jnanam*, Self-knowledge. '**All this was not a dull thought. It flashed through me vividly as living truth which I perceived directly, almost without thought process.**'

When you have any experience the knowledge of that experience arises in the mind. This knowledge needs to be grasped, owned, if you will. In this case (as the Self) he witnessed the knowledge: '**It flashed through me vividly as living truth …**'

So how does this relate to liberation?

Many people have these kinds of experiences but do not realise that they are '**spirit transcending body**'. It is this knowledge that is called liberation. Why is it liberation? Because thinking you are the body is a huge problem. It makes the world and everything in it seem to be real. But to the Self the world appears as a kind of dream, so all the experiences you have in it cannot bind you. In the next statement he addresses this issue of what is real. He says, '**"I" was something very real, the only real thing about my present state, and all the conscious**

activity connected with my body was centered on that "I".' This is knowledge. The 'I' is real. The body-mind entity isn't.

Surely, if it is the Self it has to be real, doesn't it?

That's a good point. There is a statement in *Vedanta* that says, *Brahma satyam, jagan mithya*. It means the limitless Self is real, the world (read body-mind) is apparently real. Real is defined in spiritual science as what never changes, what lasts forever. So experience and the body don't fit that definition. But experience isn't actually unreal either. It has a peculiar status, neither completely real, nor completely unreal. There is a famous *Vedantic* text, the *Vacarambana Sruti*, that explains how it is. I won't digress into it because we are just getting to the meat of Sri Ramana's experience.

There is one more thing to understand here and that is that Sri Ramana is not quite through with the process he's experiencing. He is at the intermediate stage. Before this experience came and he realised he was the Self he thought that the body was real. But this experience has shown him that with reference to the Self the body is not real. It is important that he completely negate his belief in the reality of the body. So he has to say that it isn't real. Then later, when the knowledge that he is the Self is completely firm, he can take the body back as real because it is non-separate from him. The only actual problem with the body is the belief that it is an independent entity and that the 'I' depends on it. But Sri Ramana realised that the 'I' was free of the body. He says, and this is very important, '... **all the conscious activity connected with my body was centered on that "I".'**

People who are ignorant that they are the immortal Self, what you would call materialists, believe that the 'I' is centered on the body, that it is the body that gives life to the 'I'. But scripture and direct experience reveal that the body is centered on the 'I'. In other words the 'I' is the living principle and the body is just matter. Sri Ramana realised that fact.

Now the next statement is very difficult to understand. In a way, we would have been a lot happier if Sri Ramana had just packed up his meditation carpet and stole silently away into the night. He's the Self and he knows it. Shouldn't that be the end? But as usual life always has another surprise in store. He says, '**From that moment onwards the "I" or "Self" focused attention on itself by a powerful fascination.**'

Which 'I' did what? If I'm the 'I', the one without a second, how do we get two 'I's here? Has Sri Ramana lost his realisation? How can the Self be fascinated with anything? It would only be fascinated if it felt there was something to experience or know. But we know that it is whole and complete, lacking nothing, so why is it acting as if it weren't? Furthermore, if it is Self-aware it is already 'focused' on itself.

This experience was not the end. In fact it was just the beginning of Sri Ramana's spiritual journey. He has just become Self-realised but he has not become enlightened if we take these words at face value.

What do you mean by that?

The last paragraph shows us clearly that he thinks of the Self as an object and he sees himself as separate from it. He is experiencing it, no doubt – it would remain as a 'permanent experience' – but he has yet to see himself solely as the nondual Self. He does. He gets there. We don't know when, probably sometime during his meditation phase when he was living in the caves, but he gains the last little bit of knowledge.

How do you know that he doesn't yet see himself as the nondual Self?

The language. Let's take the language at face value. Sri Ramana was a very straightforward person. He says, '**Absorption in the Self continued unbroken from that time on.**' So the natural question is, 'Who is absorbed in what?' Was the Self absorbed in the Self or was Sri Ramana absorbed in the Self? We understand what he means a couple of sentences later when he says, '**… I was still centered on the "I"**.' And one gets the impression that the first 'I' was different from the second. This is a statement of the Self-realisation phase of the spiritual journey. If there was no duality left, why doesn't he just say, 'I, the Self, was centered on myself.' This is how it is in nonduality, not that the Self is centered on anything. I is self-knowing by nature and requires no centering.

What do you mean when you say that the Self is not centered on anything?

It is very perceptive to pick up on what seems to be a contradiction. This is a crucial point for understanding enlightenment. Think of it this way. The Self is like an uncreated light bulb that is so huge that it can contain trillions of universes millions the times the size of the one we live in. All these universes would not even add up to a tiny fly speck compared to the Self. And this light bulb is not connected to any source of electricity. When we see a light we know that it is drawing electricity from an electricity grid. But the Self requires no external source of power. It effortlessly generates the light to shine forever solely from within itself. It knows itself by itself. And this Self is the Self of every living being. So when you realise that you are the Self, it is not Sri Ramana realising the Self, it is the Self realising the Self.

The ignorance that formerly covered the Self's appreciation of itself disappeared when the Self as Sri Ramana made the enquiry and there was no one there to be centered on anything. This is why enlightenment is not experiential, not a special experience for an ego, a 'small' self. The experiencer is cancelled when the Self realises its nature. And from this point on there is no duality. The Self is self-experiencing, self-knowing. In this statement he says, '**Absorption in the Self continued unbroken from that time on.**' It is entirely possible that Sri Ramana was unable to formulate this in words properly, and it is even more likely that the person who recorded his words and/or translated them did not understand this self-experiencing, self-knowing fact about the Self and therefore formulated his enlightenment in the language of experience from the conventional human point of view.

We do not know. But because he was so young and this was his first experience 'of' the Self and his knowledge that he was the Self was firm, this statement seems to be about the Self-realisation phase of the spiritual journey. It ends, as I mentioned, when the final subject-object duality disappears. Then if you speak of it you can only speak of it by illustration. You cannot formulate it directly, except to say that the Self is self-knowing, self-revealing, self-luminous, self-realised. There is no other Self to realise the Self because reality is nondual and there is only one Self.

So what is the next phase? How does it happen?

You keep watching the Self. You stay alert, which is not hard because the Self is very beautiful. And the more you watch it the more it sets you to thinking. It fits in with the Self-enquiry that Sri Ramana taught, which was based on his own experience and backed by scripture. One of the definitions of Self-enquiry that Sri Ramana gives in another text is '**Holding the mind on the Self is enquiry.**' So here he is, a young boy of sixteen who didn't have a clue about the Self, with his mind fixed permanently on the Self. You become fascinated. The words Sri Ramana uses are '**a powerful fascination**'. When you're in this phase you need a cave, or something like it. You do not want to be in the world. If you stay in the world there is a danger that your connection might be broken.

You fall in love. When you are in love you do not stop thinking. One thing that we need to point out here is very important. You know how I have been saying that this belief that the mind has to stop completely is not true, that it does happen but it need not happen, that having a dead mind can be a big problem?

Yes.

Well, it's clear by Sri Ramana's own admission that his mind had not stopped completely. He says, '**Other thoughts might come and go like the various notes of music …**' This 'state' he is 'in' is *savikalpa samadhi*, to use the *Yogic* term. It is a state of clear seeing in which *vikalpas*, thoughts, arise and fall. But the thoughts do not obscure your vision of the Self. This is very important. Sri Ramana says so.

Anyway, where was I? Yes … love. You fall in love. When you are in love you do not stop thinking. On the contrary, you think more, you want to know what your beloved is, what he or she is doing. This thinking is enquiry. Sri Ramana already had the knowledge from his experience to guide him in his enquiry. He knew about himself and the 'I' beyond the body.

You are getting it all straight about who you are and what your relationship is to this beautiful being. And then one day something happens. We cannot say when. It just happens if you stay focused on the beloved. There is an 'Aha!' and at that moment the you that was looking at the Self 'becomes' the Self. There is actually no becoming. You were it all along. The 'becoming' is a recognition, a knowing. But the 'becoming' changes your perspective. You are no longer the individual looking in at the Self, awareness, you are awareness looking out at the individual. And what do you know? That awareness and the individual are one. Or in the words of the scripture, *Tat Tvam Asi*, That (Self) you are. Formulated from the Self's perspective the words are *Aham Brahmasmi*, I am limitless. Sri Ramana the form is limited. Sri Ramana the Self is unlimited.

This is what *Vedanta* calls enlightenment. From that point on you do not abide 'in' the Self you abide 'as' the Self. You have only one nondual identity.

Thank you. That's a very important analysis that will help many people who are nearing the end of their spiritual journey.

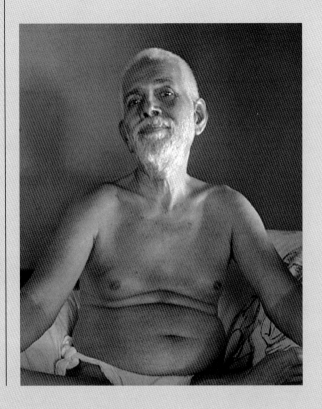

Enquiry in the form 'Who am I?'
alone is the principal means.
To make the mind subside, there
is no adequate means other than
Self-enquiry. If controlled by other
means, mind will remain as if
subsided, but will rise again.

Sri Ramana Maharshi

COMMENTARY

Above: Classic full Arunachala south face

Left: Sri Ramana with children

Below: Temple cart
Ramana Ashram peacock

Right centre: Celebration in the New Hall

Right bottom: Sri Ramana with rabbit and visitors in Old Hall about 1930

CHAPTER 6

Commentary on Sri Ramana's Teachings 'Who Am I?' (Nan Yar) from a Vedanta point of view

*James Swartz in dialogue
with Premananda*

[Sri Ramana's direct words are in bold]

James begins by introducing us to **Vedanta.** *He points out that Sri Ramana had respect for the* **Yoga** *and* **Vedanta** *traditions even though he wasn't a traditional teacher. James explains that as we are not able to remove the world, what is meant by removal is the removal of our ignorance. Our beliefs have to go, not our mind. He points out that Sri Ramana knew he was the Self, hence his realisation. There was no duality in his understanding of himself.*

James, I would like to ask you to comment, from a Vedanta *point of view, on Sri Ramana's teachings as he wrote them in the booklet* Who Am I? *Could you explain a little about* Vedanta *to begin?*

The portion of the *Vedas* that reveals the knowledge of consciousness, your innermost Self, is called *Vedanta*. '*Veda*' means knowledge and '*anta*' means end. Exoterically it refers to the texts at the end of each *Veda* that deal with the topic of Self-knowledge. Esoterically it refers to Self-knowledge. It is 'the knowledge that ends the search for knowledge'. Or, it is 'that, knowing which everything else is as good as known'. This means that if you think you are small and limited and incomplete and are chasing security or pleasure or fame or power – or anything else for that matter – because you think they will make you happy, you need to know that you are already whole and complete. If you know this fact you will no longer look for happiness in objects. You will live happily with whatever objects you have.

So how does *Vedanta* work? It does not promise to give you an experience of the Self because whatever you are experiencing at any time is the Self. The Self is just your being, your existence. It is not meant to prove that you exist either. Awareness projects all objects, gross and subtle. There is nothing other than it to objectify it. Everything shines in its light but nothing shines light on it. No proof is required to establish its existence. If you need someone or something to establish the fact that you exist, you need a psychiatrist, not *Vedanta*, the Science of Self-Enquiry.

If you investigate your being along the lines established by the Science of Self-Enquiry you will see very clearly that you are limitless, not separate from anything, and eternal. But because most of us are so busy trying to make life work we forget to ask who the 'us' is. In the process we pick up all sorts of strange notions that cover up our core identity. A list of these notions would fill volumes.

Knowledge is nothing but the removal of ignorance. Although the basic methodology of *Vedanta* is the same as it has always been, it has developed over the centuries into a very sophisticated body of teachings that strip away Self-ignorance. Every time one of its truths is revealed you say, 'I already knew that' because it brought to light something that was there in you but which you had overlooked for some reason.

The Science of Self-Enquiry expands your mind, lifts it up and gives it the big picture. When you discover just how consciously the creation is structured, how the *karma* (result of all actions) machine works, how ignorance works, how the body and mind function, how it all relates to the Self and how you can transform your life with knowledge, you can no longer hold on to your small ideas about who you are and the nature of reality.

For it to work you need to accept the following logic. I want lasting happiness. Lasting happiness is freedom from dependence on objects. I cannot get it through the pursuit of objects. I cannot get it through spiritual practice because practice produces limited results. Knowledge is the only other option. For knowledge I need a means. *Vedanta* is a proven means. Therefore, if I want help I should expose my mind to the teachings.

Vedanta actually works in a very dynamic and practical way to remove the student's ignorance about who he or she is. And very often enlightenment happens right in the classroom as the teacher is unfolding the teachings. This is possible because *Vedanta* says that as the Self you are already enlightened and that all that prevents you from knowing it are the erroneous notions you have about yourself and the world. So assuming you want to be free of your limiting views you expose yourself to the teaching and let it remove your ignorance.

What about this idea that Sri Ramana taught in silence, that all you had to do was to sit in his presence and the silence would enlighten you?

I suppose that if you were completely qualified, absolutely ready to pop, you could just sit in the presence of someone like Sri Ramana and maybe figure out that you are whole and complete limitless awareness. But this is highly unlikely. Usually people who are highly qualified only have one or two very subtle doubts separating themselves from *jnanam*, Self-knowledge. And usually they already know the answer, they just don't have one hundred percent confidence in it. Experientially they have everything they need and all that is missing is the knowledge of who they actually are. So when they offer their ignorance to a sage like Sri Ramana, who is an authority and for whom they have respect and devotion, he can, with a few very well chosen words, remove their ignorance. Sometimes the person puts the question and gives the answer and the teacher just nods, and that is it. Or sometimes the teacher just asks a question in response to the student's statement and the student understands, without giving a verbal answer.

So you're saying that words are better than silence?

Not better than but at least as good. A thing and its opposite may both be true and useful. There is a kind of romantic myth about silence that does not really serve people spiritually. People are tired of words and they want relief and this is understandable but if you are already enlightened and don't know it, then silence is not going to help. Silence will not remove your ignorance.

What do you mean by that?

Silence is not opposed to ignorance. It can exist side by side with it quite nicely. But knowledge is opposed to ignorance and it will destroy it. You start out thinking you're limited but the fact is that you are not limited. It may be that in silence you will realise it but it wasn't the silence that made you realise it, it was the fact that you were doing some kind of enquiry, looking into the nature of the silence and seeing that it was you. This seeing is *jnanam*, knowledge. You find people who spend years sitting in silence alone or in the presence of a mahatma and nothing happens. Sure, you can argue that they are not ready to get it but if they were able to formulate their doubt and express it to a *jnani* (one who has realised the Self) they might have it removed in a second. So the right words spoken by the right person at the right time can be just as effective as silence.

Sri Ramana wasn't a traditional teacher but he had a great respect for the teaching tradition. Let me give you a little background for his statements. There are two great traditions under the umbrella of *Sanatana Dharma*, the *Vedic* culture: *Yoga* and *Vedanta*, the Science of Self-Enquiry. *Yoga* deals with the experiential side *(karma)* of spiritual life and is actually meant for the purpose of purifying the mind. It is not a valid means of Self-knowledge because its stated aim is a particular type of experience called *samadhi* (immersed in the Self). *Yogis* do sometimes attain enlightenment, not directly through their practice of *Yoga* but because they develop curiosity about consciousness, the Self, as a result of the subtle experiences that their practices generate. They may intuitively draw the correct conclusion about the Self and their identity as consciousness during one of their *samadhis* – like Sri Ramana did during his 'death' experience (see Chapter 5) – or by reflecting on their experiences over a period of time.

Many people have epiphanies similar to Sri Ramana's. I've heard hundreds of such stories. But almost no one becomes enlightened during a particular experience (although it may feel like that) because the meaning of the experience or the significance of the one to whom the experience is occurring is not assimilated. The hard and fast understanding that 'I am the Self' needs to come out of Self-experience to set you free. You need to come away from the experience with the clear understanding that you are whole and complete limitless awareness.

Vedanta acknowledges the importance of experience but deals with 'meaning'. Any experience is only useful spiritually if it shows you that you are whole and complete limitless awareness. If the experience leaves you incomplete and separate, craving another Self-experience, what use is it?

The knowledge that the 'I' is actionless awareness, as Sri Ramana says, is called *Vedanta*, the knowledge that erases one's ignorance. What is that ignorance? The belief that the 'I' is limited, inadequate, and incomplete, the belief in oneself as a doer.

So chasing experience isn't the way to go? You're saying that you should be looking for knowledge?

Yes, absolutely. It is quite rare to have a single experience like Sri Ramana and come away with the firm knowledge that 'I am the Self'; a one-in-a-million chance. He was either exceptional or lucky, although there really isn't any particular advantage to waking up at a young age. He may have been graced but this does not mean that his enlightenment was exceptional. He certainly didn't behave as if it were. Enlightenment is just enlightenment and over time countless people have attained enlightenment in many unusual circumstances. When you realise that you are the Self it destroys your sense of being special or unique.

The joke is that enlightenment is not an experience, nor is there any permanent experience. Furthermore, to make an experience permanent one would have to be a doer, an agent acting on the experience, maintaining it or controlling it or staying in it – which is a dualistic state, not enlightenment.

The idea that enlightenment is not a particular experience is quite revolutionary, isn't it?

It is and it isn't. People are experience oriented because they feel they need to get something. After years of picking up various experiences along the way they get totally conditioned to seeing everything in terms of experience, how they feel about things. But experience is limited. And very dumb. It does not teach them anything. It can't teach them anything unless they are out to learn something. So when they start to get disillusioned with experience and turn within to seek the Self they naturally continue seeking in terms of experience.

But a few rare people understand that seeking experience, particularly the experience of enlightenment, is not the way to go. In the old days many more people sought understanding, perhaps because of the nature of society, who knows? The reason Sri Ramana emphasises Self-enquiry is because the problem is ignorance. Experience does not remove ignorance. It is motivated by ignorance. Only knowledge removes ignorance. And you get knowledge by making an enquiry or by being taught. Everybody starts out chasing experience but the clever ones switch off it at some point and head for knowledge.

So how would you express that knowledge?

The negative way to express Self-realisation is 'I am not the doer. I am not the enjoyer.' In Sri Ramana's case he realised 'I am not the body' because he found himself to be quite aware even as the body lay on the floor 'dead'. 'I am not the body' is the equivalent of 'I am not the doer' because the body is the doer. Sri Ramana was called a *jnani* because he gained knowledge of who he was during the experience. The experience finished after some time but the knowledge of who he was remained permanently. It was there operating in the background regardless of what experience he was having. At the end of his life he must have been experiencing serious pain, but his Self-knowledge was unaffected. And he was unaffected because he was the Self. But the body-mind complex suffered.

If you know the real spiritual India you will understand that while enlightenment is rare with reference to the total number of people on the planet, there are tens of thousands of 'fully' enlightenened people worldwide, and particularly in India. I've lived here many years and was introduced to the highest levels of Indian spirituality when I was quite young and I've lived with a number of enlightened people of the same caliber as Sri Ramana.

That sounds like heresy and contradicts the conventional wisdom.

Yes, I suppose it does. But conventional wisdom is often wrong. It is rare but not as rare as it is made out to be. One source of ignorance accounting for this belief is the ego's lack of spiritual self-confidence. It always resists the truth and in fact often does everything it can to sabotage one's efforts to attain it. So to keep it from doing the work, it imagines that only supermen are capable of it.

Sri Ramana seems to be more of a jnani *than a* Yogi.

Sri Ramana's teachings can be confusing if one does not understand the difference between *Yoga* and *Vedanta* because he used both languages when he was speaking. The language of *Yoga* is well-known and most people who came to him were not qualified for enlightenment so he used that language. If you are not qualified it does no good to try to enlighten someone with either words or silence because they are simply incapable of getting it. So what Sri Ramana did was to encourage them to purify themselves by following a path which typically involved some sort of *Yogic* discipline and surrender to God.

What do you mean by 'qualified for enlightenment'?

Many Western people have no idea what *sadhana* (spiritual practice) is. They actually think that they can just get a ticket to India and get on the spiritual circuit and attend a *Satsang* (meeting in Truth) or two and they will get 'awakened'. They may have some experiences but if they get 'awakened' they will certainly fall back to sleep, usually because there is no *sadhana* in place. And there are gurus who themselves did *sadhana* but are loath to insist that their disciples do it – for fear of losing them, I suppose. You see many people who have been to Ramesh Balsekar coming through Tiruvannamalai and what they seem to have got is the idea that they are not 'doers'. So their *sadhana* is 'no *sadhana*'. Why? Because they have been told there is nothing you can do because your enlightenment is not up to you. It's all up to 'grace'. I'm not sure why the resolve to do vigorous *sadhana* is not the grace of God, but there you are.

It's true that you are not a doer, but the you that is not a doer is the Self. The ego doesn't become a non-doer by trying not to 'do' anything. This sort of teaching is very misleading because it is tailor-made for the ego.

Sri Ramana is completely in line with traditional *Vedanta* on this issue of *sadhana*. Purification is at least as important as knowledge, perhaps more so, because without a clear mind, you will not get knowledge, *jnanam*. This idea does not sit well with people nowadays. They want it handed to them on a platter. This accounts for the popularity of the *shaktipat* (spiritual energy transmitted from guru to student) gurus like Amachi, and the miracle makers like Sai Baba. Around them you have a whole class of people who actually believe that the guru is doing the work for them!

But Sri Ramana didn't do sadhana *to get enlightenment.*

That's true, but he certainly did *sadhana* after it. Knowing who he was, he need not have sat in meditation in caves for many years; he could have gone home and eaten his mum's *iddlys* (rice cakes) and played cricket. It was all the same to him. But he didn't. He decided to purify his mind. The glory of Sri Ramana is not his enlightenment. It was just the same as every other enlightenment that's ever been. His glory was his pure mind. He polished his mind to such a degree that it was particularly radiant, a great blessing to himself and everyone whom he contacted. That kind of mind you only get through serious *sadhana*, or *Yoga*, if you will. These modern gurus, particularly the so-called crazy wisdom gurus who seem to revel in gross mind, refuse to encourage people to develop themselves because they do not understand the tremendous pleasure that comes from a pure mind.

Who Am I? (Nan Yar) *is a small booklet containing the core teachings of Sri Ramana. See Chapter 4 for the complete original text. The numbers of the original questions are written in brackets. James, I would like to ask you to comment on these teachings.*

Who am I? [Q1]

Sri Ramana answers with a typical *Vedantic* teaching, called the *pancha kosas* or the five sheaths. This teaching is found in the *Upanishads*. He negates the five sheaths (erroneous notions about one's Self).

If I am none of these, then who am I? [Q2]
He replies **'After negating all of the above-mentioned as "not this", "not this", that Awarness which alone remains – that I am.'**

What is the nature of Awareness? [Q3]
'The nature of Awareness is Existence-Consciousness-Bliss.'

When will the realisation of the Self be gained? [Q4]
'When the world which is what-is-seen has been removed, there will be realisation of the Self which is the seer.'

The question *'When will the realisation of the Self be gained?'* is a *Yogic* type of thought. *Yoga* is for doers, achievers. He or she believes the Self is something that is not available all the time, something to be gained. It is natural to want what you do not have if you think it will benefit you in some way. One of the meanings of the word *Yoga* is 'to obtain'. Obviously you can only obtain something you do not already possess.

Vedanta, the Science of Self-Enquiry, contends that the Self cannot be gained at some time in the future as a result of action. It is called the path of understanding and it employs a language of identity. For example, it says, 'You are consciousness.' It says that the Self cannot be gained because you are the Self already. If there is anything to gain it will be Self-knowledge, and Self-knowledge is only a loss of ignorance because you actually do know who you are.

This teaching is called the discrimination between the subject (the seer), and the objects (the seen). It establishes the understanding that what you 'see' meaning experience – including all mystic experiences – is 'not Self', and the one who sees them is you, the Self. He says that you will realise who you are, meaning understand that you are the Self, when you have separated you from your experience.

Sri Ramana's response is completely in harmony with traditional *Vedanta* – the *Upanishads*, *Bhagavad Gita*, and *Shankara's Drk-Drksha Viveka*, for example. Sri Ramana had the greatest respect for the knowledge enshrined in *Vedanta*. Contrary to the popular notion, he was very scripturally astute. He even wrote a scripture that has been granted the status of an *Upanishad* by the traditional *Vedanta* community, a great honour.

One thing I admire about Sri Ramana is his refusal, unlike many of the modern teachers, to cook up a fancy personal teaching on the subject of Self-realisation. His statements were in harmony with the scriptures on either *Yoga* or *Vedanta*. Even though Sri Ramana died a half century ago he was a very 'modern' sage if you consider the fact that the *Vedic* spiritual tradition is thousands of years old.

Why did he refuse to do so? Because no fancy, modern teaching is required. The whole 'what is enlightenment and how to attain enlightenment' business was worked out a long time ago. Enlightenment is a very simple understanding of the Self and its relationship to experience, the ego-experiencer and the forms the ego experiences. In a nutshell it is the understanding that while the forms depend on the Self, the Self does not depend on the forms. This freedom from experience is called *moksha*, liberation. This wisdom had been clearly stated long before Sri Ramana came on the scene and needs no interpretation or new terminology.

Sri Ramana probably knows that the question 'When will the realisation of the Self be gained?' is actually imprecise and that the person who is asking it will not understand if he attacks the question, so he takes it at face value and puts it in a traditional way. You have a copy of the booklet. Can you refresh my memory about how he answers?

He says, '**When the world which is what-is-seen has been removed, there will be realisation of the Self, which is the seer.**'

This statement is pure *Vedanta*. The operative words are, '**has been removed**'. How is one supposed to understand the words '**has been removed**'? What kind of removal is it? Is it the *Yogic* view that complete destruction of the unconscious tendencies, *vasanas*, allows you to 'gain' the 'Self'? Or is it the *Vedantic* view – removal of the notion that the world is separate from the Self?

In Sri Ramana's teachings you will find both ideas. The first is called the *vasana kshaya* theory of enlightenment by *Vedanta* and *manonasha* by *Yoga*. The word 'world' is actually a psychological term in *Yoga*. It does not mean the physical world. The physical world – in so far as it is physical – is the Self. No individual created it and no individual is going to remove it. But the 'world' that Sri Ramana says has to be removed consists of the psychological projections that make up our personal 'worlds', that is, ignorance. These projections are based on an incorrect understanding of the Self, on a belief that the Self is separate, inadequate or incomplete.

Sri Ramana's teaching, which is *Upanishadic* teaching, is called *vichara*, enquiry. The purpose of enquiry is knowledge, not the 'physical' removal of the mind. If he had been teaching *Yoga* as a means of liberation he would not have encouraged enquiry because *Yoga* is committed to the experience of *samadhi*, not to understanding that one is the Self.

This is interesting. I never heard it stated this way before.

Well, it isn't really revolutionary. People read into Sri Ramana whatever fits with their beliefs. So from that point of view it may seem controversial. But if you know the tradition from which Sri Ramana comes this statement is pure *Vedanta*. *Yoga* is very popular and it always has been. I started out as a meatball businessman practising *Hatha Yoga* for muscles, and I worked my way up to some very high *samadhis* through meditation. Then I realised that the Self wasn't a state and with a bit of luck a guru came into my life and sorted me out. Mind you, I'm not attacking *Yoga*. *Yoga*, purification through *sadhana*, is essential for enlightenment but it is an indirect means.

But I thought the goal of the practices was sahaja samadhi.

This is what the *Yogis* say but it is only a means to liberation. Liberation is freedom from experience and *samadhi* is an experience. Contrary to conventional wisdom, the *samadhis* are not the final goal. *Sama* means equal and *dhi* is a contracted form of *buddhi*, intellect. So it means a mind that values everything equally. *Sahaja* just means 'continuous' and 'natural' so it is a mind that has continuous nondual vision. Perhaps you can gain this kind of mind by the long and difficult practice of *Astanga Yoga*. But why go to all this trouble when you actually have this *samadhi* naturally all the time without doing a lick of work?

Oh, how is that?

As the Self. This vision is not continuous because the Self is out of time, but it is natural to the Self. It is your nature.

Anyway, no *samadhi* is equivalent to enlightenment because *samadhis* are only states of mind or no mind, no mind being a state of mind. *Nirvikalpa samadhi* (highest transcendent state of consciousness) is nondual but unfortunately it is a state that can easily be destroyed. And there is no individual there in that state. So when it ends, ignorance about the nature of the Self is not removed and a sense of limitation is experienced once more.

Samadhi helps to purify the mind by burning subconscious tendencies and is a great aid to enquiry, but if you remove the mind how will you make an enquiry? Who will make an enquiry? You make an enquiry with the mind for the mind, so it can shed its ignorance and no longer trouble you. The mind is a very useful God-given instrument. Would God have given a mind if He had intended for you to destroy it? And, in fact, *Yoga* isn't about killing the mind either because how will you experience a *samadhi* if you don't have a mind? The mind is the instrument of experience.

If you argue that you are aiming at *nirvikalpa samadhi* where there is no mind, fine, but the problem with *nirvikalpa samadhi* is that a fly landing on your nose can bring you out of it, not that there is anyone there to come 'out'. And when the 'you' who wasn't there does 'come back', as I just mentioned, you are just as Self-ignorant as you were before because you were not there in the *samadhi* to understand that you are the *samadhi*. If you are the *samadhi* you will have it all the time because you have you all the time. Therefore, there will be no anxiety about making it continuous or permanent.

Okay. You're saying that samadhi *is not the goal, that it is just the means?*

Yes. Not 'the' means, 'a' means. There are other ways to purify the mind. Misunderstanding this teaching is perhaps responsible for more despair, confusion, and downright frustration than any other. It is commonly believed that this 'removal' means that all the *vasanas* (tendencies of the mind) need to be physically eradicated for enlightenment to happen. And many people believe that Sri Ramana had 'achieved' that state.

If you study Sri Ramana's life you will see that by and large he was a very regular guy – a large part of his appeal – head in the clouds, feet firmly planted on the earth. He walked, talked, cooked, read and listened to the radio. I love the story of him returning to the ashram at one in the afternoon to see a sign saying the ashram was closed from noon till two. So he sat down outside and waited for it to open. If he did not have a mind, who or what was doing all these things? No *vasanas* means no mind because the *vasanas* are the cause of the mind. How did he go about the business of life? So I think we need to look at the word 'removal' in a different way.

Sri Ramana was called a *jnani*, a knower of the Self, because he had removed the idea of himself as a doer – it is called *sarva karma sannyasa* – which happens when you realise you are the Self. Or you realise you are the Self when you realise you are not the doer. 'Not the doer' means the Self. It doesn't mean that the ego becomes a non-doer. The ego is always a doer. As the Self he understood that while the few non-binding *vasanas* he had left (which are not a problem even for a worldly person) were dependent on him, he was not dependent on them. So for him, as the Self, they were non-binding. How can a thought or a feeling affect the Self? For a person who thinks he or she is the doer, allowing the *vasanas* to express or not is not an option. Actions happen uncontrollably because the ego is pressurised to act in a certain way by the *vasanas*. For a *jnani*, *vasanas* are elective, for a normal person they are compulsory.

So the 'removal' that Sri Ramana talks about is only in terms of knowledge. He often uses another metaphor which he borrowed from *Vedanta*, the snake and the rope. In the twilight a weary, thirsty traveller mistook the well rope attached to a bucket for a snake and recoiled in fear. When he got his bearings and his fear subsided he realised that the snake was actually only the rope. There was no reason to take a stick and beat the snake to death (which is equivalent to trying to destroy the mind) because the snake was only a misperception. When he calmed down and regained his wits (did some enquiry) he enquired into the snake and realised that it was just a rope. And in that realisation the snake was 'removed'.

My understanding is that when he said 'When the world which is what-is-seen has been removed ...' *he meant the removal of all the attachments to the conditioned mind.*

How would that come about?

In his ashram his disciples would sit doing nothing for years. His own attendant, Annamalai Swami (see Chapter 3), spent ten to fifteen years in daily contact with Sri Ramana and every minute when they were not working, they would be sitting quietly. Then, one day Sri Ramana said to Annamalai Swami, 'Now, you stop working and you go away and sit quietly.' He then sat for fifty years in his room never again setting foot in Ramana Ashram. Sri Ramana himself sat for almost fifteen years in Virupaksha Cave, with very few people around. So it involved a lot of sitting, presumably witnessing whatever thoughts were coming up.

Well, sitting doing nothing is doing something. And you can get very attached to a meditation lifestyle. You can get attached to anything, even *sannyasins* (renunciates) get attached to their sticks and begging bowls. But yes, this idea is completely in line with traditional *Vedantic sadhana.* The texts support it. First you get the mind quiet and then you are capable of realising that you are the Self. There is no better way to get the mind quiet than staying in close proximity to a person like Sri Ramana whose mind was exceptionally quiet. It sets the tone and the disciple's mind becomes like it. The longer you do apparently nothing, the more you realise that you don't have to do anything to be what you are. So this practice gradually kills off the doer.

One of the misconceptions people have about *Vedanta* is that the talk somehow obscures the silence and therefore the words are just 'intellectual' and therefore of no use spiritually. But this is not true. My guru, Swami Chinmaya, was a famous *Vedanta* master who had many enlightened disciples and he spoke incessantly. But the words were all coming out of the silence, the Self, and pointed the person's mind at the Self. Words and silence are not necessarily opposed. Sri Ramana had a mind. He spoke. He used it efficiently all his life.

Yes.

So, he wasn't removing *vasanas*.

Perhaps he was removing the attachment to them? He must have had a pull to go back to his family. He didn't do that and when his mother first came he sent her away. He wasn't caught up in that anymore.

That was because he understood he was the Self. The way you lose attachment in one go is to understand you are the Self.

It is often called 'a constant experience'.

Sure, but the Self is 'constant experience' anyway. Or put it this way, if this is a nondual reality and this reality is the Self then each and every experience is the Self. So nobody is short of Self-experience, the ignorant and the enlightened alike. The problem is that very few people understand that everything is the Self. So they seek for all these incredible 'Self' experiences.

The Self is a constant experience?

No, the Self is constant experience, if there is such a thing. In fact 'constant experience' is a contradiction. The Self becomes experience but it does not sacrifice it's nature as a non-doing, non-experiencing witness to do it. That means you actually are free of your experiences. Let's put it a better way: experience is the Self but the Self is not experience.

When one says 'constant experience' would that mean remembering the Self constantly?

Yes, remembrance is helpful, up to a point. But you can never make remembrance constant. Knowledge is constant. When knowledge takes place, that's it. Remembering is a kind of mental activity that implies forgetting. Once you know you are the Self there is nothing to remember any more. How can you remember what you are? You are the one who is doing the remembering. You are prior to the act of remembrance. You cannot forget because you are always present. If you were somewhere else you could forget.

> *Will there not be realisation of the Self even while the world is there (taken as real)?* [Q5]
> **'There will not be.'**

What is meant by, '... the world is "there"?' Where is 'there'? And what is 'the world'? Doesn't it mean that if you believe that 'out there' is real then you cannot realise the Self at the same time?

I think that is what is meant. The words make it sound as if the world needs to be removed. But this is not likely, so what does 'world' mean? It means the belief that something in the world will make you happy or can take away your happiness. It is the belief that needs to be removed. That belief counts as Self-ignorance because the Self is unaffected by anything in your mind.

You can say it's an understanding of the true nature of the world.

Correct. *Vedanta* says you only need to know what the world is and what the Self is. Neither is the source of suffering if you know what they are. When I know that contact with the world will not produce lasting happiness, then I've had it with the world. There is no way it can burn me. It's a problem when I seem not to know that it is endlessly changing. Or put it this way – I want it to last, at least when things are going good, and I want it not to last when things are going badly. What is wrong with this picture?

Enlightenment does not mean that there are two kinds of happiness, one worldly and one spiritual. The small bits of happiness that I'm able to pick up in the world are actually only my own Self too. If I understand that happiness gained through the world will not last, I can certainly enjoy it for as long as it lasts. When it ends, it ends. I just say, 'Okay, party is over – great!'

Sri Ramana was a *jnani* because he removed his ignorance. I don't think he sat there all day trying to break his attachments, although he may have done some of that in the years immediately following his enlightenment when he was a cave dweller, although he doesn't mention it. I would think that because he was so young when he woke up his *vasanas* had not had a chance to get entrenched. And Indian culture was pretty pure in those days and he came from a decent family so he would not have had many deep negative attachments like sex and money and so on.

When Sri Ramana was a nineteen or twenty year old boy sitting for long hours in samadhi *in the temple he was taken care of, so the people there recognised him to some extent.*

That is pretty common in India when an incarnation appears. Indians have an innate appreciation of spiritual people.

Yes, so they could have felt something and so supported him. But how about him? Would he really have known what was happening to him? He had never read any spiritual books, never had a teacher.

That's a good question. He probably did know because there were all these mahatmas running about, role models if you will. So, he knew how they lived and he probably got lots of teaching from the *sadhus* (ascetics) who he came in contact with. You need to know that the Indian spiritual scene is a vast network, and word of someone's enlightenment gets around very fast. Many great men must have come to see him and speak with him, share with him certain things that would have been helpful to him. After all, he was sitting at the hub of one of India's most holy sites, Arunachala, which has been attracting mahatmas for thousands of years.

I stayed with a great mahatma in Kerala, Swami Abhedananda, who was a guru's guru. Many enlightened people came to see him and he would invite them up to his room and I'm sure that they got something very valuable. Many of the Westerners who come to India, even the ones who have been here a long time and who have only been associated with the 'export' gurus, often have peculiar notions about saints like Sri Ramana. They believe that he was a kind of lonely figure, the only one of his kind, head and shoulders above the crowd, lived in a cave like a hermit and sat in silence most of the time and didn't have a social life. Probably he was quite distant and emotionally reserved like most Tamil men, but he had love in spades and if you have love people come and give you what you need.

And then too you have to understand that his sense of himself being the Self never left him, so he wouldn't be that concerned about his emotional needs.

What I am getting at is how would he really have known that his experience was the Self and not something else? How would he have known that?

How do you know that you are Premananda rather than someone else?

I don't. I don't know that anymore. That's exactly my situation.

Do you know that you don't know that?

Yes, I know that whatever Premananda was doesn't work anymore for me. So I know that much.

Yes, that's what knowledge is: 'Premananda doesn't work for me anymore.' When you see the Self, you know what the Self is. Self-realisation is the recognition of a fact. There is no doubt involved in it. If you are stranded on a desert island deprived of human contact for fifty years and somebody rescues you and they ask you your name, you answer 'Premananda' immediately, even though you had never been asked for it for fifty years. That's knowledge.

Did Sri Ramana know the Self?

Yes, it seems he did. He may have thought of it as an object at first, which is natural. It's hard to tell. Perhaps the reason he sat in the caves alone was to erase whatever sense of duality there was left in his understanding, which would show remarkable maturity. But then this kind of enlightenment will only come to a very mature person regardless of his age. Usually, the Self appears first as an object and then, keeping the mind on the Self and repeatedly enquiring into it, the bedrock understanding eventually comes that one is the Self that one is enquiring into. This is certainly what he taught. And he taught it with authority based on personal experience.

The problem of language comes in here at this level. Sri Ramana uses the language of experience more than he does the language of identity. If you read that statement in the ashram describing Sri Ramana's enlightenment experience (see Chapter 5) you can get the sense that he knew he was it, perhaps a little vaguely in the beginning, but more clearly as time passed. Again it is very difficult to tell from the words.

It's probably not correct to say that he knew the Self. It is much more accurate to say he knew he was the Self. That is the meaning of the word Ramana.

That seems like a very subtle distinction.

It is, but there is a world of difference. To say you 'know the Self' means that you see the Self as an object, as something separate. To say that you 'are the Self' means that there is no duality in your experience or understanding of yourself.

When will the world which is the object seen be removed? [Q7]
'When the mind, which is the cause of all cognition and of all actions, becomes quiescent, the world will disappear.'

Now this is pure *Yoga*. *Vedanta*, on the other hand, says that when the world disappears, you do not disappear. For you to know that it has disappeared you have to be there. Seeing that you exist independently of the world is the purpose of this kind of experience. If the world disappears and you do not understand that you are the Self, then what is the point of having this experience?

When the world '**disappears**' the Self is revealed as it is and with it should come the knowledge that 'I am the Self'. From this point onward you do not need to experience the Self. You do not have to do anything to be the Self. The Self is a given. It's already here, already accomplished.

What is the nature of the mind? [Q8]
'When the mind comes out of the Self, the world appears. Therefore, when the world appears (to be real) the Self does not appear; and when the Self appears (shines) the world does not appear.'

It's a very tricky statement. We need to dig beneath the surface. We have to know what is the meaning of '**appears**' and '**does not appear**'. It sounds like the world or the mind has the power to obliterate the Self.

The world is the Self and I am the Self. The problem is my understanding is confused. I need to know what the world is and what I am and what my projections are. That is all. I need to destroy the confusion I have about each of these three aspects of my being.

So he must mean the mind's attachment to the world.

What he's doing is giving the mind and the Self the same order of reality which is not correct. Is this a problem of Sri Ramana's understanding or is this a problem of the translation?

Well, this has all been edited by Sri Ramana himself.

Somebody knew that it was a misleading statement and put 'to be real' in parentheses (perhaps it was Sri Ramana himself who did this?) because without this qualifier you have nonsense. There should also be the same modifier at the end of the first sentence '... **the Self does not appear (to be real)**' and at the end of the second sentence '... **the world does not appear (to be real)**'.

Without the phrase 'to be real' we have what appears to be a statement that the world disappears when the Self is known and the Self disappears when the world is known. Which we know cannot be true. But if we amend it with the phrase 'to be real' included in the appropriate places it jibes with scripture and makes sense, even though it is only partially true. The operative word in this answer is '**appears**'. '**Appears**' means that the mind is misunderstanding something.

Mind you, this is not a statement of enlightenment. It is a bit of knowledge that needs to be applied at the intermediate stage, the stage of enquiry. It is meant to help to distinguish between the mind and the Self. The person has the belief that his mind, his 'world' is real. So when he is caught up in that and focused on experience, he does not see the truth, his Self. There is a verse in the *Gita* that says the same thing: 'What's day for the sage is night for a worldly person.' It means you can't have it both ways, you can't see the mind and the Self both as real. You have to come down on the side of the Self as the sole reality. Once you have done that then you can see that the mind is also real but that it enjoys a lower order of reality, an apparent reality, a time-bound reality. So it isn't a problem. There is no conflict between different orders of reality. When you're on the path to enlightenment you have to completely negate the world, the mind, etc. So this statement is meant to help you do that.

Can you explain what he means by **'When the mind comes out of the Self, the world appears.'***?*

This teaching comes from *Samkhya* (a school of Hindu philosophy) and was incorporated into *Vedanta* and *Yoga*. It's called *karana-karya vada*, the cause and effect teaching. 'When the mind comes out of the Self ...' means that the mind is just an effect of the Self, the Self transforming itself into a form, a mind. For example this Coke bottle is an effect of glass. Glass is the cause and the effect is the bottle. You break the bottle and the bottle is no more – but glass still exists. So the mind is just the Self in a form. It depends on the Self but the Self is independent of it. As I've said repeatedly, the removal or destruction of the mind, unlike the bottle, is all in terms of understanding. There is no actual destruction. You see how it is and that finishes your attachment to the belief that the mind is an independent entity.

This understanding is what you're calling freedom.

Yes. There are two kinds of superimposition. When either of them is destroyed the result is freedom. Both take place in the mind and have nothing to do with physical reality. One is where you see the snake and when you understand that it is a rope it doesn't come back. This is unconditioned superimposition. There is nothing left to condition the perception of the rope after knowledge has taken place. The other is the mirage – which you negate through knowledge too – but the perception of water remains. There is still something creating the appearance of water but you know the water isn't real. This is called conditioned superimposition.

Ignorance makes both *vasanas* and the mind a problem. If you can see that they are superimposed on the Self out of ignorance, they become non-binding. Let the sex *vasana* come, the money *vasana*, whatever is meant to be unspiritual – it's just me. Like the web of a spider it comes out of me and is drawn back into me and is made of my own consciousness. The *vasanas* are like a mirage and enjoy only an apparent reality. Of course if I act on them thinking that I will gain something it means that I do not know who I am.

Sri Ramana continues answering question 8: What is the nature of the mind?

'When one persistently enquires into the nature of the mind, the mind will end, leaving the Self (as the residue).'

This is what is called enlightenment by default and is compromised by the language of experience, the belief that the spiritual path takes place in time. It seems to but it doesn't really because the problem is ignorance and it doesn't take any time for light to destroy darkness – it's immediate.

It's true but it's not the truth because the Self is there all along, even when the mind is there. The mind is known to be a problem because the Self illumines it. So the Self never just appears at the end of a long *sadhana*. The Self, awareness, is there all along, observing the seeking, motivating the seeking, doing the practice and it is there available for understanding at any point during the quest. Sometimes the person hasn't even done *sadhana* – like Ramana – and they wake up to the Self. Well, he did one small practice. He pretended to die (see Chapter 5).

Is this because of their innate purity?

Nobody knows.

But it would tend to be somebody who is not much in the world, wouldn't it?

Sure, or somebody who has just suffered a lot, like Saul on the road to Damascus. That's what happened to me. I was an awful person, a real devil. Life was a living hell. Then one fine morning on the way to the post office I was just lifted out of it and instantly became aware of this divine factor. It took me years to get clear what it was – and that I was it – but I did the work.

Let's go back to the statement that the mind obscures the Self and that it needs to be destroyed for the Self to shine and the subsequent statement that '… the mind will end leaving the Self (as the residue).' Maybe there are two kinds of mind?

Good! Yes, we need to ask what type of mind he is talking about. Because if that's true, Ramana wasn't enlightened because his mind kept working. He says so. The mind that needs to be destroyed is the conditioned mind, the extroverted mind. The mind created by *sadhana*, the subtle mind, the *sattvic* (calm and peaceful) mind, remains. It is the mind that makes the enquiry. Remember, the mind is actually the Self. It is not the enemy.

Vedanta's view is that the mind 'ends' when you understand that the mind is not you. In reality the mind keeps functioning but you have divorced it. It may not have ended from its point of view, but it has ended from yours. You just don't take it seriously any more.

So it seems that the absence of thought isn't enlightenment.

If the absence of thought is enlightenment then we're all enlightened, because who hasn't slept?

You can use this *Yogic* language if you want – Sri Ramana wasn't actually in the scriptural tradition, he just picked it up slowly as he went along. He may have eventually understood the limitations of the language of *Yoga* but we need to also keep in mind who he's talking to. Probably most of the people who came to him were more familiar with the language of *Yoga* than with the language of *Vedanta*. It's always like that so there is a tendency to use the language that appeals to your audience.

It's the same today, perhaps worse because now you have a lot of people who are switching from *bhakti* (devotion) and *Yoga*, and even Buddhism, to *Advaita Vedanta*. Part of this is just a fad because the *Satsang* gurus are all using the word '*Advaita*', often without much comprehension. But it is understandable, particularly if the person has been on one of those paths for years. Why? Because all their experiences have not solved the problem of limitation and they like *Vedanta's* idea that you are limitless and that this is something to be understood, not gained as an experience.

Most of these people are quite confused because they are entering new terrain, the language of identity, but they haven't left their old country, the language of experience, so they have conflicting concepts about enlightenment. They have no idea how you can know the Self and that would set you free. They all know 'of' the Self but they do not know what it means to 'be' the Self. They do not understand that they are already free and that the only thing standing in the way is the belief that they aren't. They also do not understand that beliefs can be destroyed by knowledge. Like religious people, they are very attached to their beliefs. They think they are actually knowledge. This dead mind idea is one of the biggest beliefs in the spiritual world.

You have said that enquiry is about getting discrimination, that you only do Self-enquiry when there are thoughts in the mind because enquiry is about getting discrimination, the knowledge of the Self and its relationship to the mind. That doesn't fit with what I know about enquiry and Self-knowledge. Can you explain what you mean by it? I thought that Self-knowledge was non-discriminating wisdom.

From the Self's perspective wisdom is non-discriminating because there is only the Self. But when the mind is in the picture discrimination operates. The mind is the Self appearing as an apparently changing reality. The technical Sanskrit term is *mithya*. It isn't completely real but it isn't completely unreal. It really isn't an illusion, except in the sense that an illusion has some basis in fact. Without the fact supporting the illusion, the illusion can't exist.

Could you give an example?

Sure, the famous snake in the rope. You won't see the snake unless there is a rope there. So you won't see the mind unless there is a substrate for it to be sitting on. That substrate is you, the Self.

The world is the mind because the world arises in the mind?

Yes. And the mind is the Self because it arises out of the Self. This is why the world is the Self. The mind is not independent of the Self. But – and this is freedom – you, the Self, are independent of the mind. It is the reason you don't have to kill the mind to be free of it. You are already free of it.

If this is a nondual reality, as the scripture says, and there is such a thing as the mind, the mind has to be the Self. So the only question is what kind of self is it? It's the Self apparently changing. When you know this you aren't afraid of the mind because you understand that whatever you are getting out of your mind is not going to last. So you just enjoy or suffer the mind as it is. The big problem is thinking that the things in the mind and the world should be unchanging. If you do then you suffer periodic disillusionment. When somebody falls in love they need to know that it will not last. If you can enjoy it knowing that it will not last, fine.

So how do you get this discrimination?

Well, you pay attention to your experience and respect it. It's funny how people know that nothing lasts yet they perversely expect it to, at least when things are going well. When they aren't, that's another case. Your experience shows that nothing in the world-mind lasts. The scripture harps tirelessly on this subject … *anitya, anitya, anitya.* *Anitya* means impermanence. If the mahatmas confirm it, you can bank on it.

Sri Ramana makes a strong statement when asked:

> *Will there not be realisation of the Self even while the world is there (taken to be real)?* [Q5]
> *He says,* '**There will not be.**'

We spoke about this before. The statement means it will seem to be real if you see the world as an independent reality. They put the phrase 'taken to be real' in because 'is there' makes it seem that the world has to be physically not seen for realisation to happen. One might believe that perceptually, experientially, the world is going to disappear. It's a common belief among spiritual types.

That's right. And that makes it even worse. It makes it scary.

168

They think that if it hasn't disappeared they aren't enlightened.

They also think that the enlightened are walking around in some sort of deep grey void.

Language is very important because these people are getting their ideas from somewhere. Failure to understand explains why so many seekers do not become finders. There are many people in the spiritual world who have had considerable experience of the reflection of the Self in the mind when the mind was in a *sattvic* condition and who would be classified as Self-realised. This is what Ramana calls *antar mukha*, turning the mind inward – watching or realising or experiencing the Self.

But, rightly, these people are not satisfied and continue to entertain doubts about their 'state'. Usually the doubt has to do with making the state permanent, which is impossible since the person and his pure mind are still in the realm of time. In other words there is always the realistic fear that the experience will not last. And even though they are so close to enlightenment experientially, it still eludes them. And the reason?

Because they are prisoners of the language of experience. The language we use indicates the way we think. At this stage, when the experience is more or less continually available, the only barrier to converting the experience to a 'permanent' state, not that enlightenment is a state, is the way one thinks. What needs to happen at this point is that the individual needs to convert the language of experience to the language of identity. The language of identity states that the experiencer and what is being experienced are not two separate things, that they are in fact the same. When any object is experienced, the knowledge of that object arises simultaneously in the intellect. And if the mind in which the Self is reflected is pure, the knowledge of the Self will arise with it in the intellect. This knowledge is in the form of a thought, an *akandakara vritti*, an unbroken idea that I am the whole and complete actionless awareness that I am experiencing. (Wow! That's me! Whoopee! I'm it!!!) If the person is accustomed to thinking of the Self as an object he or she will be reluctant to surrender the experiencer, and the Self will continue to remain as an experienced object. The surrender is in terms of letting go of the idea of oneself as an experiencer and embracing one's limitless identity. This is the destruction of the mind that the *Yogis* talk about.

Were the person to be trained in the language of identity, this problem would not arise. In fact the person would immediately recognise the content of the experience as 'I' and that would finish the work. What all this clinging to experience is about is hanging on to the container and therefore sacrificing the content. It's like a person pouring the Coke out of the bottle and eating the bottle. We can throw away the container. It is non-essential. We need the contents, the Self.

The whole of *Vedanta* can be reduced to one simple equation found in the *Upanishads*: 'You are That.' 'That' is the Self and 'you' is the Self in the form of the experiencer and the verb 'are' indicates the identity between the two.

I've been saying that you are the master of the universe, meaning that without you, the I, experience is not possible. I'm saying to hell with the experience; you make it anything you want, because you're the boss. Without me, the I, experience is not possible. Experiencing isn't bossing me. I'm bossing it. Without me it doesn't amount to a hill of beans. That's freedom. I don't have to erase it. I just take it how I please. This is why bad days are good days for the enlightened. They can see themselves in everything. Looking to experience for validation is the tail wagging the dog. We're trying to set things straight – get the dog wagging the tail. That's how it is; dogs wag their tails, not the other way around like *Yoga* says. It says if you get this experience, *nirvikalpa samadhi*, then you are enlightened. *Vedanta* says that you are enlightened no matter what experience you are having.

Is it any use reading books for those who long for liberation? [Q23]
'All the texts say that in order to gain liberation one should render the mind quiescent; therefore their conclusive teaching is that the mind should be rendered quiescent; once this has been understood there is no need for endless reading. In order to quieten the mind one has only to enquire within oneself what one's Self is …'

This statement may lead a person to conclude that no scriptural information would be useful in Self-enquiry. But you can't make an enquiry without knowledge. In fact Sri Ramana supports scripture with the statement **'All the texts say …'** You can't perform enquiry without the knowledge that I am not the body, mind, etc. You can't just sit there without any information like a dodo and say, 'Uh … Who am I? Duh … Hey God … Who am I?' This is not going to work, even if the heavens are rent asunder with the booming voice of God: 'YOU ARE PURE CONSCIOUSNESS!!!'

Even if He tells you to your face, you will have no way to evaluate this information. 'Uh? I am? What does that mean?' I need knowledge. I need to know how who I am relates to my body and mind and the world around. It has to be contextualised or it is useless. Scripture does an excellent job of contextualising the 'I', telling you what it means to be the Self.

What is wisdom-insight, jnana drishti? [Q25]
'Remaining quiet is what is called wisdom-insight.'

I think I'll argue with that statement. It's the language of experience trying to co-opt the language of identity. Let's use one of Sri Ramana's most frequent teachings to unmask this statement. Let's ask, 'Who is remaining quiet?' There are only two possibilities, the Self and the ego. It won't be the Self because the Self is silence; and it is not a doer so it can't 'remain'. 'Remain' implies 'not remaining' or 'noise'. So an ego remaining quiet is wisdom insight? I don't think so. I go to my room, get in bed and close my eyes and go to sleep and I'm quiet as a mouse – and that makes me wise?

Papaji's main teaching was 'be quiet'. By this he didn't mean being silent but being still. Then in this stillness enquiry just happens by itself.

Yes. It is natural for the mind to become curious and ask questions when it is still. But I think this is quite a relaxed view of Sri Ramana's teaching. He seemed to advocate a more aggressive discrimination.

The term *jnana drishti* is much more easy to deal with when we take it as a statement in the language of knowledge. One way to define *jnana drishti* is that when the mind is quiet and a thought arises in it, I gain knowledge of that thought. And if that thought, based on my perception of the Self shining on my quiet mind, was 'I am limitless awareness' and I took that thought for my own and let it become my identity, then *jnana drishti* means enlightenment, liberation.

Or (which amounts to the same thing) it could be translated as 'the knowledge (*jnana*) that comes from seeing (*drishti*)'. Seeing what? Seeing what is. And what is? The Self. And what is the Self? The I. So *jnana drishti* means Self-knowledge. This is quite different from 'remaining quiet'. Of course if you are the Self you are silence but there is no one there to 'remain' silent.

It could also mean that *jnanam* (knowledge) is *drishti* (seeing). The seers, the *rishis* who gave us the *Vedas*, saw *(drishti)* the truth *(jnanam)*, and enshrined it in the form of the *Vedas*. It could also mean 'to see is to know'. You really need to have all of these teachings contextualised. They all fit into the wonderful bouquet of ideas that is called *Vedanta*.

By 'quiet' doesn't he mean not be caught up in all the thoughts? To have a sattvic *mind?*

Dispassionate.

And to be focused inside.

Yes.

He doesn't mean 'not talk'.

No.

What is the relation between desirelessness and wisdom? [Q26]
'Desirelessness is wisdom. The two are not different; they are the same.'

Why is desirelessness wisdom? Because the Self is whole and complete. It doesn't want anything.

He goes on: '**Desirelessness is refraining from turning the mind towards any object.**'

This is a good one too. Here he's defining it as a quality of the ego. He's saying that an ego that doesn't allow the mind to go to objects is wise. No, that's not strictly correct. The mind naturally goes to objects. He probably means that one who doesn't react to the mind's contact with objects – just witnesses it and lets it be – is wise. That is, when you see a pretty girl you know you'd like to get into bed with her, but you don't go over and chat her up. You just let the thought die. Why is this wise? Because you are love, you are pleasure, you have it all already. A few sense ticklings are not going to make you happier.

What is liberation? [Q28]
'**Inquiring into the nature of one's self that is in bondage and realising one's true nature is liberation.**'

You are already the Self, even when you think you aren't. Enlightenment is not gaining something that you didn't have. So when you say you found it, you are actually saying that you were a fool for a long time.

So it's saying that you are always the Self. You cannot not be the Self. So the question of bondage and freedom does not arise.

Right. It's a myth. 'Realising' one's true nature does not mean experiencing one's true nature because you are always experiencing your true nature. It means knowing that I am the Self, knowing that I am limitless awareness.

What is called mind is a wondrous power existing in Self. It projects all thoughts. If we set aside all thoughts and see, there will be no such thing as mind remaining separate; therefore, thought itself is the form of the mind. Other than thoughts, there is no such thing as the world.

Sri Ramana Maharshi

Above: Sri Ramana with visitors

Left: Samadhi Hall scene

Below: New Hall and Samadhi Hall

Right: Sri Ramana standing 1940s

Right bottom: Arunachala south-west face

CHAPTER 7

Commentary on Sri Ramana's Teachings 'Self-Enquiry' from a Vedanta point of view

James Swartz in dialogue with Premananda

[Sri Ramana's direct words are in bold]

James comments on Sri Ramana's book, Self-Enquiry. *He explains that a still mind is needed to practise Self-enquiry. Hence the value of the traditional practices like meditation. To achieve Self-realisation there needs to be no longer any hope that something in the world will make us happy. There needs to be a great longing to be free of one's mind. James discusses a very interesting quote from Lakshmana Swamy which highlights the importance of the guru. James also offers an alternative explanation about a 'dead mind' to the one David Godman puts forward in Chapter 2.*

James, you have commented on Sri Ramana's booklet, Who Am I? *How do you feel about discussing some additional points concerning his teachings from another book,* Self-Enquiry?

What are called Sri Ramana's teachings are just the tip of the *Vedic* iceberg. Because of who he was he did not run all over India and the world selling his books and videos, giving *Satsangs* (meetings in Truth) and seminars to see that 'his' teachings reached a spiritually starving world. So we only have some conversations, questions and answers and pithy statements he made naturally in the course of his life, most of which were not recorded. In one way it's a shame in so far as Sri Ramana had an exceptionally clear mind and went right to the essence. But in another it doesn't matter because he was firmly within the *Vedic* tradition and never, to my knowledge, said anything that contradicted either the *Yoga* or the *Vedanta* scriptures. So if someone wanted a more comprehensive view one could study the scriptures.

Yes, it was a different time, no website, no DVDs. Anyway, I've mentioned several times that we should talk about Self-enquiry as a practice and I came across an interesting question and answer that addresses this issue.

Sri Ramana is asked, 'What is the method of practice?' and he replies, '**As the Self of a person who tries to attain Self-realisation is not different from him and as there is nothing other than or superior to him to be attained by him, Self-realisation being only the realisation of one's own nature, the seeker of liberation realises, without doubts or misconceptions, his real nature by distinguishing the eternal from the transient and never swerves from this natural state. This is known as the practice of knowledge. This is the enquiry leading to Self-realisation.**'

He seems to be saying that Self-enquiry is more than just asking, 'Who am I?'

That's right. From speaking with people who are looking for Self-realisation I've learned that many think all one has to do is say 'Who am I?' and somehow the answer will be revealed. But this isn't how it is. The fact is that the nature of the 'I' is well known. If you have a doubt just read the *Upanishads* or *Shankara* or any *Vedantic* text. It is very clear. There are literally hundreds of words that indicate the Self and there is a brilliant proven methodology that can destroy your Self-ignorance.

There is a peculiar belief that the Self is some mysterious unknown presence only apprehended through mystic means about which one can say nothing. Unspeakable. Indefinable. Beyond words, etc. But actually, the Self is the only thing one can speak about with precision and certainty, because it is the only reality. All the rest of it, what people think of as real, cannot really be described because it is neither completely real nor is it completely unreal. In this statement Sri Ramana uses perhaps the most common word to indicate the nature of the Self. He says it is eternal. This distinguishes it from the body-mind-ego complex and the world around which is constantly changing. We think of the body as real and have a word for it but when you look into the body you can't come up with anything substantial. It keeps resolving into subtler and subtler elements until it disappears altogether. But no matter how much you analyse it, you cannot reduce the Self to anything else. It cannot be dissolved.

So enquiry is not a matter of getting knowledge then, it is a matter of applying it?

Yes, Sri Ramana says that enquiry is separating the real from the unreal, the eternal from the transient. So it is a practice. Before you can practise you need to know what is real and what isn't. Twelve centuries before Sri Ramana, *Shankara* uses the exact same words, 'practice of knowledge (*jnanabyasa*)' to describe this process. And it was already part of the tradition when *Shankara* came along. The practice is called *viveka* and it is the proven method of liberation.

It seems quite intellectual. How does it work?

180

It isn't 'intellectual' in the pejorative sense that one hears the word used today. But it definitely relies on an astute use of the intellect. There is this notion that Sri Ramana taught in silence and that only by sitting in silence, not by using the mind in any way, can one realise the Self. This is patently untrue. Here Sri Ramana is not recommending silence. Mind you, meditation, sitting in silence, is a very useful practice but Sri Ramana himself makes it very clear that in Self-enquiry the intellect is the instrument of realisation.

In his description of his own awakening one can see that he was obviously conscious and thinking. And there is no reason why one can't think when the mind is silent. In fact, in that state conscious thinking is beautiful, a real joy. There is even a *Yogic* term for it, *savikalpa samadhi*. It means *samadhi* (immersed in the Self) with thought. *Vikalpas* are thoughts.

This is quite surprising. The common notion is that the intellect needs to be shut down for the Self to be realised.

That is the view of *Yoga*. Controlling the mind is useful to prepare the mind for Self-realisation but it is not tantamount to Self-realisation. We need to remember that the mind is transient and therefore unreal. So how are you going to control something that is non-eternal? The one who is trying to change, the ego, is non-eternal; what is meant not to change is eternal. Therefore, how can there be any permanent change? Even if there is change as a result of your efforts you will have to keep up the effort to keep the changes operational. So you find yourself having to do all these things to be what you want to be. This is always the problem when you try to change the mind, or stop the mind. Enquiry is not a question of controlling the mind. It is a question of observing the mind.

So how does this discrimination work?

Well, first we need to know that any Tom, Dick or Harry cannot just practise enquiry. In the first line of the very next paragraph Sri Ramana says, 'This is suitable only for the ripe souls.' You need to be prepared. Prepared means mature, indifferent to the blandishments the world has to offer. And secondly, one needs a burning desire to be free of his or her own mind. This is different from saying that one needs a dead or different mind. The mind is going to be with you in one form or another whether you like it or not, so the only sensible question is how to live happily with it. When you realise what the Self is and that you are it, you see that you have always been free of the mind.

And this does not mean that any experienced person is qualified to practise Self-enquiry and attain enlightenment. Many, perhaps most, experienced people haven't learned anything important from their experiences.

That's a rather sweeping generalisation.

Perhaps that is a clumsy way of saying what I wanted to say. By that I mean they haven't learned that experience is not going to solve the happiness issue and that liberation is possible. So they just keep chasing the same things. I read the other day that Ted Turner, who is a billionaire, and his wife, Jane Fonda, a beautiful rich actress, divorced. In the article the interviewer asked what was the cause of the breakup and Jane said that Ted just couldn't stop doing business, meaning he didn't spend enough time with her. Now here is a very successful, accomplished person who literally has everything, except love, and he is unsuccessful in getting love because he can't stop his addiction to making deals. Not only is he unsatisfied with the amount of money he has, his obsession keeps him from enjoying the love of a woman, much less from understanding that his view of himself is the problem. So no matter how accomplished you are in your field of experience, without coming to the right conclusion about oneself you will not qualify for enlightenment.

And discrimination does qualify you?

Absolutely. And to get to the point, discrimination or enquiry is the moment-to-moment practise of the understanding that the experiencer and what one is experiencing are not real, and that witness, the awareness because of which the experiencer is capable of experience, is real.

And how it works is that whenever an impulse to do something or have something or feel something or change something comes up in the mind, as it does all the time, one does not just mindlessly set out to manifest the desired result, but one thinks 'What lasting benefit will I get by doing, getting, experiencing this? Will I be more, better, different? Will I gain lasting happiness or will I still be what I am?' Assuming that the one doing the practice is the ego – which it would necessarily be – will that person be any wiser with reference to his or her own Self by doing/thinking/feeling/experiencing something? And the answer is always no. True, you may be wiser with reference to a specific idea, but will you actually become whole and complete and free of your mind by doing what you are contemplating doing? For example, you may invest in the stock market and lose a bundle because the corporate fat cats are cooking the books. So you learn to not take people's word for things concerning money, but are you fundamentally different because you don't have the money you once had? Or are you fundamentally different because you are more wary? No. You are still what you are.

So self-transformation is not Self-realisation.

It may be useful to clean up your ego a bit before you set out to set it free but the very fact that you are trying to change means that you are not free.

A friend and I rented a house we found on the internet recently from a woman who was going on vacation and when we moved in I noticed a collage on the wall celebrating her recent spiritual awakening. Pasted on the collage were different sized words from various periodicals that said, 'One day I got tired of being the same so I made the BIG JUMP.'

What you have here is a spiritual awakening, but not Self-realisation. This is a person who has been stuck with some bad values and consequently caught up in some unhealthy habits who finally gets the courage to confront herself and make changes in the way she lives. And this is very good, an important first step. But this is not Self-realisation.

Awakening is not Self-realisation, although during an awakening you may come to experience and understand that there is a Self.

This is an important distinction, I think.

Yes it is. This is not Self-realisation because the one who landed is the same one who made the jump. Once the proper values and good habits are in place a new problem will surface: Is this all? Because you haven't addressed the fundamental problem. You have just corrected some karmic mistakes the ego made. I'm not saying that spiritual awakenings aren't good but once you are awake to how foolish you are and the possibility of getting out of it, then you can perhaps start to seek wisdom which at some point will entail asking who made the jump.

Now, if Sri Ramana is saying that the Self never changes and you are the Self and the Self is endless bliss, then you will never want to jump out of yourself. So what we have in the case of this woman is an ego changing itself. And no matter how much the ego changes for the better it is never going to change into the Self. When you realise that you are the Self it doesn't matter to you what the ego is. You accept it as it is. You understand that it wouldn't be the way it is if it could help it and you let it be. Or you work on it dispassionately if that is your *karma* (result of all actions). When you no longer see yourself as it, it will gradually become more like the Self but it will never become the Self. So thinking that you are going to become different is not the way to go.

So you're saying that working out your karma *or trying to be different will not produce wisdom?*

Yes, definitely.

Surely it must have some value.

You're right. It made me realise that I was chasing the wrong thing – experience. It made me begin to think in terms of understanding. And shortly after I came to that conclusion I met my master.

What I needed was to see that no matter what kind of experience I had I was still the same. This is discrimination. It is very difficult to practise because the ego can't stand its incompleteness and is passionately committed to getting what it wants or avoiding what it doesn't want to feel good.

So you're saying that enquiry is always choosing not to go with your vasanas (tendencies of the mind)?

No, not really. It is knowing that if you go with them you will not get lasting satisfaction from them. In a way you can't avoid doing certain things, there is too much internal pressure. To fight them would cause too much stress and personality distortion. But you can go through the experiences that life has to offer minus the belief that life is capable of making you happy. You can aim for a clear balanced mind. This is the purpose of discrimination and the fruit of enquiry. It neutralises your likes and dislikes. This is the difference between a worldly person and an enquirer.

Sri Ramana defines enlightenment in the first part of this quote and it is important to know what enlightenment is if you are seeking it.

> *He says,* 'As the Self of a person who tries to attain Self-realisation is not different from him and as there is nothing other than or superior to him to be attained by him, Self-realisation being only the realisation of one's own nature ...'

I think this statement should be required reading for anyone who wants to understand what enlightenment is. Sri Ramana makes it very clear that it is not about being different from what you are or of getting something that is better than what you already have, like a high state of consciousness. He uses a very interesting word here – only – to make the point that incredible spiritual experiences or altered states of consciousness or transforming oneself are not enlightenment. He says it is 'only' realising what you are.

But isn't this realisation something unique?

No. What is being realised might be considered unique if you had been ignorant for a long time but this realisation is no different from realising or understanding or knowing anything. When it happens there is always a sense of irony because it is something that has always been known. What could be more familiar to you than you? It may seem like a big deal because something that is so obvious can easily be taken for granted and forgotten. So Self-realisation is always a re-discovery, not a discovery.

So this is the whole cosmic joke idea.

Yes. To solve the riddle you need a trick, a technique, which Sri Ramana calls enquiry or *viveka*. You need to be reminded that you are eternal, that you have always been, that nothing can be added to or subtracted from you, that experience is impermanent, and that you need to start paying attention to your own mind and its ideas to the contrary and get to work dismissing them. As long as you hold erroneous views about yourself you will not hold the right view about yourself.

Which is that you are whole and complete.

Yes, that experience depends on you, but that you do not depend on experience.

That nothing can affect you.

That you don't need anything at all to make yourself happy.

> *At the end of the book Sri Ramana says,* 'The experience of the Self is possible only for the mind that has become subtle and unmoving as a result of prolonged meditation. He who is thus endowed with a mind that has become subtle, and who has the experience of the Self is called a *jivanmukta*.'

Here's a vindication from Sri Ramana's mouth of what I've been saying about the mind: that the mind does not have to be killed. When enough of the gross *vasanas* are exhausted the mind becomes subtle. It still has thoughts in it but the thoughts do not unbalance it. This kind of mind comes about through simple restrained living and clear thinking. It is capable of Self-realisation.

But I have to take issue with this part of the statement '**… and who has the experience of the Self is called a *jivanmukta***'. Experience of the Self is not enlightenment. When is the Self not experienced? It may be Self-realisation but it is not enlightenment for the simple reason that there is an experiencer other than the Self. It is enlightenment when the experiencer realises that he or she is what is being experienced, i.e. the Self. Enlightenment is knowledge, *jnanam*, not experience of anything. People erroneously believe that enlightenment is gaining some permanent, incredible experience 'of the Self'. But a *jivanmukta* is free of everything, especially experience. *Jivanmukta* simply means someone who has realised he or she is the Self and has no sense of duality.

'It is the state of *jivanmukta* that is referred to as the attributeless *Brahman* and as the turiya. When even the subtle mind gets resolved, and experience of self ceases …'

Well, this is not a correct understanding of *jivanmukta*. In the first place it is not a 'state'. States are experience-based and come and go. Attributeless *Brahman* would not have any states in it, nor would it be a state. A state is an attribute. Attributeless *Brahman* are two words that describe the Self. It has no attributes and is limitless, which is the meaning of the word *Brahman*. The resolution of the mind is simply a resolution in understanding. The mind understands that it is the Self and that makes it peaceful and finishes it as an independent entity. It does not mean that the mind dies never to think a thought again.

'… and when one is immersed in the ocean of bliss and has become one with it without any differentiated existence, one is called a *videhamukta*. It is the state of *videhamukta* that is referred to as the transcendent attributeless *Brahman* and as the transcendent *turiya*. This is the final goal.'

So is he saying this is enlightenment?

That's the way it seems. He is describing enlightenment in both the language of *Vedanta* (identity) and the language of *Yoga* (experience). If you analyse the language you can find the problem. He is experiencing limitless bliss, yet he is talking about it being a goal. Something to be gained. But in the language of identity it is something that you are.

We have to resort to linguistic analysis because Sri Ramana is dead and we have no idea if the translator knew what he meant and used the correct words. Even if he was speaking to us directly it would be possible to misunderstand the meaning. The only way to get the proper idea of the meaning of these words is to hold them up to scripture and see how well they fit. This will be a useful interview for seekers but it will not make me a lot of friends among the Sri Ramana devotees because Sri Ramana has attained the status of deity of late and you can't have your gods with feet of clay.

He was a realised soul and a human being of the highest caliber. But we only have his words to go on and I don't want this to be my opinion on his teachings, although it will certainly be taken as such. My idea is to discuss Sri Ramana in light of the spiritual context in which his enlightenment took place.

Let's pick apart this statement a little more. In the first place what do the words 'immersed in' mean? These are experiential words. They indicate a person having a particular kind of experience, in this case bliss. The next words of interest are 'has become one with it'. What do they mean? What kind of 'becoming' is it? If the 'becoming' is experiential the experience of bliss stops because the one who was experiencing it is no more. In oneness, nonduality, the subject and object necessary for experience are not present. So if somebody is going to lose the experience of 'the ocean of bliss' why will they merge into the Self? It doesn't make a lot of sense.

This is why the *bhakti* (devotion) tradition scoffs at the liberation tradition. The *bhaktas* (practitioners of *bhakti*) say, 'Why would I want to be God when I can experience God all the time?' It's a valid point. However, it doesn't take into account the fact that you can be God and experience God. There is only a contradiction when you have a flawed understanding of the nature of God and the ego.

But what if this 'becoming' is the coming of understanding? By understanding I mean the recognition that the subject (the mind-ego, the one experiencing the bliss), and the object (the bliss), are one. Bliss is a common but inaccurate word used to describe the Self because of its experiential implications. One way to describe this understanding experientially is that it is a shift during which the foreground, the ego, which has been experiencing the Self in the form of bliss, becomes the background, and the Self, which has been the object of experience, becomes the foreground, 'I'. So now the 'I' is the Self looking out at the ego looking 'in' at it. And when this shift takes place there is an instant recognition that 'I' is the Self. One's identification of 'I' with the ego-mind ends once and for all. From that point on there is no foreground or background, no in or out. The mind is purified of these 'spiritual' concepts.

Videhamukti exoterically is usually taken to mean 'liberation when the body dies'. Why would you have to wait until the body dies to realise the Self since the Self is always present when you are alive? This liberation at death is just a belief. Death is just a belief. The actual meaning is 'freedom from the body'. *Vi* means without and *dehi* means the body and *mukti* means liberation. So it is not an experiential term; it is a statement of knowledge. It means that when you realise that you are not the body you are free. The realisation that one is not the body, if it is a hard and fast knowledge, is enlightenment. We can include the mind-ego in the word 'body' too because it is a body, albeit a subtle one. Body means embodied. This experience and the understanding that arises with it mean that from this point on you are no longer embodied. The bodies are in the Self but the Self is not in the bodies. This is why it is called liberation.

You have always been the Self; it's like a recognition.

That's right.

It's an embracing.

Yes, one owns it.

It's the moment the wave sinks into the ocean. It's when the wave stops being this wave.

Yes, but – here's that famous 'but' – the wave can be there. If there is a wave in the ocean you know that it is not just an independent wave but it is the ocean too. It won't be a wave unless it is the ocean. The wave depends on the ocean but the ocean does not depend on the wave. So even if there is a wave it has no effect on the ocean. Enlightenment does not destroy dualistic experience. One just realises that experience depends on me, the Self, but that I am always free of experience. Acting in the world with this knowledge is quite different from acting in the world without it.

Right. What you are saying now is very important. It's completely contrary to what many have been led to believe. It's a vital point. Recently a woman came to me quite disturbed because she could not do anything about her mind. She had the idea she must kill her mind completely.

All that 'teaching' does is deflate people, it doesn't give them any encouragement and it is patently untrue. Mind you, you need to get some mind out of the way – your neuroses, your binding likes and dislikes – and for that you need to do some work. That's why Sri Ramana encouraged *sadhana* (spiritual practice). That's what *Vedanta* says too. The mind needs to be quiet but that does not mean that the world has to go and the mind has to disappear completely. It may disappear completely. But it always reconstitutes itself.

If Self-realisation only happens when the mind is non-existent, then the Self and the mind enjoy exactly the same order of reality, like sickness and health. When you are healthy you are not sick. The scriptures say that is not so. Experience shows that it is not so.

The Self is knowable directly when the mind is functioning. The Self doesn't need any knowledge. The mind needs it so it has to be functioning clearly. But when the mind is overcome with heavy *rajas* (activity) and *tamas* (dullness) it is impossible to know the Self.

So the mind does experience the Self, then? This seems contrary to what you were saying before.

That's good, picking up on an apparent contradiction. The answer is yes and no. What is experienced is the reflection of the Self in a *sattvic* (calm and peaceful) mind. The *sattvic* mind is like a highly polished mirror and the Self illumines it so it is experienceable there. There can be no 'direct experience' because the mind and the Self enjoy different orders of reality – the Self is subtler than the mind. Sri Ramana defines enquiry as **'holding the mind on the Self'** which means keeping your attention on the reflection of the Self in the *sattvic* mind.

The reason you hold your attention on it is to get knowledge. When you get knowledge you can relax. You are trying to figure out what it is and what it has to do with you. And if you are faithful, meaning if you do not involve yourself with the occasional *vasanas* arising in the mind, there will eventually come a point – it is inevitable – when there is the 'Aha!' And that 'Aha!' is simply the recognition that what I am experiencing is me, not some consciousness other than my own.

When you grasp this knowledge that 'I am the Self' you are no longer excluding yourself from the experience of the Self. As long as you are experiencing the Self then you are excluding yourself from the Self. You are saying, 'I am here and the Self is there and I am experiencing it.' In the *Gita*, *Arjuna* has fear when he sees *Krishna's* cosmic form because he is not included in it. He has separated himself from the vision. If he sees himself in the vision then it is not a problem for him.

Lakshmana Swamy was a direct disciple of Sri Ramana (see Chapter 3) He still lives here in Tiruvannamalai. This is what he says on the subject of Self-realisation and enlightenment:

'Devotees by their own effort can reach the effortless, thought-free state. That is as far as you can go by yourself. In that state there are no more thoughts, desires or memories rising up. Then go and sit in the presence of a realised being, the power of the Self will make the residual "I" go back to its source from where it will die, never to rise again. This is the complete and full realisation. This is the role of the guru who is identical with the Self within – to pull the desire-free mind into the heart and destroy it completely.'

This again is the language of *Yoga* and needs to be looked into. Mind you, I'm not for or against any language. One just needs to know what the words are actually referring to, and see whether or not the words are the best ones for revealing what is. The *Yogis* are probably talking about the same thing as the *Vedantis*. But the way a *siddha* (one who has attained a paranormal ability) like Lakshmana Swamy uses words is going to be different from an ordinary person because he understands what the words actually refer to. And for someone who is not enlightened, who is using the words to guide his or her *sadhana*, the words need to be very carefully considered. Because at these subtle levels of experience the way you think about things can make or break your endeavour.

I'm going to take the words literally and be a bit hard on this statement of Lakshmana Swamy's, without meaning any disrespect. Speaking of a pure *sattvic* state he says, 'In that state there are no more thoughts, desires or memories rising up.' Fair enough. Then he says, 'Then go and sit in the presence of a realised being …'

What is wrong with this statement? If there are no desires rising up how could you go and 'sit in the presence of a realised being'? You would have to have a desire to do that. If there were no desires you wouldn't do anything at all because action is motivated by desire. You wouldn't even scratch the mosquito bite on your nose. Sri Ramana has said that it is quite possible to do Self-enquiry when there are thoughts in the mind. In fact you only do Self-enquiry when there are thoughts in the mind because enquiry is about getting discrimination, the knowledge of the Self and its relationship to the mind. If you have no thoughts you have no mind; if you have no mind, there is no instrument with which to enquire.

Desires are only a problem spiritually if they are binding. Non-binding desires are just fine. Even the *Yoga Sutra*, which is the authority on this subject, distinguishes between binding and non-binding *vasanas*. But the point is well taken. It is basically saying what the scriptures say – that you need to have a certain kind of prepared mind. We will not quibble about whether there are no thoughts or whether there are only a smattering of light, non-distracting thoughts. And it is saying that a pure mind is not enough, that you need a guru. *Vedanta*, The Science of Self-Enquiry, would agree.

Once you are in the presence of a realised being he says '… the power of the Self will make the residual "I" go back to its source from where it will die, never to rise again.' When the mind is full of passion and dullness it is in the presence of the Self but it doesn't know it. But when you have purified the mind to the point that Lakshmana Swamy is speaking about, the mind is already in the presence of the Self. That would be the only thing there aside from the mind and the mind would be so subtle that it would brilliantly refract the light of consciousness making Self-realisation inevitable. Even if one had the desire to be enlightened why wouldn't simply having that desire invoke the power of the Self and cause it to make the mind '… go back to its source from where it will die, never to rise again'? Presumably one would only have gone through such an arduous *sadhana* if one were going for liberation, so the Self would have been well aware of the desire of the aspirant.

So why would you seek a realised soul? Sri Ramana didn't have a guru and his mind was active, yet he realised the Self. If his mind wasn't active he would not have been able to simulate death and report the thoughts and feelings he had about it (see Chapter 5).

Another problem with this thought-free mind idea is that the mind is already the Self. If this is a nondual reality and there is such a thing as a pure mind, then that pure mind is going to have to be the Self. So what is meant here is not that the mind is destroyed never to rise again, but that the mind's ignorance – the belief that it is something other than the Self – never rises again, and is destroyed in the presence of the guru. It is ignorance that makes the mind a problem, not the mind itself. If by mind Swamy means ignorance then I have no quarrel with his statement.

What I'm going to say next is very important. It shows that the problem is ignorance, not lack of Self-experience. There is a reason why they called Sri Ramana a guru. And the reason is because the guru removes ignorance. You only need to look at the word itself to divine the meaning. 'Gu' means 'darkness' and 'ru' means 'to remove'. Darkness is a symbol of ignorance. What removes darkness? Light. Light is a symbol of knowledge. So you go to a guru to get knowledge, not to get some sort of permanent experience of the Self. The way this statement stands it seems as if a realised soul has some special power that will just sort of magically enlighten you. We can never be sure because we do not have Lakshmana Swamy here to help us with the meaning.

I asked Lakshmana Swamy for confirmation and he wouldn't answer me nor meet me.

If this statement of Lakshmana's were to be taken literally we could dismiss it as untrue because here he is using his mind to tell us about enlightenment. If it were dead, 'never to rise again', then who is making this statement? Presumably he is making the statement because he has a desire to enlighten us about enlightenment. If his desire-free mind was destroyed by the power of the Self he would not be able to make this statement on two accounts. First, a desire-free mind would have no desire to enlighten anybody and secondly, if the desire-free mind has been destroyed how will it say anything? People speak because they want to speak. Perhaps it was destroyed and reconstituted itself, but with a different understanding. How are we to know?

I'm not arguing with Lakshmana's statement. I agree that you need a guru if you are going to realise who you are. So the question becomes, 'What does the guru have to do with it and what is the nature of the experience he calls enlightenment?'

When I look at any statement, even one that on the face of it seems strange, rather than dismiss it out of hand I try to see how it could be true. Very few people study language and this probably applies to most enlightened beings. So a person like Lakshmana Swamy, who is respected as a realised soul, probably knows what he is talking about. At least maybe this is what happened to him when he went to Sri Ramana. Or maybe it is the best he can do to express how he got his realisation.

Let's take a look at the following: '… the power of the Self will make the residual "I" go back to its source from where it will die, never to rise again. This is the complete and full realisation.' What power is he talking about? Is it some special mystical power that only enlightened beings have?

In *Vedic* spiritual science three kinds of *shakti* or power are mentioned: *jnana shakti, iccha shakti,* and *kriya shakti. Iccha shakti* means desire. *Kriya shakti* means action and *jnana shakti* means the power of knowledge. It won't be the power of desire because we have been informed that the seeker has worked long and hard to free himself of desire. It won't be the power of action because the mind is dead already. So, let's take it that he means the power of knowledge. This would be something that someone going to a guru would lack. If liberation is liberation from ignorance that the Self is limited, then knowledge is what is needed. A blissful, dead, desireless mind is still not an enlightened mind.

There are a few more questions that need to be answered before this statement makes sense. What does 'residual "I"' mean? What does 'go back' mean? How will the power of knowledge make the residual 'I' go back to its source? And what kind of death is it?

I think the only reasonable interpretation of 'residual "I"' is an ego that does not know that it is limitless awareness. So the 'going back' is not a physical journey, an experiential journey, but the erasing of ignorance. The erasing of ignorance is not a mystical experience, but it has huge ramifications in terms of experience. It has important ramifications because what you experience has no meaning apart from how you interpret it. Your interpretation depends on your values and your values depend on what you know or do not know i.e. your ignorance.

So when your ignorance concerning your identity is removed, you interpret experience as it is, not according to your ignorance i.e. beliefs or opinions. When you see things as they are, your suffering stops.

In any case 'the source' means the Self. So the going back is the realisation of the identity of the residual 'I' and the Self. This 'destroys' the residual 'I'. What kind of destruction is it? It is the removal of the belief in the ego, the residual 'I', as your only identity. You can still function as an individual in the world when your sense of duality is gone. In fact you function perfectly without it. Even if it remains it remains like a mirage remains when you realise that it is not water. The ego is effaced completely. Scripture says it is like a burnt rope. It looks like a rope but it can't bind anything.

There is one more point that I'd like to make that concerns the last sentence. He says that the guru will '... pull the desire-free mind into the heart and destroy it completely'. Again we need to look at the meaning of the words. But before we do we need to address one glaring contradiction: why would the desire-free mind need to be destroyed? One can understand why one would want to rid oneself of a desire-filled mind – but a desire-free mind? A desire-free mind is thought by many to be the goal. Buddhism, for example, defines enlightenment as a desire-free mind. The word *nirvana* means a desire-free mind. Furthermore, why would you want to get rid of a desire-free mind only to gain a desire-free Self? The Self is *nirvana*, free of flame, desire. '*Nir*' means not and '*vana*' means flame.

The only way this could possibly make sense is that even a pure mind stands in the way of enlightenment. *Vedanta* does say that attachment to a pure mind is an obstacle to enlightenment, but how can the power of some external guru remove your attachment to anything? Only you can remove it because it only belongs to you.

This statement is a fine example of the problems that come with the language of experience. Let's give Lakshmana Swamy the benefit of the doubt and assume that he was misquoted or mistranslated and that he means the guru will remove your ignorance about who you are. If that is so then there is only one other possible source for a potential misunderstanding: that the guru is going to do this. It does look like the

196

guru is doing it but there is one lesson that needs to be learned from Sri Ramana's own enlightenment that applies across the board to all enlightened beings. And that is that the guru may show you the Self, but you have to realise it yourself. If the guru could do it, every qualified person who had an enlightened guru would be immediately enlightened. But it would effectively finish off the tradition of enlightenment. You would not have the confidence to enlighten others because you would not have enlightened yourself – like Sri Ramana and every other enlightened being did.

So the destruction of the mind that he is talking about is actually the destruction of ignorance?

Vedanta says that it is a destruction of ignorance, not desire. True, ignorance of the fact that one is whole and complete generates a lot of foolish and unnecessary desires. And these need to be gotten rid of if you are going to get a clear mind, and you need a clear mind if you are going to realise who you are. But certain desires are quite fine. In the *Bhagavad Gita*, which is a liberation scripture with the status of an *Upanishad*, *Krishna*, who is the enlightened person, says, 'I am the desire which is not opposed to *dharma* (path of Truth).' So there you have an enlightened mind that has desires in it.

Lakshmana Swamy is saying that if you have desire there is no way you can realise the Self.

Well, he does and then he contradicts himself. If you have a dead mind like he is saying, you won't have any desire in it – so why would you go off to an enlightened person to get something? Desire is what makes the mind alive.

Shankara and the whole of the *Vedantic* tradition says that you need a discriminating, dispassionate, quiet mind with a burning desire for liberation. If you have that you can realise that you are consciousness, and the knowledge will stick. You need the quiet mind so that you can grasp the knowledge. You need discrimination so you can sort out the subtle parts of the inner Self and you need dispassion so your emotions and prejudices won't derail your enquiry. So it seems to me that you need quite a bit of mind – just not a disturbed mind. Sri Ramana realised the Self with a very active mind. He made a little ritual and used logic while it was going on.

Are you saying that a person following the no-mind idea can't get enlightened?

No. I'm saying that it is not the only option. This whole argument is rather like the religious argument advanced by the Christians: you can only come to God through Christ. No other way works. I'm saying that the whole idea of a path, following a certain idea, has to be transcended at a certain point, particularly this idea that the mind has to be completely dead. People often try to kill it, eventually they give up and sometimes turn to the path of understanding.

It suggests things that are in the way must be gotten out of the way.

That's what Buddhism also says. They have this same *Yoga* idea. You have to remove all your unconscious tendencies. When they are gone, that is enlightenment.

But that can take years and years, even lifetimes.

Sure can. You have no idea how much stuff is in there. Are you going to set out to get rid of it all when you don't even know how big a task you're setting for yourself?

But people do it. Or think they are doing it.

They are actually doing something else but aren't aware of it. People can't just go sit in a room and do nothing. It's too 'weird'. They need a justification. It's like fishing. A lot of fishermen don't give a damn about fish, they just like to go out and stand in a cool stream looking at the lovely mountains and observing life in the wild. But it doesn't look that good. If somebody comes by and asks why they are standing there in waist deep water staring out into space they will be hard-pressed to come up with a sensible answer. So they take a fishing rod with them.

Vedanta says all you need to do is to destroy the ignorance that makes you believe that you are the ego, the small 'I'. Then the *vasanas* become non-binding. So it is ignorance that causes the thoughts to bind, rather than the thoughts themselves. You see that water tower?

Yes.

That means that you have a water tower thought in your mind.

Okay, I'm with you so far.

What are your feelings about it?

Feelings?

Right. You don't have any. You don't give a damn about it. You have no relationship to it at all. It is just a thought in your mind. It doesn't help you or hurt you. It just is what it is. It doesn't bind you in any way. What insulates you from it is the knowledge that you are not it, just like Sri Ramana realising he wasn't the body. He did not have to destroy his body to realise it. He just destroyed it in his mind.

So it is incredibly rare to find someone with a dead mind?

It's rare to find a duck-billed platypus. But what conclusion should we draw from that? The fact is that if you have a dead mind you are either in *nirvikalpa samadhi* (highest transcendent state of consciousness), asleep, in a coma, or actually dead. We have already seen that *nirvikalpa samadhi* is not liberation. And the others certainly aren't. There is a great statement by the Buddha that applies: 'Believe nothing you have read nor anything you have heard, even if I have said it, unless it agrees with common sense and reason.' This dead mind belief totally defies common sense and reason.

Sri Ramana says that the Self can only destroy the mind when the mind no longer has the tendency to move outward.

It means destroy the belief that there is something 'out there' that will make the mind permanently happy. When you no longer believe there is anything 'out there' the mind automatically turns inward. It's called *vairagya*, dispassion. You become indifferent toward the world. This is not the end of it. True, the mind is 'Self-realised'; that is to say it is experiencing the reflection of the Self in the pure mind but it still needs to determine if it is what it is experiencing or if it is something other than what it is experiencing.

This getting rid of *vasanas* is a good teaching. It is necessary, up to a point, for liberation. But to say that they all need to be gone is simply not true. The real problem is attachment to the *vasanas*.

That makes sense.

I'm not arguing against an introverted mind or Self-experience. Not at all. And please do *Yoga* and enjoy all the incredible mind-blowing Self-experiences you want. It's fine. But why sit there and just endlessly have Self-experience? Self-experience is not something you do. It is not an experience. It is your nature. No effort is required.

If it's a discrete experience, unlike any other, it will naturally exclude every other experience and you will not be able to enjoy the world because you can't have two experiences simultaneously if the world and the Self are mutually exclusive. In reality you have constant Self-experience, whether the mind is 'experiencing the Self' or not – you just don't know that whatever you are experiencing at every moment is the Self. So what the teachings of *Vedanta* try to do is to deal with a bit of ignorance – the tendency to exclude yourself from what you are experiencing – by pointing out that all experiences share something in common, an 'I'.

I don't take myself into account. So I don't understand that I'm the content of the experience. Without me there is no possibility of an experience. So I'm what's valuable, not the experience. Without me there is no possibility of having any experience, including the experience of an empty mind, the situation that Lakshmana Swamy talks about where all *vasanas* are exhausted leaving only the ego. Then, according to him, what is required is that this person should go and sit in the presence of a master to get his ego destroyed. But let's not get too frightened until we understand what is actually being destroyed. Does that mean there is no ego ever again? If that's the case then Sri Ramana wasn't enlightened, was he? He had an ego, a body, a mind. He walked and talked and acted like a normal person. In fact when you say 'Sri Ramana' you think of a person, an embodied being, an ego. You do not think of the Self although that is the meaning of his name. The reason Sri Ramana was so great was because he realised he was not just the little Ramana and embraced his identity as Sri Ramana the Self.

Yes. He worked in the kitchen and had very distinct ideas about how the food should be prepared and how things should be done in a particular way.

Yes. He had his preferences, his likes and dislikes.

He also had a mind that could design buildings and get them constructed.

Yes. The world is the Self and I'm the Self. The problem is my understanding is confused. I need to know what the world is and what I am and what my projections are. That is all. I need to destroy the confusion I have about each of these three aspects of my being. And Lakshmana Swamy is right that in the presence of the guru this understanding can come.

What does 'in the presence of a realised being' mean? What actually happens there? How does the presence of the guru remove my confusion? Sometimes it works through words. If you have an open mind and you only want liberation this is the easiest. Sometimes it works by just sitting there and observing, seeing from where the guru sees and seeing how the guru operates his life from that position. Then seeing that you are that position and that that position is free of everything – the world and your ego-mind. There are a number of different ways that this can come to you. It doesn't mean that the guru gives you a certain kind of glance, or some incredible 'energy' just wipes your ego out once and for all.

Lakshmana Swamy said that you can go so far on your own and then you need contact with a mahatma.

I agree with that.

But it is said that enlightenment is very rare.

Ananda, who was thought to be the Buddha's most highly qualified disciple, didn't get it when he was with the Buddha. When you are attached to your *vasanas* you will have beliefs like this. Your ego, which is nothing but your *vasanas*, does not want you to believe that it is easy. So you have the belief that there is some impossible experiential situation, in this case a totally dead mind, that will make you whole and complete, happy, whatever you think enlightenment is. Or you are holding out for something you think the world has to offer, the love of somebody, for example, and won't entertain the belief that you are love. The ego is that part of you that wants but doesn't want you free. So it encourages you to pick up beliefs that conclude that enlightenment is unbelievably rare. Sure, the scripture says it is very hard and it also says it is very easy. It is easy if you are rightly resolved and well qualified. It is very difficult if you are just playing at seeking. You can't have your cake and eat it too!

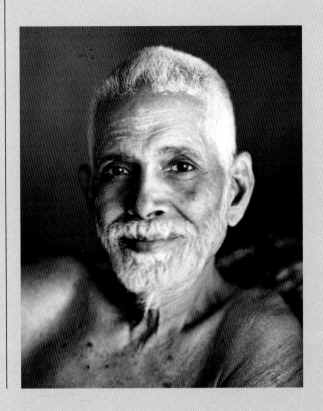

Keeping the mind fixed in the Self at all times is called Self-enquiry, whereas thinking oneself to be *Brahman*, which is *sat-chit-ananda* [being-consciousness-bliss], is meditation. Eventually, all that one has learnt will have to be forgotten.

Sri Ramana Maharshi

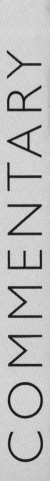

COMMENTARY

Above: Lion statue on Outer Path, bathing pool

Left: Sri Ramana and calf

Below: Sri Ramana with palmleaf 1940s
Group portrait 1930s

Right: Celebration

Right bottom: Arunachala north-west face from Vadayappanur village

CHAPTER 8

Commentary on Sri Ramana's Teachings 'Who Am I?' (Nan Yar)

By David Godman

[Sri Ramana's direct words are in bold]

In this essay written by David Godman, he carefully examines most of the questions and answers from Who Am I? (Nan Yar) *With his thorough knowledge of the subject, David's commentary provides wonderful interpretations and extra background information which really assist the reader to understand Sri Ramana's words. He brings together quotes and excerpts from other texts of Sri Ramana's to illustrate the* Who Am I? *text.*

This essay, composed by Bhagavan in the mid-1920s, is the work that originated with answers written in the sand in 1901. For many years it was the standard introduction to Bhagavan's teachings. Its publication was subsidised and copies in many languages were always available in the ashram's bookstore, enabling new visitors to acquaint themselves with Bhagavan's practical advice.

Although it continues to be a standard primer for those who want to know what Bhagavan taught, parts of *Who Am I?* are quite technical. Since Sivaprakasam Pillai, the devotee who asked the questions in 1901, was well acquainted with philosophical terminology, Bhagavan freely used technical terms in many of his answers. I have explained many of these in notes that alternate with the text. Bhagavan's answers from the original essay and other texts are printed in **bold type**. Everything else is my own commentary or explanation.

Since these explanations were originally answers to Sivaprakasam Pillai's questions, I have included some of the original questions in my own notes. Before each new section of *Who Am I?* begins, I give, if possible, the question that prompted it. Towards the end of the essay Bhagavan took portions from different answers and amalgamated them into single paragraphs, making it hard to know for sure whether he is answering a particular question or merely giving a teaching statement.

The paragraph that begins the essay was not given out in response to a question. It was composed by Bhagavan when he was rewriting the work in the 1920s. Many philosophical works begin with a statement about the nature of happiness and the means by which it can be attained or discovered. Bhagavan has followed this tradition in this presentation.

Every living being longs to be perpetually happy, without any misery. Since in everyone the highest love is alone felt for oneself, and since happiness alone is the cause of love, in order to attain that happiness, which is one's real nature and which is experienced daily in the mindless state of deep sleep, it is necessary to know oneself. To achieve that, enquiry in the form 'Who am I?' is the foremost means.

Who am I? [Q1]

'Who am I?' The physical body, composed of the seven *dhatus*, is not 'I'. The five sense organs ... and the five types of perception known through the senses ... are not 'I'. The five parts of the body which act ... and their functions ... are not 'I'. The five vital airs such as *prana*, which perform the five vital functions such as respiration, are not 'I'. Even the mind that thinks is not 'I'. In the state of deep sleep *vishaya vasanas* remain. Devoid of sensory knowledge and activity, even this [state] is not 'I'. After negating all of the above as 'not I, not I', the knowledge that alone remains is itself 'I'. The nature of knowledge is *sat-chit-ananda* [being-consciousness-bliss].

Vasanas is a key word in *Who Am I?* It can be defined as, 'the impressions of anything remaining unconsciously in the mind; the present consciousness of past perceptions; knowledge derived from memory; latent tendencies formed by former actions, thoughts and speech'. It is usually rendered in English as 'latent tendencies'. *Vishaya vasanas* are those latent mental tendencies that impel one to indulge in knowledge or perceptions derived from the five senses. In a broader context it may also include indulging in any mental activity such as daydreaming or fantasising, where the content of the thoughts is derived from past habits or desires.

The seven *dhatus* are chyle, blood, flesh, fat, marrow, bone and semen. The five sense organs are the ears, skin, eyes, tongue and nose, and the five types of perception or knowledge, called *vishayas*, are sound, touch, sight, taste and smell. The five parts of the body that act are the mouth, the legs, the hands, the anus, and the genitals and their functions are speaking, walking, giving, excreting and enjoying. All the items on these lists are included in the original text. I have relegated them to this explanatory note to facilitate easy reading.

The five vital airs *(prana vayus)* are not listed in the original text. They are responsible for maintaining the health of the body. They convert inhaled air and ingested food into the energy required for the healthy and harmonious functioning of the body.

This paragraph of *Who Am I?* has an interesting history. Sivaprakasam Pillai's original question was 'Who am I?', the first three words of the paragraph. Bhagavan's reply, which can be found at the end of the paragraph, was '**Knowledge itself is "I". The nature of knowledge is** *sat-chit-ananda.*' Everything else in this paragraph was interpolated later by Sivaprakasam Pillai prior to the first publication of the question-and-answer version of the text in 1923. The word that is translated as 'knowledge' is the Tamil equivalent of '*jnana*'. So, the answer to that original question 'Who am I?' is, '*Jnana* is "I" and the nature of *jnana* is *sat-chit-ananda.*'

When Bhagavan saw the printed text he exclaimed, 'I did not give this portion. How did it find a place here?'

He was told that Sivaprakasam Pillai had added the additional information, including all the long lists of physical organs and their functions, in order to help him understand the answer more clearly. When Bhagavan wrote the *Who Am I?* answers in an essay form, he retained these interpolations but had the printer mark the original answer in bold type so that devotees could distinguish between the two.

This interpolation does not give a correct rendering of Bhagavan's teachings on Self-enquiry. In the following exchange (*Talks with Sri Ramana Maharshi*, talk no. 197) Bhagavan explains how Self-enquiry should be done, and why the 'not I, not I' approach is an unproductive one:

Q: I begin to ask myself 'Who am I?', eliminate the body as not 'I', the breath as not 'I', the mind as not 'I' and I am not able to proceed further.

B: Well, that is as far as the intellect can go. Your process is only intellectual. Indeed, all the scriptures mention the process only to guide the seeker to know the truth. The truth cannot be directly pointed at. Hence, this intellectual process. You see, the one who eliminates the 'not I' cannot eliminate the 'I'. To say 'I am not this' or 'I am that' there must be an 'I'. This 'I' is only the ego or the 'I'-thought. After the rising up of this 'I'-thought, all other thoughts arise. The 'I'-

thought is therefore the root thought. If the root is pulled out all others are at the same time uprooted. Therefore, seek the root 'I', question yourself 'Who am I?' Find the source and then all these other ideas will vanish and the pure Self will remain.

Will there not be realisation of the Self even while the world is there [taken as real]? [Q5]
There will not be.

Why? [Q6]
If the mind, which is the cause of all knowledge and all actions, subsides, the perception of the world will cease. [If one perceives a rope, imagining it to be a snake] perception of the rope, which is the substratum, will not occur unless the perception of the snake, which has been superimposed on it, goes. Similarly, the perception of one's real nature, the substratum, will not be obtained unless the perception of the world, which is a superimposition, ceases.

What is the nature of the mind? [Q8]
That which is called 'mind', which projects all thoughts, is an awesome power existing within the Self, one's real nature. If we discard all thoughts and look [to see what remains when there are no thoughts, it will be found that] there is no such entity as mind remaining separate [from those thoughts]. Therefore, thought itself is the nature of the mind. There is no such thing as 'the world' independent of thoughts. There are no thoughts in deep sleep, and there is no world. In waking and dream there are thoughts, and there is also the world. Just as a spider emits the thread of a web from within itself and withdraws it again into itself, in the same way the mind projects the world from within itself and later reabsorbs it into itself. When the mind emanates from the Self, the world appears. Consequently, when the world appears, the Self is

not seen, and when the Self appears or shines, the world will not appear.

If one goes on examining the nature of the mind, it will finally be discovered that [what was taken to be] the mind is really only one's Self. That which is called one's Self is really *Atman*, one's real nature. The mind always depends for its existence on something tangible. It cannot subsist by itself. It is the mind that is called *sukshma sarira* [the subtle body] or *jiva* [the soul].

What is the path of enquiry for understanding the nature of the mind? [Q9]

That which arises in the physical body as 'I' is the mind. If one enquires, 'In what place in the body does this "I" first arise?' it will be known to be in the *hridayam*. That is the birthplace of the mind. Even if one incessantly thinks 'I, I', it will lead to that place. Of all thoughts that arise in the mind, the thought 'I' is the first one. It is only after the rise of this [thought] that other thoughts arise. It is only after the first personal pronoun arises that the second and third personal pronouns appear. Without the first person, the second and third persons cannot exist.

Hridayam is usually translated as 'Heart', but it has no connection with the physical heart. Bhagavan used it as a synonym for the Self, pointing out on several occasions that it could be split up into two parts, *hrit* and *ayam*, which together mean, 'this is the centre'. Sometimes he would say that the 'I'-thought arises from the *hridayam* and eventually subsides there again. He would also sometimes indicate that the spiritual Heart was inside the body on the right side of the chest, but he would often qualify this by saying that this was only true from the standpoint of those who identified themselves with a body. For a *jnani*, one who has realised the Self, the *hridayam* or Heart is not located anywhere, or even everywhere, because it is beyond all spatial concepts. The following answer (*Day by Day with Bhagavan*, 23.5.46) summarises Bhagavan's views on this matter:

I ask you to see where the 'I' arises in your body, but it is not really quite true to say that the 'I' rises from and merges on the right side of the chest. The Heart is another name for the reality, and it is neither inside nor outside the body. There can be no in or out for it since it alone is ... so long as one identifies with the body and thinks that he is in the body, he is advised to see where in the body the 'I'-thought rises and merges again.

A hint of this can also be found in this paragraph of *Who Am I?* in the sentence in which Bhagavan asks devotees to enquire '**In what place in the body does this "I" first arise?**'

Ordinarily, *idam*, which is translated here as 'place', means only that, but Bhagavan often gave it a broader meaning by using it to signify the state of the Self. Later in the essay, for example, he writes, '**The place [*idam*] where even the slightest trace of "I" does not exist is *swarupa* [one's real nature].**'

So, when Bhagavan writes '**In what place ...**' he is not necessarily indicating that one should look for the 'I' in a particular location. He is instead saying that the 'I' rises from the dimensionless Self, and that one should seek its source there.

As he once told Kapali Sastri, (*Sad Darshana Bhashya* pp. xvii-xix) '**You should try to have rather than locate the experience.**'

How will the mind become quiescent? [Q10]
The mind will only subside by means of the enquiry 'Who am I?' The thought 'Who am I?', destroying all other thoughts, will itself be finally destroyed like the stick used for stirring the funeral pyre.

What is the means for constantly holding on to the thought 'Who am I?' And what is jnana drishti? [Q11]
If other thoughts arise, one should, without attempting to complete them, enquire, 'To whom did they occur?' What does it matter if ever so many thoughts arise? At the very moment that each thought rises, if one vigilantly enquires

'To whom did this appear?' it will be known 'To me.' If one then enquires 'Who am I?' the mind will turn back to its source and the thought that had arisen will also subside. By repeatedly practising in this way, the mind will increasingly acquire the power to abide at its source. When the mind, which is subtle, is externalised via the brain and the sense organs, names and forms, which are material, appear. When it abides in the Heart, names and forms disappear. Keeping the mind in the Heart, not allowing it to go out, is called 'facing the Self' or 'facing inwards'. Allowing it to go out from the Heart is termed 'facing outwards'. When the mind abides in the Heart in this way, the 'I', the root of all thoughts, [vanishes]. Having vanished, the ever-existing Self alone will shine. The state where not even the slightest trace of the thought 'I' remains is alone *swarupa* [one's real nature]. This alone is called *mauna* [silence]. Being still in this way can alone be called *jnana drishti* [seeing through true knowledge]. Making the mind subside into the Self is 'being still'. On the other hand, knowing the thoughts of others, knowing the three times [past, present and future] and knowing events in distant places – these can never be *jnana drishti*.

The word *swarupa* is another key word in the text. It means 'one's real nature' or 'one's real form'. Each time the phrase 'one's real nature' appears in this text, it is a translation of *swarupa*. Bhagavan's repeated use of the word as a synonym for the Self indicates that the Self is not something that is reached or attained. Rather, it is what one really is, and what one always has been.

Mauna is another of the synonyms Bhagavan used to describe the Self:

Q: *What is* mauna *[silence]?*
A: That state which transcends speech and thought is *mauna* … That which is, is *mauna*. Sages say that the state in which the thought 'I' does not rise even in the least, alone is *swarupa*,

which means *mauna*. That silent Self is alone God … (*Be As You Are*, p. 13)

In *jnana*, the state of Self-knowledge or Self-realisation, there is no one who sees, nor are there objects that are seen. There is only seeing. The seeing that takes place in this state, called *jnana drishti*, is both true seeing and true knowing. It is therefore called 'seeing through true knowledge'.

In *Day by Day with Bhagavan* (17.10.46), Bhagavan points out that this seeing is really being and should not be confused with or limited to the sensory activity that goes under the same name: **'You are the Self. You exist always. Nothing more can be predicated of the Self than it exists. Seeing God or the Self is only being God or your Self. Seeing is being.'**

The same concept was elegantly formulated by Meister Eckart, the medieval German mystic, when he remarked, during one of his sermons, 'The eye by which I see God is the same eye by which God sees me. My eye and God's eye are one and the same, one in seeing, one in knowing.'

What is the nature of the Self? [Q16]
The Self, one's real nature, alone exists and is real. The world, the soul and God are superimpositions on it like [the illusory appearance of] silver in mother-of-pearl. These three appear and disappear simultaneously. Self itself is the world; Self itself is the 'I'; Self itself is God; all is *Shiva*, the Self.

At the beginning of this paragraph Bhagavan says, in effect, that the world, the soul and God are illusory appearances. Later he says that all three are the Self, and therefore real. This should be seen as a paradox rather than a contradiction. The following answer (*Guru Ramana* 1974 ed., p. 65) clarifies Bhagavan's views:

Shankara was criticised for his views on *maya* [illusion] without understanding him. He said that (1) *Brahman* [the

Self] is real (2) the universe is unreal, and (3) *Brahman* is the universe. He did not stop at the second because the third explains the other two. It signifies that the universe is real if perceived as the Self and unreal if perceived as apart from the Self. Hence *maya* and reality are one and the same.

The seeing of names and forms is a misperception because, in the Self, the one reality, none exist. Therefore, if a world of names and forms is seen, it must necessarily be an illusory one. Bhagavan explains this in verse 49 of *Guru Vachaka Kovai*:

Just as fire is obscured by smoke, the shining light of consciousness is obscured by the assemblage of names and forms. When, by compassionate divine grace, the mind becomes clear, the nature of the world will be known to be not illusory forms, but only the reality.

Are there any other means for making the mind quiescent? [Q12]
To make the mind subside, there is no adequate means except enquiry. If controlled by other means, the mind will remain in an apparent state of subsidence, but will rise again. For example, through *pranayama* [breath control] the mind will subside. However, the mind will remain controlled only as long as the *prana* [see the following note] is controlled. When the *prana* comes out, the mind will also come out and wander under the influence of *vasanas*. The source of the mind and the *prana* is one and the same. Thought itself is the nature of the mind, and the thought 'I' which indeed is the mind's primal thought, is itself the *ahankara* [the ego]. From where the ego originates, from there alone the breath also rises. Therefore, when the mind subsides, the *prana* will also subside, and when *prana* subsides, the mind will also subside. However, although the mind subsides in deep sleep, the *prana* does not subside. It is arranged in this way as a divine plan for the protection of the body and so that others do not take

the body to be dead. When the mind subsides in the waking state and in *samadhi*, the *prana* also subsides. The *prana* is the gross form of the mind. Until the time of death, the mind retains the *prana* in the body. When the body dies, the mind forcibly carries away the *prana*. Therefore *pranayama* is only an aid for controlling the mind; it will not bring about its destruction.

According to the *Upanishads*, *prana* is the principle of life and consciousness. It is the life breath of all the beings in the universe. They are born through it, live by it, and when they die, their individual *prana* dissolves into the cosmic *prana*. *Prana* is usually translated as 'breath' or 'vital breath', but this is only one of many of its manifestations in the human body. It is absorbed by both breathing and eating and by the *prana vayus* (mentioned earlier) into energy that sustains the body. Since it is assimilated through breathing, it is widely held that one can control the *prana* in the body by controlling the breathing.

According to *Yoga* philosophy, and other schools of thought agree, mind and *prana* are intimately connected. The collective name for all the mental faculties is *chitta*, which is divided into:

(a) *manas* (the mind), which has the faculties of attention and choosing
(b) *buddhi* (the intellect), which reasons and determines distinctions
(c) *ahankara*, the individual feeling of 'I', sometimes merely translated as ego

Chitta, according to *Yoga* philosophy, is propelled by *prana* and *vasanas* and moves in the direction of whichever force is more powerful. Thus, the *Yogis* maintain that by controlling the breath, which indirectly controls the flow of *pranas*, the *chitta* can be controlled. Bhagavan gives his own views on this later in the essay.

The reference to *samadhi* needs some explanation. According to Bhagavan, (*Guru Vachaka Kovai*, verse 898) '**Samadhi** is the state in which the unbroken experience of existence is attained by the still mind.' Elsewhere he has said, more simply, '**Holding onto reality is samadhi.**' (*Talks with Sri Ramana Maharshi*, talk no. 391)

Though Bhagavan would sometimes say that a person in *samadhi* is experiencing the Self, these *samadhis* do not constitute permanent realisation. They are temporary states in which the mind is either completely still or in abeyance.

The next section is a continuation of the answer to the previous question.

Are there any other means for making the mind quiescent? [Q12]
Like breath control, meditation on a form of God, repetition of sacred words and regulation of diet are mere aids for controlling the mind. Through meditation on a form of God and through the repetition of sacred words the mind becomes focused on one point. An elephant's trunk is always moving around, but when a chain is given to it to hold in its trunk, that elephant will go on its way, holding onto the chain instead of trying to catch other things with it. Similarly, when the mind, which is always wandering, is trained to hold onto any name or form of God, it will only cling to that. Because the mind branches out into innumerable thoughts, each thought becomes very weak. As thoughts subside more and more, one-pointedness [of mind] is gained. A mind that has gained strength in this way will easily succeed in Self-enquiry. Of all regulations taking *sattvic* food in moderate quantities is the best. Through [this], the *sattvic* quality of the mind gets enhanced and becomes an aid to Self-enquiry.

A *sattvic* diet is one which is vegetarian and which also excludes stimulating substances such as chillies, tobacco, alcohol and food that is excessively sour, salty or pungent.

Some Indian systems of thought maintain that the mind is composed of three fluctuating components called *gunas*:

(a) *sattva*, purity or harmony

(b) *rajas*, activity

(c) *tamas*, inertia or sluggishness

Since the type of food eaten affects the quality of the mind, non-*sattvic* foods promote *rajas* and *tamas*. The *sattvic* mind is the most desirable. One of the aims of spiritual practice is to increase the *sattvic* component at the expense of *rajas* and *tamas*.

Is it possible for the vishaya vasanas, *which come from beginningless time, to be resolved, and for one to remain as the pure Self?* [Q14]

Although *vishaya vasanas*, which have been recurring down the ages, rise in countless numbers like the waves of an ocean, they will all perish as meditation on one's real nature becomes more and more intense. Without giving room even to the doubting thought, 'Is it possible to destroy all these *vasanas* and remain as Self alone?' one should persistently and tightly hold onto meditation on one's real nature. However great a sinner one may be, one should, instead of lamenting, 'Oh, I am a sinner! How can I attain liberation?' completely give up even the thought of being a sinner. One steadfast in meditation on one's real nature will surely be saved.

How long should enquiry be practised? What is non-attachment? [Q15]

As long as there are *vishaya vasanas* in the mind, the enquiry 'Who am I?' is necessary. As and when thoughts arise, one should, then and there, annihilate them all through Self-enquiry in the very place of their origin. Not giving attention to anything other than oneself is non-attachment or desirelessness; not leaving the Self is *jnana* [true knowledge]. In truth, these two [non-attachment and desirelessness] are one and the same. Just as a pearl diver, tying a stone to his waist, dives into the sea and takes the pearl lying on the bottom, so everyone, diving deeply within himself in a detached way can obtain the pearl of the Self. If one resorts uninterruptedly to remembrance of one's real nature until one attains the Self, that alone will be sufficient. As long as there are enemies within the fort, they will continue to come out. If one continues to cut all of them down as and when they emerge, the fort will fall into our hands.

Is it not possible for God or the Guru to effect the release of the soul? [Q20]

God and Guru are, in truth, not different. Just as the prey that has fallen into the jaws of the tiger cannot escape, so those who have come under the glance of the Guru's grace will never be forsaken. Nevertheless, one should follow without fail the path shown by the Guru.

Remaining firmly in Self-abidance, without giving the least scope for the rising of any thought other than the thought of the Self, is surrendering oneself to God. However much of a burden we throw on God, He bears it all. Since the one supreme ruling power is performing all activities, why should we, instead of yielding ourselves to it, think, 'I should not act in this way; I should act in that way'? When we know that the train is carrying all the freight, why should we, who travel in it, suffer by keeping our own small luggage on our heads instead of putting it down and remaining happily at ease?

In the last three sections Bhagavan has used three terms, meditation on one's real nature *(swarupa dhyanam)*, remembrance of one's real nature *(swarupa smaranai)* and the thought of the Self *(atma chintanai)* to indicate the process by which one becomes aware of the Self. They should not be understood to mean that one should try to focus one's attention on the Self, for the real Self can never be an object of thought. The benedictory verse of *Ulladu Narpadu* explains what Bhagavan meant by such terms. It asks the question, 'How to meditate on that reality which is called the Heart?' since that reality alone exists, and it answers by saying, 'To abide in the Heart as it really is, is truly meditating.' That is to say, one can be the Heart by 'abiding as it is', but one cannot experience it as an object of attention.

This interpretation is confirmed by the sentence in the last extract from *Who Am I?* in which Bhagavan equates *atma chintanai* (the thought of the Self) with *atma nishta* (Self-abidance).

In a similar vein Bhagavan remarks later in the essay that '**always keeping the mind fixed in the Self alone can be called Self-enquiry**'.

What is happiness? [Q24]

What is called happiness is merely the nature of the Self. Happiness and the Self are not different. The happiness of the Self alone exists; that alone is real. There is no happiness at all in even a single one of the [many] things in the world. We believe that we derive happiness from them on account of *aviveka* [a lack of discrimination, an inability to ascertain what is correct]. When the mind is externalised, it experiences misery. The truth is, whenever our thoughts [that is, our desires] get fulfilled, the mind turns back to its source and experiences Self-happiness alone. In this way the mind wanders without rest, emerging and abandoning the Self and [later] returning within. The shade under a tree is very pleasant. Away from it the sun's heat is scorching. A person who is wandering around outside reaches the shade and is cooled. After a while he goes out again, but unable to bear the scorching heat, returns to the tree. In this way he is engaged in going from the shade into the hot sunshine and in coming back from the hot sunshine into the shade. A person who acts like this is an *aviveki* [someone who lacks discrimination], for a discriminating person would never leave the shade. By analogy, the mind of a *jnani* never leaves *Brahman*, whereas the mind of someone who has not realised the Self is such that it suffers by wandering in the world before turning back to *Brahman* for a while to enjoy happiness. What is called 'the world' is only thoughts. When the world disappears, that is, when there are no thoughts, the mind experiences bliss; when the world appears, it experiences suffering.

Is not everything the work of God? [Q17]
In the mere presence of the sun, which rises without desire, intention or effort, the magnifying glass emits hot light, the lotus blossoms and people begin, perform and cease their work. In front of a magnet a needle moves. Likewise, through the mere influence of the presence of God, who has no *sankalpa* [intention to accomplish anything], souls, who are governed by the three or five divine functions, perform and cease their activities in accordance with their respective *karmas*. Even so, He [God] is not someone who has *sankalpa*, nor will a single act ever touch him. This [untouchability] can be compared to the actions of the world not touching the sun, or to the good and bad qualities of the elements [earth, water, fire and air] not affecting the immanent space.

Sankalpa means 'resolve', 'will', or 'intention'. God has no personal *sankalpa*. That is to say, He does not decide or even think about what He should do. Though mature devotees 'bloom' on account of His presence, it is not because He has decided to bestow His grace on these fortunate few. His presence is available to all, but only the mature convert it into realisation.

The three divine functions are creation, sustenance and destruction. The five divine functions are these three plus veiling and grace. According to many Hindu scriptures, God creates, preserves and eventually destroys the world. While it exists, He hides His true nature from the people in it through the veiling power of *maya*, illusion, while simultaneously emanating grace so that mature devotees can lift the veils of illusion and become aware of Him as He really is.

For those who long for release, is it useful to read books? [Q23]
It is said in all the scriptures that to attain liberation one should make the mind subside. After realising that mind

control is the ultimate injunction of the scriptures, it is pointless to read scriptures endlessly. In order to know the mind, it is necessary to know who one is. How [can one know who one is] by researching instead in the scriptures? One should know oneself through one's own eye of knowledge. For [a man called] Rama to know himself to be Rama, is a mirror necessary? One's self exists within the five sheaths, whereas the scriptures are outside them. This self is the one to be enquired into. Therefore, researching in the scriptures, ignoring even the five sheaths, is futile. Enquiring 'Who am I that am in bondage?' and knowing one's real nature is alone liberation.

In self-enquiry one is enquiring into the nature and origin of the individual self, not the all-pervasive *Atman*. When Self appears in capitals, it denotes *Atman*, the real Self. When self it appears in lower case, it refers to the individual.

The five sheaths or *kosas* envelop and contain the individual self. They are:

(1) *annamayakosa*, the food sheath, which corresponds to the physical body
(2) *pranamayakosa*, the sheath made of *prana*
(3) *manomayakosa*, the sheath of the mind
(4) *vijnanmayakosa*, the sheath of the intellect
(5) *anandamayakosa*, the sheath of bliss

Sheaths two, three and four comprise the subtle body (*sukshma sarira*) while the fifth sheath, called the causal body, corresponds to the state of the individual self during sleep.

The individual 'I' functions through the five sheaths. Practitioners of the *neti-neti* (not this, not this) type of *sadhana* (spiritual practice) reject their association with the five sheaths in the way described in the second paragraph of *Who Am I?* The idea behind this practice is that if one rejects all thoughts, feelings and sensations as 'not I', the real 'I' will eventually shine in a form that is unlimited by or to the sheaths.

> **Keeping the mind fixed in the Self at all times is called self-enquiry, whereas thinking oneself to be *Brahman*, which is *sat-chit-ananda* [being-consciousness-bliss], is meditation. Eventually, all that one has learnt will have to be forgotten.**

One can distinguish different levels of experience in the practice of self-enquiry. In the beginning one attempts to eliminate all transient thoughts by concentrating on or looking for the primal 'I'-thought. This corresponds to the stage Bhagavan described earlier in the essay when one cuts down all the enemies, the thoughts, as they emerge from the fortress of the mind. If one achieves success in this for any length of time, the 'I'-thought, deprived of new thoughts to attach itself to, begins to subside, and one then moves to a deeper level of experience. The 'I'-thought descends into the Heart and remains there temporarily until the residual *vasanas* cause it to rise again. It is this second stage that Bhagavan refers to when he says that 'keeping the mind fixed in the Self alone can be called self-enquiry'. Most practitioners of self-enquiry will readily admit that this rarely happens to them, but nevertheless, according to Bhagavan's teachings, fixing the mind in the Self should be regarded as an intermediate goal on the path to full realisation.

It is interesting to note that Bhagavan restricts the term 'self-enquiry' to this phase of the practice. This unusual definition was more or less repeated in an answer he gave to Kapali Sastri:

> *Q: If I go on rejecting thoughts, can I call it* vichara *[self-enquiry]?*
> **A: It may be a stepping stone. But real *vichara* begins when you cling to yourself and are already off the mental movements, the thought waves.** (*Sad Darshana Bhashya*, 1975 ed., p. ix)

The following optimistic answers by Bhagavan, on keeping the mind in the Heart, may provide encouragement to those practitioners who often feel that such experiences may never come their way:

Q: How long can the mind stay or be kept in the Heart?

A: The period extends by practice.

Q: What will happen at the end of that period?

A: The mind returns to the present normal state. Unity in the Heart is replaced by a variety of perceived phenomena. This is called the outgoing mind. The Heart-going mind is called the resting mind.

When one daily practises more and more in this manner, the mind will become extremely pure due to the removal of its defects and the practice will become so easy that the purified mind will plunge into the Heart as soon as the enquiry is commenced. (*Be As You Are*, p. 66)

Bhagavan noted that 'thinking oneself to be *Brahman* ... is meditation', not enquiry. Traditional *Advaitic sadhana* follows the path of negation and affirmation. In the negative approach, one continuously rejects all thoughts, feelings and sensations as 'not I'. On the affirmative route one attempts to cultivate the attitude 'I am *Brahman*' or 'I am the Self'. Bhagavan called this latter approach, and all other techniques in which one concentrates on an idea or a form, '**meditation**', and regarded all such methods as being indirect and inferior to self-enquiry.

Q: Is not affirmation of God more effective than the quest 'Who am I?' Affirmation is positive, whereas the other is negation. Moreover, it indicates separateness.

A: So long as you seek to know how to realise, this advice is given to find your Self. Your seeking the method denotes your separateness.

Q: Is it not better to say 'I am the Supreme Being' than ask 'Who am I?'

A: Who affirms? There must be one to do it. Find that one.

Q: Is not meditation better than investigation?

A: Meditation implies mental imagery, whereas investigation is for the reality. The former is objective, whereas the latter is subjective.

Q: There must be a scientific approach to this subject.
A: To eschew unreality and seek the reality is scientific.
(*Talks with Sri Ramana Maharshi*, talk no 338)

Is it necessary for one who longs for release to enquire into the nature of the tattvas? [Q21]
Just as it is futile to examine the garbage that has to be collectively thrown away, so it is fruitless for one who is to know himself to count the numbers and scrutinise the properties of the *tattvas* that are veiling the Self, instead of collectively throwing them all away.

Indian philosophers have split the phenomenal world up into many different entities or categories which are called *tattvas*. Different schools of thought have different lists of *tattvas*, some being inordinately long and complicated. Bhagavan encouraged his devotees to disregard all such classifications on the grounds that, since the appearance of the world is itself an illusion, examining its component parts one by one is an exercise in futility.

Is there no difference between waking and dream? [Q22]
One should consider the universe to be like a dream. Except that waking is long and dreams are short, there is no difference [between the two states]. To the extent to which all the events which happen while one is awake appear to be real, to that same extent even the events that happen in dreams appear at that time to be real. In dreams, the mind assumes another body. In both the dream and the waking [states] thoughts and names-and-forms come into existence simultaneously.

I will finish this commentary with an answer to a question that has already been given:

Is it possible for the vishaya vasanas, *which come from beginningless time, to be resolved, and for one to remain as the pure Self?* [Q14]

There are not two minds, one good and another evil. The mind is only one. It is only the *vasanas* that are either auspicious or inauspicious. When the mind is under the influence of auspicious tendencies, it is called a good mind, and when it is under the influence of inauspicious tendencies, a bad mind. However evil people may appear, one should not hate them. Likes and dislikes are both to be disliked. One should not allow the mind to dwell much on worldly matters. As far as possible, one should not interfere in the affairs of others. All that one gives to others, one gives only to oneself. If this truth is known, who indeed will not give to others?

If the individual self rises, all will rise. If the individual self subsides, all will subside. To the extent that we behave with humility, to that extent will good result. If one can continuously control the mind, one can live anywhere.

Self-enquiry directly leads to
Self-realisation by removing the
obstacles which make you think
that the Self is not already realised.

Sri Ramana Maharshi

COMMENTARY

Above: *Arunachala from Perumpakkam Road, south face*

Left: *Sri Ramana with Kariyanur Natesa Swamigal of Esanya mutt (left)*

Below: *Ashram Dining Hall today*

Right: *Sri Ramana in the ashram with monkey*

CHAPTER 9

How to conduct Self-Enquiry

*Practical commentary on part of
'Who Am I?' (Nan Yar)
from a Satsang with Premananda*

[Sri Ramana's direct words are in bold]

This chapter is taken directly from Premananda's
Satsang. *He draws our attention to the fact that we are
always occupying our minds with some story. When we
make the space by becoming still and quiet, the Self is
revealed. He asks us to become aware of our conditioning
and our attachment to our thoughts – my thoughts, my
life. Questions and answers from* **Who Am I?** *(Nan Yar)
where Sri Ramana talks about Self-enquiry are discussed
and clarified. Premananda clearly explains how to do
Self-enquiry, leaving no doubt as to how to proceed.
Quotes from Sri Ramana on Self-enquiry are scattered
through the chapter.*

Always keeping the mind fixed in Self alone is called 'Self-enquiry'.

Sri Ramana Maharshi

We are Truth, we are what we are looking for. It's right here, so close. Not even close. We are this Truth. When people actually discover this Truth, they laugh, because they look around at everybody doing their drama, which they call 'my life', and it's so incredibly funny. It's a bit like a dog chasing its own tail. The dog never realises that the tail is part of itself, and the more it runs the more the tail also runs!

This is an incredible misunderstanding. People think the tail is somehow separate and if they just get the right teaching, they will find out where the tail is and then they can stick it back on the dog. What you're looking for is you and it's always there. It's always been there, even when you were a baby, and now as an adult you have lost touch with it. This is something you must never forget. You are what you are seaching for.

Satsang (meeting in Truth) is all about how to come back to where you were when you were born. When we're born we're just there, absolutely present, without any baggage of 'my life', the past and future. Life is just happening moment by moment. When we are hungry we need milk and when things come out the other end, they come out. When there is light the eyes are attracted to it – it is very simple.

It is important to realise that the only thing that prevents us from simply being here is what we call 'me', all this stuff on our computer hard drive, in our video projector – all those old films that we're always watching. They're the only things which prevent us from knowing our true nature. We need something simple to remind us to come back to the source, to come back to our origin. We just need a little reminder. We don't need any big teaching.

When my teacher, Papaji, was asked, 'What is your teaching?' he said, 'Be quiet!' His whole teaching was 'Be Quiet!' When you be quiet, then without really doing anything, thoughts become less and less. When you focus on an emotion or a body sensation and you just accept it, don't try to fight it, don't try to change it, simply accept it, 'poof', it disappears like magic. You haven't done anything. You bring your focus inside to that place. You don't do anything, you just accept it. 'Poof!' It's gone.

When Sri Ramana Maharshi was a schoolboy of sixteen he had a spontaneous awakening. He ran away from home to the holy mountain, Arunachala, and spent the rest of his life there. He never left the mountain (see Chapter 1). In the beginning, after the awakening, he didn't know what had happened to him. He was very young, there was nobody to tell him what had happened and he didn't even know to ask about it. Later, he said that he thought perhaps he had some terrible disease, but if he did, he liked it! He couldn't resist the pull to the holy mountain, Arunachala.

At the base of the mountain there's a huge *Shiva* temple, one of the five most important temples in South India. When he first arrived in Tiruvannamalai he came to the temple, threw away the last of his possessions and became totally immersed in the Self, oblivious to the outside world. The people in the temple supported him; they gave him food and protected him.

Some years later Sivaprakasam Pillai, a scholarly devotee, approached the young Sri Ramana on Arunachala when he was living in Virupaksha Cave and asked him for his teachings. He approached Sri Ramana when Ramana was about twenty-two years old, by which time he'd been living on the mountain, alone and in silence, for about three years. What resulted was this small booklet with twenty-eight questions and answers.

It's very small and will fit in your pocket. It's called *Who Am I? (Nan Yar)*. At the end of all the different spiritual traditions, with all the different techniques, you come to this question about the 'I'. It's about the fact that we believe in the false 'I', this video, 'my life'. We believe I am these strange beliefs, judgments and desires, this whole package I call 'my life'. But it's simply not true. It's just a wrong idea.

Self-enquiry begins with changing the focus from outside in the world to the inside. We become Self aware. We watch. This is only possible when our mind has become quiet. If the mind is constantly full of thoughts we cannot get anything from Self-enquiry. Sri Ramana has outlined a clear method for using Self-enquiry intensely in our everyday life to bring the mind to rest at the source.

> **You have to ask yourself the question 'Who am I?' This investigation will lead in the end to the discovery of something within you, which is behind the mind. Solve that great problem and you will solve all other problems.**
>
> *Sri Ramana Maharshi*

We will look at the questions and answers from the booklet which have a direct bearing on how to conduct Self-enquiry. Sri Ramana's words are printed in bold. The complete booklet is reproduced in Chapter 4.

What I'm calling the True Nature is called the Self in the booklet. You can call it the Higher Self. You can call it God. You can call it the Soul. 'The world' means the thoughts and feelings and all the objects, including people, which can be perceived by the five senses.

Sri Ramana was asked:

When will the realisation of the Self be gained? [Q4]
When the world which is what-is-seen has been removed, there will be realisation of the Self which is the seer.

Will there not be realisation of the Self even while the world is there (taken as real)? [Q5]
There will not be.

This is very clear and very shocking because he's saying that if you want to know the Self, then the world has to be recognised for what it really is, an illusion. He is also saying that if the world is there you don't know the Self. It suggests that what we take as the world is not really as solid as it appears. Our whole conditioning has always been that the world is real as it is, that it is solid and that we are a separate part of that world. This world, which we take as real, must be seen as an illusion in order to know the Self.

People who have had a taste or a glimpse of the Self or who have found the Self, know this to be true. It doesn't actually mean, for example, that Premananda doesn't see any trees in the garden. I see the trees in the garden. I even see you sitting here. In that way the world looks like it used to look, but something changes. When we merge with the Self then it's as if our whole awareness is just there in this stillness. It's as if the world then disappears. We only know the world through our senses but when we come deeply into the Self we're not so busy with our senses and it's as if the world fades or becomes like a shadow.

Any words I might say about this don't make sense because the mind can't understand. If you are quite new to this, your mind can only freak out. It can't catch it, yes? There's no way for the mind to make sense of this. The understanding has to be from your own being, from deeper than the mind.

When people come to *Satsang* they become quiet, they leave their stories and dramas behind for two or three hours. They drop their attachment to these stories and come to stillness. They go back to work, families, relationship, everyday life. Just walking in the street there's a collective sense about life that we've been conditioned by for so many years. We pick up again all those invisible structures and we're back in the movie called, 'my life'. Immediately this stillness seems to fade away and then we say 'Oh! *Satsang* didn't work.' But it can't not work because we are that stillness. That is our nature. It has to work. It's always working, we just don't know it.

A prerequisite to know the Self is to have achieved a still mind though a spiritual practice. Most people have such a busy mind and are so identified with their story that there is simply no space in which Self-enquiry can work. There needs to be some work, some time spent to get to know the mind and to quieten it. It is important to come to a *sattvic* mind, a clear and peaceful mind. This is a mind that is available to understand the Truth.

So *Satsang* absolutely works. It's absolutely beautiful because it's so simple. It's so incredibly simple and it's a complete change, a revolution, because you don't need anything from the outside. You don't need anything from anybody. You've got it all there, everything, all the wisdom of the universe, all the knowledge, all the love, everything is just there, right there inside you. I say 'inside'. Actually it's not inside. It's all around and through you.

So how to stay in touch with this stillness? There's a suggestion from Sri Ramana who was asked:

How will the mind become still? [Q10]
By the enquiry 'Who am I?'. The thought 'Who am I?' will destroy all other thoughts, and like the stick used for stirring the funeral pyre, it will itself in the end get destroyed. Then, there will be Self-realisation.

In India, when they burn the body, they use one stick for making sure everything burns and in the last minute they also throw that stick into the fire and then nothing is left. It is the same with Self-realisation. The question 'Who am I?' acts like the stick in the fire and it will destroy all the other thoughts. He says, '**Then, there will be Self-realisation.**' When all the thoughts are destroyed then Self-realisation is simply there.

Persist in the enquiry throughout your waking hours. That would be quite enough. If you keep on making the enquiry till you fall asleep, the enquiry will go on during sleep also. Take up the enquiry again as soon as you wake up.
Day by Day with Bhagavan, (D. Mudaliar)

Yesterday, when we did this enquiry together, almost everybody arrived for the meeting with some excitement in the body. Perhaps there was a little bit of pressure in the chest or some other bodily sensations, maybe some fear or other emotions, or lots of thoughts. You'd been busy driving a car or arranging something on the telephone. Then we all just became quiet.

We sat together for twenty or thirty minutes and we became more and more quiet. There was no talking, no discussing. Then I asked everyone to look: What is there? In the beginning people found a thought, they found a feeling, because we are always looking for something. When we look at the sky we always see clouds, an aeroplane, the sun, the moon or the stars at night. We never even notice the blueness of the sky because our minds are programmed to always look for something. It's the same when we look inside. We're always looking for something – a thought, a feeling, a body sensation, something.

Actually what we're really looking for, the Self, is simply an empty nothing. It's just a huge space of nothing, like the sky without any boundaries, without any colour, without anything in it. It's just emptiness. It's like a vast dark ocean. Sometimes people experience it as light, but most people experience it as a kind of shiny black ocean. Once you come into this shiny black ocean even a few thoughts don't matter. There can be a few thoughts coming and going and they're just bubbles in the ocean. They don't disturb anything.

But we so easily get attached to the world. There's some drama with the children, or suddenly there's heavy rain and the roof starts leaking. Then there's the drama of getting the builder to come. Where's the money to pay for it? A big telephone bill arrives. It's so easy to get caught up in the world. We need some way to come from the world back to this ocean, back to the source.

> *What is the means for constantly holding on to the thought 'Who am I?'* [Q11]
> When other thoughts arise, one should not pursue them, but should inquire: 'To whom do they arise?' It does not matter how many thoughts arise. As each thought arises, one should inquire with diligence, 'To whom has this thought arisen?' The answer that would emerge would be 'to me'. Thereupon if one inquires 'Who am I?', the mind will go back to its source; and the thought that arose will become quiescent. With repeated practice in this manner, the mind will develop the skill to stay in its source.

'When other thoughts arise, one should not pursue them ...' What does he mean by 'not pursue them'? Usually when some thought appears in our head, 'Lunch!' then we think, 'What kind of lunch?'

'Fish.' 'Where to buy the fish?' Okay, then, 'How to get to the fish shop?' 'Oh! My bicycle is broken.' Before long, this first thought about lunch has suddenly taken us a long way and we're thinking about how to borrow our friend's bicycle. (Laughter) It started just with a thought about lunch and now we're thinking, 'Well, how can I borrow my friend's bicycle?' You see? Don't pursue the thought. The thought comes, 'lunch'. It's okay, no problem, and then it will disappear.

If you get really quiet you can see the thoughts popping out of nothing. There's this stillness, there's this ocean and suddenly out of the ocean comes a thought. Usually we take this thought and we say, 'It's my thought. I thought that. I'm thinking about lunch.' But actually it's just a thought. We're very attached to all these thoughts. 'They're my thoughts.' But actually it's not true. They're just thoughts. So Sri Ramana is saying don't pursue the thoughts. The thought of lunch comes and then it will go, and then another thought, 'football'. Then that one goes.

Question from the audience: When do you eat?

When you're hungry.

When you're hungry. That's different from thinking of lunch?

Yes. You just go through your day and when the body needs food you'll feel hungry. It's all arranged. The body is arranged like an alarm clock and when it's hungry you know it. But of course, we human beings have made all these things into a programme. Lunch is at one o'clock, tea is at four o'clock and dinner is at seven o'clock. But in fact you can simply trust your own body. When the body is tired then you sleep. Maybe you want to sleep at four o'clock in the afternoon. Maybe you sleep at eleven at night. Maybe it changes. When the body is tired you can sleep. When the body is hungry you eat.

Sri Ramana says, '**When other thoughts arise, one should not pursue them …**' That's very important. Don't go into the thoughts, don't become attached to the thoughts. Don't follow lunch back to the friend's bicycle. Treat the thought just as a thought, not my thought. No attachment. Rather, he says, '**As each thought arises, one should inquire with diligence, "To whom has this thought arisen?"**' You're not interested in the thought. You are not interested if it's about lunch, money or a new girlfriend. You're not interested in the quality of the thought or the content of the thought. You're just interested to ask, '**To whom has this thought arisen?**' The answer is 'to me'. It's always 'to me' because our whole attachment is to this 'me – my life'.

Then he said, '**Thereupon if one inquires "Who am I?"** [or "Who is this me?"] **the mind will go back to its source …**' So it is two questions: you ask, '"**To whom has this thought arisen?**" The answer that would emerge would be "to me". Thereupon if one enquires, "**Who am I?**" [or "Who is this me?"] **the mind will go back to its source; and the thought that arose** [it doesn't matter what it is] **will become quiescent. With repeated practice in this manner the mind will develop the skill to stay in its source.**' If you continue to enquire intensely, after some time the mind will become quieter; there will be fewer thoughts and the mind will get into the habit of simply being still.

In the beginning there is a bit of a battle, but after some time it works by itself. If you do this intensely, after some time you don't have to ask the two questions. It comes to the point where just to remember the questions is enough, or even a shorthand like 'who'. Just the remembering, and you are back into stillness.

Sri Ramana also suggests that when you start Self-enquiry you sit and with your eyes closed. As soon as you close your eyes sixty percent of the world disappears. Then you've only really got the thoughts, the sounds, some emotions and body sensations. In the beginning you can make it like a practice, sit and look inside and do the Self-enquiry. Once you have mastered Self-enquiry with your eyes closed, then you're ready to take Self-enquiry and put it in your ordinary day.

From where does this 'I' arise? Seek for it within; it then vanishes. This is the pursuit of wisdom. When the mind unceasingly investigates its own nature, it transpires that there is no such thing as mind. This is the direct path for all.

> **The mind is merely thoughts. Of all thoughts the thought 'I' is the root. Therefore the mind is only the thought 'I'.**
>
> *Sri Ramana Maharshi*

Sri Ramana is suggesting a very ancient wisdom and it's very simple. He says that when we are going through our ordinary day we don't have to change anything. Everything that happens in our ordinary day can be used to come back to the source. If you are driving your car, if you are washing the dishes, if you're thinking, you can use all these situations to come back to the ocean. Perhaps there are some emotions: somebody didn't treat me right, I feel angry, I don't feel love. Again, all these can be used to come back to the source. We don't need to take anything as real. Anyway, these emotions are always changing. One minute we're angry and the next minute it's gone. We feel sad, it's gone.

He is suggesting you don't have to change your life. You can just accept that your life is an opportunity to constantly come back to the source. It's a completely different way to look at your life. Usually we look at our life as the point; he is suggesting the point of our life is to use the everyday things in the world to come back to the source. If you haven't had much experience of this it can all sound a bit difficult.

I will clarify the steps again. To do Self-enquiry you ask: 'Who is driving the car?' 'Me.' 'Who is this me?' This second question doesn't have a mental answer because it doesn't make any sense to say, 'A man is driving the car.' You just be quiet and see how it takes you back to stillness. Maybe not in the beginning, but if you persevere the mind comes back to stillness. 'Who is cooking the lunch?' 'Me.' 'Who is this me?' And you come back inside. 'Who is feeling tired?' 'Me.' 'Who is this me?'

Question from the audience: You don't stick to the second question? You don't push it?

You just leave it. Just look inside and you'll find that with some practise you'll come to an empty space, nothing is happening. The source is, in fact, an empty space. Our true nature is not all these thoughts, ideas and desires, but just emptiness. It's like a potential and then when something happens in our life, out of this potential we act, we speak, we think. There's nothing wrong with the mind in the sense of functioning. If we have to go from A to B we need a mind to navigate through the city. When we need it, the mind just activates and navigates through the city. What we are interested in is not being attached to the conditioned mind that's always thinking endlessly about nothing important, about the past or the future.

Yes, it's misleading because it seems the options are either having a mind or not having a mind.

Yes, when you hear about no-mind you could have the idea that suddenly you've got no mind, there's nothing there. Well, then you'd be dead. For functioning you need a mind. To walk up the stairs you need a mind that figures out how high to lift your legs. We don't need a mind that goes from the thought of lunch back to my friend's bicycle, and we don't need a mind that's walking in the park thinking about last year's holiday when it rained every day, the food was terrible and my girlfriend went off with my best friend. It was a terrible holiday! We don't need the conditioned part of the mind, full of old stories.

The other thing I can say is that when one does this enquiry intensely it seems to have the effect of creating a much thinner mind, a light-weight mind rather than a thick, heavy mind, and so it brings people closer to this moment of awakening. I'm not saying that if you do Self-enquiry for six months then you'll awaken, but it might help your chances.

Let me give you an example. A woman started coming to *Satsang* a year ago. What she heard agreed with her own ideas, even though her parents had tried to get these ideas out of her for many years through therapy. She felt a resonance with *Satsang* and she was interested. She began to practise Self-enquiry. She's a very focused person and she has a very intelligent, detailed mind and so when she went on holiday to the Canary Islands she sat on the rocks doing Self-enquiry for two weeks, every day, very intensely.

Also, very importantly, she had a strong longing inside to wake up, to come out of the dream. She never really believed the dream, but her parents were always telling her, 'This dream is real; have a bit more therapy, then you can believe it like we believe it.' Then suddenly on the rock one day there was an experience like death, like the end. Everything became black and it was as if she was dying. What actually happened in this death was that her conditioned mind, 'my life', crashed. It just stopped. After that she brought the focus of her life to *Satsang*.

Here's another story, about a very intelligent guy. He designed software for computers, so he had a very analytical kind of mind. He had been doing meditation and Reiki for two years. Then he met me, became connected and came to the retreat in India. During this retreat the focus is on Self-enquiry. He came back to Germany where he has a wife and a son in Nuernberg. He had lots of stories he wanted to tell his wife from India. When he got back she said, 'Wait a minute! I have something to tell you. While you've been in India I've been having a love affair with one of your friends.' He was really shocked. So all these very strong emotions came – feeling abandoned, feeling he was going to lose his son and family, feeling upset.

He came to a moment where he was sitting on the couch in the living room holding a cup of tea. He was just sitting on this couch and then he remembered the Self-enquiry from the retreat. Using Self-enquiry he was able to see that there was a body which was sitting on the couch, holding a cup of tea, with a mind that was freaking out, and that was all. In that moment of clear seeing his conditioned mind simply dropped. I can't say if you use Self-enquiry you will become Self-realised, but it seems to be a tremendous support.

Question from the audience: What about when I do Self-enquiry and I become very judgmental of myself? For example, when I ask 'Who am I?' an answer comes such as, 'I am an arrogant man.'

I'm arrogant, yes. Well this is the kind of thing that your mind believes about you. You believe you are an arrogant man, but is that true?

I don't know.

Well, of course it's not true. It's true only in your conditioned mind. You have been conditioned by your family to believe that you are this kind of person. But it's not true.

Then do you say to yourself that it's not true, or do you do something different?

You begin with a simple question such as, 'Who is sitting on the chair?' 'Me.' 'Who is this me?' And you leave the second question. You don't say 'I'm a man', or 'I'm an arrogant man.' You just leave it without words. Because what we're trying to find, this source, is beyond words.

Yes, but my mind is so fast, the words just pop up.

Yes. In the beginning it's like that but it gradually becomes quieter and quieter.

Okay, that's a relief!

Sri Ramana was then asked:

> *Are there no other means for making the mind quiescent?* [Q12]
> **Other than inquiry, there are no adequate means. If through other means it is sought to control the mind, the mind will appear to be controlled, but will again go forth.'**

There are all kinds of spiritual practices. There is meditation, *mantra* (sacred sound) singing, breath techniques. If you meditate you can appear to have stillness. Many people who meditate for twenty years become very quiet. It looks like stillness. It looks like the source. But if they stop doing the meditation, whatever was there comes back again. It's not real. It's only that the mind has been controlled. They are not really free.

> Meditation requires an object to meditate upon, whereas there is only the subject without the object in *Vichara* (Self-enquiry). Meditation differs from *Vichara* in this way.
>
> *Sri Ramana Maharshi*

When people came to Sri Ramana's ashram and met him, he would ask them if they had a practice, and if they said it was meditation he would say, 'Very, good, very good.' He knew that if you started doing meditation, at some point you would come to this question, 'Who am I?' so he never interfered with what people were doing. But if somebody came and had no practice, then Sri Ramana would advise them to try Self-enquiry. He said that Self-enquiry is the most direct way to Self-realisation.

Over the last two years I've been noticing that people who have many spiritual ideas might not get this as easily as those who've hardly ever been to *Satsang*, who are quite innocent, humble and open. Yesterday we had a visit from a guy who has been to every teacher in the world for the last thirty years. He can write about all these things very beautifully; so many ideas. He knows this, so he doesn't mind me speaking about it. He really has a longing for Truth, but he has read so many books and he's been to so many teachers that he has all kinds of ideas. Many seekers are like this. You take them down the right turn and then their mind says 'Ah, what about turning left?' There is always this apparent knowing happening inside – a sophisticated spiritual mind. Not so easy actually. Sometimes it's easier when people are just innocent and available. Then they can really see this very simply. Jesus even said the humble would inherit the Kingdom of God.

A few years ago there was a man who was coming regularly to *Satsang* weekends. He would go back to his wife and she had the idea he must have a girlfriend because he was always looking so happy when he came home. She decided she would come and check out what was going on. She came with him to the next weekend. She really liked it and she realised there was no girlfriend. She enjoyed the energy of the *Satsang* and the energy of the community. She came to a second weekend. She'd never done any spiritual things. She worked in a bakery; a very simple woman. On the second weekend I saw her face was glowing and asked, 'What's happening to you?' She said, 'My mind has gone. I've got no mind. Just empty inside. My mind's completely empty.' It was very sweet and she only came there to look for her husband's girlfriend! (Laughter) Really beautiful.

Solitude is an attitude of the mind; a man attached to the things of life cannot get solitude, wherever he may be. A detached man is always in solitude.

Sri Ramana Maharshi

Above: On Arunachala

Left: Sri Ramana

Below: Arunachaleswara Temple view from Arunachala

Right top: Sri Ramana group Sri Ramana reclining by Welling 1948

Right centre: Dancing Shiva Sri Ramana at the Mother's Shrine

Right bottom: Arunachala north-west face

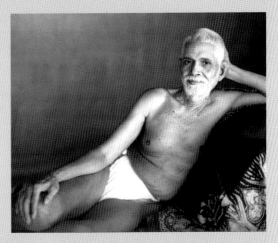

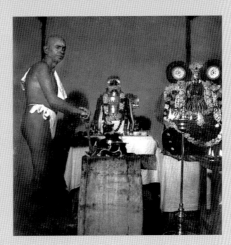

CHAPTER 10

David Godman's Life Story

David Godman interviewed
by Premananda

David tells how he left Oxford University in 1974 and found his way to India and to Ramana Ashram in 1976. He came for a visit and never left! In these last thirty-three years he has met many of the close devotees of Sri Ramana and spent much of his time researching and writing about them, in particular Lakshmana Swamy, Annamalai Swami and Papaji. His most recent book is a translation of the poems of Muruganar. In this chapter David goes into details about his spiritual masters and especially the cat-and-mouse game that Papaji played with him for several years from 1992 to 1997 while David was writing Papaji's biography, Nothing Ever Happened.

David, would you tell us a about how you came to be here at Arunachala?

In 1974 I was at Oxford University feeling very disenchanted with the reductionism of standard academic methods. I was spending very little attention on my academic course and bankrupting myself financially buying spiritual books, one of which was a book on Sri Ramana's teachings. I think up until that point I can't say that I was seeking anything; I just had an insatiable spiritual curiosity. Somehow reading that book stopped my mind. Not because it answered any questions; it just put me into a place where there weren't any questions and there weren't any answers. Somehow being exposed to Bhagavan's words in that book put me in the state he was directing people to. There was a very satisfied, contented silence. If you had asked me about it I would have said that this man answered my questions, but he didn't, he took them away.

I dropped out of college a few weeks later because I thought that there was more to life than reading these books and taking exams on them. I dropped out and became a hermit in Ireland for a while. I practised Self-enquiry.

About a year and a half later I was on a kibbutz in Israel, it's quite a long story how I got there and we don't need to go into it. I realised that I had nothing to do the next year and my grandmother had just died and left me some money. I tried to work out if I had enough to go to India and visit Ramana Ashram for a brief visit and decided that I didn't. I think that I decided that I needed an extra two hundred pounds to make the trip. So I said off-hand, 'If two hundred pounds arrives, then I am off tomorrow.' The next day of course two hundred pounds dropped from the sky for no reason at all. So I said, 'That's it, I'm off to India.' I came for a visit in 1976 and never went back.

If you came in 1976 that means you have been here for twenty-five years. During that time have you personally met some of these people that you have written about?

249

I have met them all. I mean all the ones whose books are in print. I have other books about people who passed away before I could meet them, but they haven't been published yet.

So could I ask you to describe some of these meetings? How did you meet these people? When you first came here you were quite a young chap and you were a foreigner. Did you find that they were welcoming to you?

Let's start with Lakshmana Swamy. I hadn't really heard of him except from one Australian friend of mine who I knew had spent time at his ashram in Andhra Pradesh. He was just a distant figure, a fact in the periphery of my consciousness; I hadn't really gone into him at all. Then this Australian man came running up to me very excitedly saying, 'He is here. He's here. Come and have his *darshan* (being in the presence of a saint).' I wasn't particularly excited over the prospect, but I thought, 'Why not?' I think this man gave me the one little booklet which existed, a horrendously Indian hagiography that his brother had written. I have to admit it didn't inspire me.

I walked into my first meeting with this man a little bit sceptical. I would say I was not expecting much. I sat down and looked at him. There were about ten or twelve people that day. I don't think that I am being arrogant when I say that he ignored everyone else. He just looked at me for an hour, non-stop. His eyes didn't move. I think that after the first ten seconds, totally without any mental evaluation on my part, something in me said, 'This man is a *jnani* (one who has realised the Self).' When this thought arose, I remember thinking, 'Where did that come from?' In no way was I looking at him or checking him out, seeing what he said, feeling his vibes, or coming to a conclusion. Just out of nowhere these words appeared in my head, 'This man is a *jnani*.' He looked at me and I just got more and more deeply quiet the longer he looked. Prior to that I had spent about eighteen months meditating by myself in Ramana Ashram, doing Self-enquiry.

I was a very serious *sadhu* (ascetic) in those days. I got up at five o'clock in the morning, sat and didn't move till midday. I was doing eight or ten hours every day. I thought I was getting my mind under control. I mean I was getting relatively peaceful; there were not too many stray thoughts. I was pretty happy and quiet most of the time. I really thought, 'I started here. I got to here. Not much further to go.' Then this man just looked at me and within two minutes I realised that I was, at the maximum, one millimetre towards some infinite goal that this man was established in. Whatever states I had experienced sitting by myself, they were nothing compared to what this man was merely giving me a taste of, and forget what state that he might be in himself!

I think that was the point when I realised that you can't do this by yourself. Not unless you are a real freak like Bhagavan who was a rare exception. You need someone who is in this state and who can take an interest in you. Someone who is willing to look at you and quieten you down, and if you are ready for it put you in that state. You can't do it by yourself.

So did Lakshmana Swamy become your guru?

At that time, no. As I said, I was enormously impressed by him. I was toying with the idea, 'Is he my guru? Is he not my guru?' It was not a burning question and there was no resolution to it, but around that time most of the people here were sneaking off to Bombay to see Nisargadatta. He was a big thing in those days. So I went off to see him.

He was the so-called Beedi *Baba?*

I don't know who called him that, I think possibly Osho. I don't think that anyone outside Osho's circles ever called him *Beedi* Baba. That was a derogatory term Osho occasionally brought out because he was losing a lot of business to him. (Both laugh)

Everyone I know called him Maharaj. His full name was Nisargadatta. He came from a very ancient lineage of householder gurus in India. The whole tradition was that the guru who held the lineage would visit different villages in Maharashtra. He would find out, with whatever powers he had, who were the advanced devotees. He would initiate them with the Guru *Mantra* (sacred sound) and say, 'That's it.

Just keep repeating this. I am going to come back at periodic intervals and check up on your progress.' That is all the contact you ever had. There was no question of formal meditations. You just repeated this *mantra*.

Before the guru passed on he would pick out whichever of these householder devotees he thought was the best man, and he would say, 'You are the successor; carry on, and tour around.' Maharaj was a maverick in this tradition; he didn't like this idea of touring around. He thought that the *mantra* wasn't much good, although he would give it to people if they asked for it.

He was very much in the tradition of Bhagavan telling people to focus on the 'I', the 'I-I', and get established in the 'I am'. But I think that he was also in the tradition of people like Papaji who were saying that personal effort doesn't get you anywhere. In a way he was a bridge between Lakshmana Swamy and Bhagavan, who were very gung-ho on effort, and the traditional no-effort people. He was very insistent that what was needed was an immediate experience of reality. He said, 'I am going to tell you the Truth. I don't want you to think about it, I don't want you to go away and practise it. I want you to believe it and accept it here in this moment, and if you do you become that Truth.' Have you read *I Am That*?

Yes.

It is a little bit misleading. I think that there is a lot of Maurice Frydman's (the editor) discursive style in it. Nobody who I know who has ever been with Maharaj remembers him talking like that.

That book has become a classic.

Right. He would encourage you to speak when you came. There was no hiding in the back. If you were new you would sit six feet in front of him and he would start harassing you from day one. A little bit polite to begin with, 'Who's your guru? What have you read? What is your practice?' He would make you talk about yourself so you would have to reveal where you were coming from. Then in a very elegant, forceful way (he was completely uneducated, I think that he was a third standard drop-out) he would convince you that everything you had thought, believed and practised up until that point was a waste of time. Don't ask me how he did it. There were professors and brilliant academics who would come and they were totally destroyed by this man.

It reminds me of the stories about Gurdjieff.

I mean he was teaching on his arguments, he wasn't logical. But somehow by the time he was through with you, your mind had come to the conclusion that you had been wasting your time. There was a two-track approach. Track one, he would be talking to you, slowly cutting down your beliefs and ideas, but at the same time he would be transmitting some kind of power, force, *shakti*, call it what you like. So there was a contrast: in one part of you there was a set of ideas crumbling away and somewhere else, at a much deeper level, there was an experience which he had given you. There was never any question of him saying, 'Now this is real and this is not real, now choose.' But basically this is what was happening.

He would give you this experience and as you were talking to him, he demolished everything you thought you believed in. You could see it on people's faces, 'What's true? The experience or the ideas that I have had all my life?' Then you would drop the ideas and accept that the experience he had given was the truth and that all the ideas you previously held were worthless and should be thrown out.

He called that moment 'Getting the Knowledge'. It's a strange vocabulary. He said that once you get that knowledge then that is it and you are ready for a further absorption into the Self. The way he did this was by continuously talking about consciousness and the Self. You would think, 'Oh no! Not again! I have heard about this twenty times this week. Can't he talk about something new?' Then suddenly you would think, 'Wow, he is not telling me about something, he is describing myself.' He had this amazing power to be the Self, to talk the Self, and when you were looking and paying attention you suddenly became the Self simply by the forcefulness of his explanations. You didn't believe him; you didn't think about it; you listened to him; he got inside you and you became what he talked about.

So although he called this 'Getting the Knowledge', it was actually an experience of Self?

He had a different structure from people like Bhagavan. There was a level or state he called consciousness which was 'I am This' and 'God'. And prior (he didn't like to say 'beyond', he would say 'prior') to That (which was his favourite qualification of it) is this thing called awareness. He said that consciousness comes out of awareness and all manifestation is consciousness and it goes back into awareness. He had this power to stuff you back into a consciousness in which you weren't bothered by concepts and you just had a very peaceful, quiet awareness from which the consciousness rose and manifested.

Did you personally experience that?

I doubt it.

(Laughs) Probably you did as you are English!

People would come with all the standard spiritual questions. In the beginning he would be very polite and he would listen to them, but often he would say, 'I am not interested in what you have heard or in what you have read. I am only interested in your own direct experience of yourself right now. The rest doesn't matter.' This immediately would focus the conversation onto something that he would consider essential. So within this very narrowly proscribed limit he would let you talk for a little while. Then after he had done his number on you, after he had demolished your beliefs and got you flying, he would introduce a second stipulation. He would say, 'I am not prepared to answer any questions that assume you are an individual person inside the body. That for me is a totally wrong, hypothetical assumption and I am not going to waste my time answering hypothetical questions.' So immediately you have nothing to say. You can't say. 'How do I get enlightened?' Because he would say, 'What "I"? There is no "I" there.' If you didn't register the implications of the statement and started asking, he would just prove to you that every question you could possibly think of assumed that there was a 'you' trying to get somewhere. So he said, 'If you want to talk about consciousness, what it is, how it manifests, how you experience it, fine. But don't ask questions that assume you are a person. I don't accept that premise.' So that effectively shut everybody up.

His secondary excuse was that he had throat cancer and he couldn't talk all day about things that weren't important. But this was a very good technique for making people understand what they were and what they were not, limiting non-essential questions and giving him a chance to say, 'You are the Self. You are consciousness,' ad nauseam, hour after hour, day after day. People sat there listening and once in a while a light bulb would go off and someone would think, 'Yes, I am. Wonderful. Great.' That was his technique, it was how he worked.

I have only seen him on video for a few minutes but he seemed to have an amazing presence. His eyes were very piercing.

He was like that. He was very animated. He used to wave his arms a lot. Bang his fists and shout. He wasn't a polite discusser of topics. He would scream and rant. The only word of Marathi I ever learned was *culpanu*, which means concept. Generally three or four words into any speech he would bang his fists onto the ground and shout, '*Culpanu, culpanu,*' and that was the end of your question.

But he did have these piercing eyes.

He did. I am not saying that that film was a fraudulent presentation of how he was. What I am saying is that on the soundtrack of that particular film there was somebody else reading out paragraphs from *I Am That*. What he was actually saying on the film, in Marathi, was something totally different. They just looped the film; it is the same sixty seconds of film snipped together in ten different creative ways. You can tell because it has the same body language again and again. (Both laugh) So when it is the interpreter's turn to talk they cut him out completely and read parts of *I Am That*, and pretend that he is teaching, but he's not, he is just having a rant about something else.

It sounds like he was a very powerful influence, but then you came back to Ramana Ashram?

I stopped going when he got really sick. I didn't like to see him getting old and tired. He had massive throat cancer. I kept having dreams actually saying, 'Why don't you come? Why don't you come?' I remember waking up in the middle of the night one time, thinking, 'Is this just wishful thinking or should I go?' Then I would go back to sleep and he would appear saying, 'I have just told you to come. Why don't you believe me?' Somehow I didn't go. I just didn't feel the urge to go back. I felt satisfied in a way.

Were you here at Ramana Ashram at the time?

Yes. At the last talk I had there was a sense of completion. We had a very good talk (I think that it is actually in *Prior to Consciousness* which I only found out last year) concerning what I understand about Bhagavan and about him. He didn't like people hanging around. He liked people to come and get what he had to show them and then go away. He had a little room that only took a maximum of forty people, so if you tried to hang around he would kick you out after ten days. He would say, 'There are new people and it is your turn to go,' and you went.

He wouldn't leave me alone. All through the 1980s and 1990s he would keep appearing in my dreams in the way that no other teacher ever has. They were not casual dreams in everyday situations; they were always very strong *Satsang*-format (meeting in Truth) dreams. I would be in his room and he would be giving me good teachings. I think they went on for about ten or fifteen years after he died. He caught hold of me in some place.

So in some way he was your guru in the form?

I could never make up my mind when I was there if he was or he wasn't. There have been a lot of people whom I have allowed to perform the guru function, for want of a better phrase, but I have never been able to actually say, 'You are my guru.' It has never bothered me and I am immensely grateful to all of them. If you want to know who my guru is, and I ask this question to myself, I just scratch my head and say, 'Is he my guru?'

I came here because of Bhagavan in the 1970s. I think that he became my guru in the sense that his lineage took possession of me. I fell in love with Arunachala; I fell in love with him. I went to see Lakshmana Swamy and fell in love with him, and Papaji too. All these people derived their experience, power and their teachings from that same source which is somehow actually located here.

Do you mean the mountain?

Bhagavan said it was the mountain, Papaji also acknowledged this. Lakshmana Swamy would definitely say this.

All these people that you have mentioned would find the mountain very central in their lives?

Nisargadatta would be the exception. He told me that one of the regrets of his life was that he had never met Bhagavan. He wasn't in that lineage. He did come here on a tour in the 60s after Bhagavan died. He said, 'The one regret of my life is that I never came to touch his feet.'

In fact when Ganesan, Bhagavan's great nephew, came to Bombay I happened to be there at the same time. Much to everyone's amazement, Nisargadatta, who never showed any respect to anyone, he was that type and nobody impressed him, suddenly got a big stack of cushions and made Ganesan sit on this high seat, garlanded him and prostrated full length on the floor at his feet. Nobody knew what was going on. He said, 'I never had the chance to prostrate to your great uncle, so I am doing it instead to you.'

257

Am I right in thinking that Arunachala is considered to be Shiva?

Yes.

Can you say something about Shiva? *Because for us who don't really know* India *that well,* Shiva *seems to be a figure more of mythology.*

Right. Mythology is a process of concocting stories about experiences you can't explain. I think that people have always felt the power of this mountain. They have been making pilgrimages here for at least 1,500 years to my knowledge. The oldest known writings praising Arunachala are about 1,500 years old and they are all saying the same thing.

I think people came here with Saivite conditioning, for want of a better word. They came here and they had an experience of the absolute in the presence of this mountain. So out of that would grow the association that *Shiva* is God. This mountain is giving me the experience of God therefore this mountain is *Shiva*. Once that initial identification has taken place then all the myths that are associated with *Shiva* somehow get transferred to a place like this. I think that it is a way for a generation of people, who have learnt from childhood to associate God with *Shiva*, to approach a place and give it respect and veneration. They transfer the stories from one generation to the next.

This is entirely my take; the locals wouldn't go for this at all. I am just saying that there is a power in this mountain which is totally independent of anyone's stories about it, and that dozens of generations of advanced seekers have come here. They have all got enlightened, they say, through the power of this mountain; it is not just something that happened to Bhagavan. Every one or two hundred years some big famous saint comes along and gets it sitting here, for no other reason (he has no guru) than the mountain cooks him. Bhagavan said, 'It is not a matter of belief. If you go near a fire you get burnt, if you come near this mountain you get burnt.' That was his experience; it has been the experience of generations of South Indians. Somehow out of this has grown up an accretion of mythological stories that you can take or leave. The essential point is the mountain has power. It attracts people to it, people who are ready to receive that power, and in its presence they get enlightened.

We experienced that power last night when about half a million people in the pouring rain (the first huge rain of the monsoon) were walking around the mountain non-stop. There is a power even if people don't totally understand, and that power is working. For us Westerners to see this torrent of people, with the torrent of rain on them, is pretty impressive.

I live here all the time, and I am still impressed that people can knock off from work in Chennai at five, get onto a bus and get here at ten, go out in a cyclone, walk thirteen kilometres in bare feet. Then get back onto the bus for another five hours, clock in at nine the next morning at work, and think that they have spent a good night! (Both laugh)

So what we seem to be saying in different ways is this mountain is the guru.

The South Indian tradition is called henotheism. And henotheism means that whichever particular statue, temple or manifestation of God you happen to be in front of that day, that form represents the Absolute. It is not polytheism, different gods and different places. Logically, it is a totally denial of reality.

You can come to Arunachala and have the absolute conviction this is the Supreme Being. But then you can go to Chidambaram tomorrow and have exactly the same assumption when standing in front of the *lingam* (phallic symbol of the divine, *Shiva*) there. Nobody thinks that these are two odd ideas in juxtaposition. This is the way people see things around here. Whichever shrine, deity, guru, holy place that they are in front of, for that moment they are in the presence of the Absolute God.

We are a little bit different to that. We pick. We say 'This is my guru, this is my holy mountain.' We have a hierarchy and say, 'Well I got more peaceful with that guy so he is more God than the one over here.' But that is not the way the locals see it.

After you had spent time with Nisargadatta and Lakshmana Swamy, I actually met you in Lucknow. You ended up spending quite a few years with Papaji and were privy to a great deal of closeness with him. As I understand it, you had almost daily contact with him. During that time you were working on a book of his life, so you had very intimate dialogues with him about that. Would you like to talk about your association with Papaji?

This is a hard one. I still haven't figured this one out myself. Who was I in relation to him? What was I doing there? What did he want from me? What did I get from him? These questions don't really bother me; it's just that I don't have any answers to them.

I can say that through most of the late 1980s I was collecting stories from old devotees of Bhagavan who had either long contact or a spectacular but brief contact, like Papaji and Lakshmana Swamy had.

I was making a book about the way that Bhagavan's power and presence had affected people. Annamalai Swami's book somehow was an outgrowth of that. The original book got shelved and I wrote a whole book on Annamalai Swami, because his story was so good. When I went to Lucknow to interview Papaji for the book, the same thing happened. Instead of making one chapter to fit in a book I ended up writing 1,500 pages about him. It took me several years, and I have only just got back to the original project. But he had business with me, I know. Surendra, his son, told me he was with Papaji in Haridwar in the 80s and that Papaji had written me a letter saying that I had to come to Bangalore to meet him. He said that he had business with me and wanted to see me. I never got that letter. Surendra asked me once if I ever got it. I didn't.

I know a couple of people who were told to tell me to come and for bizarre reasons, which we don't need to go into, they never told me. I collected his old letters when I was doing the book. Once or twice he wrote that he had to go to South India to see David Godman. This is before I ever contacted him. Whatever business he thought he had, he never told me what it was. Occasionally he would get these promptings to see David Godman, or that David Godman had to come there.

I finally got to Lucknow in 1992 and three days after I arrived, his wife died. There was total chaos. All his relatives descended. He cut devotees out of a lot of the main functions because he didn't want his family to be upset by all these weirdos who were hanging out around him. So he went off to Haridwar to put the ashes in the Ganges. That took about a week. So I was really on the edges of all this, trying to get him to talk.

You probably did not have any real plans of staying for long?

I couldn't stay for long. I had only two weeks and told him that: 'I have absolutely to be back in Tiruvannamalai in about twelve days time.' At that point I was looking after Lakshmana Swamy's garden. This man is a recluse par excellence. He does not allow anyone inside that gate, for any reason whatsoever, unless he thinks that they are someone special. I had a two acre garden that I had to run for him. He wouldn't let any other workers in, and I had to do the whole thing by myself. So I couldn't sandbag and tell him, 'I have to go off and interview someone for two weeks and here is so-and-so and he will look after the garden for you.' I eventually found one Danish devotee who he was willing to have in the garden to do the work, and that man had to be back in Copenhagen on a particular date to register for his college term, and if he didn't return by that time, he would have to repay a three-year student loan to the government. There was absolutely no way I could overstay this visit to Lucknow. The Danish devotee would be five-figure dollars out of pocket if I didn't show up in time.

So I told Papaji this, and he said, 'Yes, Yes.' So ten out of my fourteen days disappeared on funeral chaos. He wouldn't answer any of my questions when I went there. Then one afternoon we were sitting down for tea together; I had given up even attempting to ask him questions. I just asked him, 'Do you know a woman called Andevipechai who was a devotee of Swami Shivananda and had spent a lot of time with him?' I had read a book about her and her life story interested me. She had arrived at Ramana Ashram about ten days before Bhagavan had died and had a direct experience of the Self standing in front of the room in which he died. Shivananda thought a lot of her because when she finally took *sannyas* (initiation) he gave his own robes and begging bowl to her, which he had never done before.

Since Papaji had spent years in Rishikesh, I thought that he might have come across her. I was curious to get his opinion. I valued his opinion on anyone. I just said that as she was standing in front of Bhagavan the question 'Who am I?' spontaneously appeared. She had never asked that question before and didn't know that it was his teaching, and she got enlightened on the spot.

He didn't know her, but he didn't like to admit that there were any gurus he didn't know, so he kind of slid around that question. Instead of answering it, he told me the whole story of his life, with no context at all. I couldn't work out what had prompted this.

He wouldn't let me take any notes and he wouldn't let me interrupt. It took about two hours. And for the final summation, he said, 'That's the question I should have asked when I was eight years old, the "Who am I?" question. If I had asked myself "Who am I?" when I was eight, I wouldn't have wasted those next twenty-five years.' That was his very roundabout way of answering my question and telling me about his life. After this he rushed off to Haridwar and then returned almost immediately and he just wouldn't give me time. The next morning my train was leaving, so after breakfast I went up to his bedroom door and banged on the door and said, 'You have one hour. Either this gets finished up, or it doesn't get written. I don't know when I can come back again; I am not missing this train. There is too much money riding on that train, I am leaving in an hour, take it or leave it.'

You said that to Papaji? (Both laugh) Perhaps you were a little naive in those days!

He appreciated directness and I didn't know when I was coming back. I had seventy-five minutes and then I was getting into a rickshaw, and if I came back I came back, and if I didn't I didn't. He had seventy-five minutes to finish his story or not, as the case may be. I just wanted to tell him this. Anyway he said, 'Okay, sit down.'

I don't know if you knew his bedroom, he had two single beds and it was a tiny, tiny room absolutely overflowing with stuff that he wouldn't throw away. It was like some weird science fiction movie in which every day the walls were coming in closer. He had all these closets lining the wall. There was a five-years supply of dried fruit and nuts in one closet and ten lifetimes supply of *dhotis* (lengths of cotton cloth) that people had given him in another. He wouldn't part with any of this stuff. The cupboards just got deeper and deeper and the space available to do anything got smaller and smaller.

At the centre was his bed and Jyothi, his attendant, had a bed there and the beds were crammed so close that there was hardly space in between them. We sat facing each other and there wasn't even any room to be knee to knee, the knees had to be almost interlocking. I could lean forward and we would be eyeball to eyeball with noses almost touching. It didn't matter if I leaned back a bit, he would lean forward. I started asking him all the usual boring, journalistic 'clean up the mess' questions, which he had absolutely no interest in answering. He started talking about how consciousness tries to know itself. He was off on some strange thing about *prakrithi* (causal matter), which I didn't understand, but he was looking at me with totally unblinking, unwavering eyes.

There was a little corner of me that said, 'Pay attention. You have sixty minutes to get this guy to spill the beans. If you don't get something sensible out of him, then you don't get this chapter written.' So it was like one corner of David the journalist keeping two eyes above the water and the rest of me was getting totally blown away. He wasn't remotely interested in what he was saying.

There were all these different subplots going on in the room. He was giving this monologue about *prakrithi*, which maybe he believed or didn't believe, but was just an excuse to keep his mouth moving. If you are getting dizzy you try to do something to retain consciousness, and I would ask a question that seemed to be relevant to what he was talking about and he would answer. But this was all on a level that was totally disconnected to what was really going on. It was nose to nose and he was just glaring at me.

I couldn't hold it anymore; I couldn't be sensible and couldn't ask questions. He didn't want to answer any questions anyway, so why even bother? So I tried to retain some corner of the intellect and relaxed and enjoyed it. We looked at each other for a while, and in that moment I knew who he was. I sat there totally quiet and totally blown away. In the end he said, 'Well, you came here to find out who I was, and now you know.' That was his way of saying, 'Okay, this is who I am.' It was obviously not something you can go away and tell somebody. But I think that somehow, in that moment, he caught me. He knew I was coming back, I didn't. His principal job was to get his hooks into me in some way.

So based on what he told me on this long rambling teatime story and on old tape of transcripts of him talking about himself, all of which were different and contradictory, I assembled as best I could an account which seemed to make the most sense out of what he told me – you know how he was, no story got told the same twice. It would incorporate things from other stories. The membrane between the stories was very porous. Two facts from a story would migrate to another, and then three facts from a story would go somewhere else. I put all these events in a sensible, chronological order and sent it off to him and said that was the best I could do.

That was the chapter for the original book?

Yes, that was the chapter for the original book. I said to him, 'There are so many contradictions here; I present it to you in a written form, you read it. Where everything is obviously contradicting each other then correct it. If the whole thing is wrong, just tear it up and throw it away, I don't care. This is my opening gambit in trying to make sense of what you told me. Change it, add to it whatever you like. We will just start again.' I got a letter back saying, 'Thank you very much. I enjoyed reading it. You didn't tell my best stories.' I barely got the basic story out, given the circumstances. He said, 'You must come back. I want to tell you this story.' So he obviously wanted me back for more and he said, 'Fine, I find nothing wrong with it.' That wasn't the answer I wanted, because patently there was so much wrong with the story that you couldn't print it. It was just riddled with inconsistencies. I sent him an audiotape of questions. He sent me back an audiotape of him supposedly answering these questions in one of the *Satsangs*. But all he had basically done was to repeat himself. He told all the stories all over again with the inconsistencies and didn't unwrinkle the problems, so I thought that I had better go back and sort this out.

I returned four months later. In typical Papaji fashion he said, 'What are you doing here? What have you come for?' No mention of a book or that he had sent a letter telling me to come. On the rare occasion that I broached the subject, he would say, 'Later, later.' Once in a while when I wasn't there he would say, 'David seems to have forgotten why he came here.' There was a whole cat-and-mouse game going on. He wouldn't give me any time, he wouldn't tell me any stories, he wouldn't tell me anything. I stayed. The *Satsangs* in those days were incredible; there was so much power and so much grace.

Was that in 1991?

It was in 92-93. So after about a year, as a final act of despair, Bharat Mitra and I thought we have got to get these stories somehow. As Papaji likes telling these stories in *Satsang*, Bharat Mitra and I decided to set up a situation where Papaji talks in front of the camera. We would leave it like that, a kind of video biography.

Was that when you did Call Off the Search?

No, it was before. It was an attempt to get him to talk about all his stories. So I proposed this and he said, 'I can't talk in front of a camera, I have to make lots of notes and write down all the stories I want to tell.' It sounded like, 'Don't call us, we'll call you!' I said, 'Don't worry, I will write the notes. I know every single story. I don't know the contents but I can give you a one-line summary of every single story. You can have this page in front of you and you can miss whatever story you don't want to talk about or talk an hour about the things you want to. But all the notes will be in front of you.' He muttered something, but he wasn't very kind. (Both laugh)

So I went off; it took me about a week. I gave him a sixteen-page questionnaire with a hundred and twenty questions. He looked at it and seemed very excited with page one, then he looked at how long it was and you could see him sagging and he said, 'That's a lot of stories!' 'Well you have had a long life, it's been pretty much action packed.' So he said that he would have to make notes and, even though I had made notes on the side, the questionnaire went off to his bedroom and it stayed there for some months. Every time I asked him about it he said, 'I am studying it. I am making notes.' Whenever I peeked at it in his room when he was out, I would see it gathering dust on the windowsill.

At that time, when he was in a sense playing you along, was he quietly working with you, do you think? I didn't have that much contact with you at that time, but it looked from a distance that at certain moments some shifts were happening for you in your own life. Could you tell us what was going on at that time? He was using that questionnaire as an excuse to keep you around.

He was extraordinarily Machiavellian. You didn't know what he was up to, and I don't think he knew either. His *vasanas*, his conditioning, or whatever you like, made him be very elliptical. That was his way of dealing with people. He liked people to be in the state that they didn't know what was going on; that was his style.

So you never had straightforward encounters with him. I had faith he was working on me but not in any sensible way that I could say that this was my initial step and this was his response. I think that he liked to reduce people to 'I-don't-know-what's-going-on' chaos. I think that he found people more amenable in that state. So he kind of softened me up first. But yes, he was definitely working, but I can't put my finger on a day and say, 'This is what he was doing on that day or this day.' So now it was about a year and a half since I had arrived, and he still hadn't answered a single question.

By now was somebody else looking after Lakshmana Swamy's garden?

Somebody else was looking after the garden. It was curious that before I went for the second trip I went down to the garden for a check-up and there was a whole crew of workers and everything was running fine by itself. I thought, 'Well, I don't need to be here anymore!' Before I went on that second trip to Lucknow a shift had taken place, and in less than a week there were new people who were very keen and who Lakshmana Swamy was happy to have there. I thought, 'There is no limit on this trip. I can do it properly,' not knowing that eighteen months later I would still be waiting for him to answer my first question!

So sometime in 1994 I went up to him and said, 'Look I have all these projects. The Annamalai Swami book is finished and I need to go and get it printed. You promised to answer these questions and nothing has happened for six months. You have dumped the *Om Shanti* book on me (which went through several hands, including Catherine Ingram's, and finally ended up with me). I never asked for it. You never told me directly, you just said, "Give it to David." And then there is this book you claim we are going to write one day. So if you are not willing to do any work on this biography now, I will go south for a couple of months and get this Annamalai Swami book printed.' He said, 'Yes, yes, that is a good plan. Forget about the *Om Shanti*, you go and get the Annamalai Swami book printed.'

The moment I left the house he called someone to go and buy him a big book. He got a monster foolscap ledger, took out my questionnaire, dusted it and started on page one. He spent the whole of the summer on it, and you know how hot the summers are in Lucknow! He had his neck in a brace because he had spondarlitis, so he couldn't write properly. No one was allowed to look at what he was writing, but the moment he went out of his room of course everyone would dive for the book to see what stories he was writing. I kept getting these phone calls that he was answering the questions: 'He has done ten pages, fifty pages, he has done a hundred pages.' I thought 'This is good,' and I finished up with the Annamalai Swami book and came back to Lucknow.

The moment I walked through the door the questionnaire went back into the bedroom again, and he never looked at it again. You gotta figure this man! I spent a year and a half begging him to do this work, the moment I leave he starts and the moment I come back he stops. So then he gives me all these stories and because his own brain patterns are so elliptical, when you say, 'Tell me the story about how you met that *sadhu* in Benares in 1952,' he doesn't come up with the story of meeting a *sadhu* in Benares in 1952. Suddenly he remembers something that happened in the army ten years before, or something when he was eight years old. Giving him so many questions had given him all these opportunities for his random story telling to kick in. He almost never answered the question I asked. Instead, he would remember something else from a different era which was totally unconnected to the question and he would write about that. But the scatter-shot effect of this was that by the time he had actually written a hundred and fifty pages, just about every story that was left in his brain was out there. Probably in response to the wrong question, but it was all in there somewhere, and often repeated three times. So there was a really good basis for digging deeper if you like. The stories as he wrote them were not publishable, so slowly I got more information about them. But he kept up this strange facade of not wanting to talk to me.

So you were in the house everyday?

Oh yes, absolutely.

He was totally welcoming you in fact?

He wasn't unwelcoming, but he would say something like 'I hope you are not going to say you are unclear about when my sister said such and such. Okay, I'll tell you.' But he wouldn't tell me, he would wait until I had gone out and then he would get out a pen and paper and write it, and then he would give it to me. So he really didn't want to speak to me about this stuff or want me to be around when he was writing about it. I took the opportunity and disappeared, and the next day there would be another page to add to the story. I just don't know. I had no idea what was going on with him and me. It was very strange; you never knew what was going to come next. You never knew how he was going to react. I must say though he showed enormous respect for my questions and for what I was doing.

People would ask him all sorts of questions in *Satsang*; he would shout at them and not answer them. Your chances of getting a sensible, rational answer to a question were minimal at the best of times. In *Satsang* his job was to harass you into a state of Self, it wasn't to give you explanations or to tell you what you thought you needed to know. But with me he was always impeccably to the point. I could write down ten questions and instead of writing the answers he would take them to *Satsang*. Often he would spend the whole *Satsang* answering my questions and then he would look at me and say, 'Are you happy?' And I would say, 'Yes.' Nobody else was getting answers like this. He recognised that this was a legitimate research that he was actively involved in and would answer to the best of his ability.

During this cat-and-mouse period did you always feel welcome in the house? Were you being taken care of? The impression was you were close to the family even though he might not have been answering your questions.

There were all kinds of politics going on in the house. There always are in situations like this. For example, there were people who used to sleep there and people who just used to eat there. There were monster electricity bills for the house; we are talking 30,000 rupees each bill. There were six bedrooms with air conditioners, and all the air conditioners were going twenty-four hours a day. Who was going to pay for it? There were the usual fights like, 'Well I don't keep my air conditioner on when I'm out, so you should pay more than me,' and 'Well, I only eat here, I don't sleep here.' So in the end we agreed to give the total sum to Papaji and he could divide it up any way he liked and we would all agree, no matter how bizarre his appropriations. Well, he thought that this would be great fun, 'Yes, yes, we are going to have some fun with this!' (Laughs) So this bill is parked on his table every month or so and he would say, 'Right, fine Rajiv 10,000 rupees,' or some outrageous sum, and he would work his way down the list. Never once, in the whole time I was there, did he ever charge me one *paisa* for anything that went on it the house, even though I ate three meals a day there.

Maybe he had the impression that you didn't have much money because you had lived in India for many years?

It could well be. I am just saying that in terms of being looked after I got the feeling that, 'Yes he is always welcome whenever he wants to come. We are not going to force him away by charging him a hundred rupees for each meal.' He had another scheme with meals too. There was a household budget and we would all put in so much money and when it ran out we would put in the same amount again. But this was only for people that were there fulltime. But more and more people were getting invited to lunch so that meant the number of days before the money ran out was getting less and less, so Papaji started another irrational levy scheme. (Both laugh) Everybody who got occasional invites would be given a totally arbitrary sum for their meal and it would go into the house kitty. He stopped me from contributing to the house fund. Everyone would put in two hundred rupees and when it ran out would put in another two hundred rupees and he stopped me paying that. He did not want me, in any way, to have a financial liability from being in his house.

At the same time he would totally ignore me for weeks. It wasn't, 'Welcome my son, come and sit here.' Somehow we had a very physically separate, distant relationship. I could be sitting on the floor in his living room and he would want to say something to me but he wouldn't say it. He would say, 'Tell David this,' or, 'Ask David this.' It even came to the point that I would be standing as close to him as we are now, I would be looking at him and he would turn around and ask someone, 'Does David want this?' (Both laugh) He reacted to some kind of configuration in peoples' brains and even though he was enormously respectful of my work and very welcoming in terms of hospitality, he just couldn't deal with talking to me. I can't explain this, or see any significance in this; it's just the way things were.

Although you are describing what most people experienced as distancing (you were standing next to Papaji and he would get a third party to talk to you, which for most people would feel unfriendly and remote), in your eyes and energy right now, while you are telling this story, there is a great sense of intimacy. It seems to me that there was a love affair happening between you and Papaji.

It was never an intimacy which ever manifested in personal contact. I remember we once went to dinner at somebody's house in Gompti. He said, 'Who's in the van?' Somebody in the front turned round and mentioned who was in the back and my name was last. Papaji said, 'Too many people, the van is too heavy. Throw him out, he can walk!' (Both laugh) So in the middle of nowhere, halfway to Gompti, I was told to get a bus or a rickshaw, whatever. So there wasn't this feeling of, 'Welcome my son.'

We are talking about Papaji and suddenly these wild monkeys have come up to us and it's as if they are experiencing the energy of this love which is here right now. They are actually treating you with tremendous sweetness and sensitivity, as if they are responding to the energy that is here. I don't know if you are aware of it, but today is Papaji's birthday.

I do know it. I was reminded of it yesterday.

You are talking about Papaji and your closeness to him and we are sitting in the garden at Ramana Ashram, a place where he loved to come.

I know people who get off saying Bhagavan's name. They say it once and they get happy and blissful. There are people who get off singing *bhajans* (devotional songs) or by meditating. I get off talking about these people. For me, to talk is a *Satsang* that produces the same effect as if I were sitting there being zapped-out. That's just my own little package. It's the way my brain reacts.

It comes out of love. These monkeys, who are very intuitive, can feel that. (Both laugh)

271

The monkeys have become progressively tamer over the years. When I was here in the 1980s, when the young monkeys came up and behaved like this, the old ones would make a noise and show them their teeth. Now they are all at it.

Is there some other element of the Papaji story you would like to mention?

He was utterly random. I don't know if I have made this point. He did not like disclosing information and my job was to get information from him. Everybody had his or her role and my job was to get him to tell me a reasonable version of his events.

Somehow we slotted into that role. But there was something about the way his brain worked that he could never give a straight answer. So it was a major feat to get the story straightened out. You won't believe this, but the day before I sent *Nothing Ever Happened* to the press (and this is 1,200 pages of his life story) I discover that he has two children that he has never told me about. This is the level that we are operating on! So I hastily have to mention in a footnote on page 1,100 that sorry, I forgot to mention two children. If you asked him then he would say, 'Oh, yes! I have a daughter called so-and-so,' but he would never volunteer information. Nothing ever came out of him unless somehow he felt compelled.

Did you ever meet Sanjay? Sanjay was his sister's grandson and he was brought up in Berlin and came back to India. He was in *Satsang* for a while and he had an affair with an Austrian woman. One day she came to the house and complained saying, 'I don't care if he wants to leave me or not. I don't care if he wants to marry me or not. I don't care what our relationship is going to be, I just want him to tell me. I am quite happy whatever it is, but I can't get him to tell me, so what should I do?' So this is family and Papaji is the head of the family and he told someone to go and fetch the boy. So Sanjay was fetched and sat next to Papaji and this woman tells her story again, how they had been living together and he won't say what he wants to do next, and she can't get any information from him at all. So Papaji looks at Sanjay and puts his arm around him and says, 'That's my boy. You are a real member of the family.'

You could not get any information out of any of the family. They were absolutely totally buttoned down. They never said anything unless it was absolutely essential. I went to see their daughter in Delhi to interview her. I asked her questions like, 'Tell me what happened when you met Bhagavan in the 1940s.' She is perfectly capable to tell me the story herself, but what she said was, 'What did Papaji say?' And I would give Papaji's version and she would then say, 'Yes, that is correct.'

In the end did it really matter? His whole life was about creating this immediacy, this experience of the Self which was in fact love, and that was happening in a big way all the time, right?

On the factual level he prided himself on creating as many smokescreens as he could, as many diversions as possible. When I told him, 'I have to go to South India to talk to your old devotees.' He said, 'What for?' And I answered, 'Research. I want to visit your old places, take some photographs and talk to some of the people that know you.' And he said, 'You are a writer, why can't you make it all up? I make up all my stories so why can't you make up your stories as well? Why do you have to go travelling to make up stories?' (Both laugh) So he didn´t really have much regard for facts. If there weren't any to hand he would just make some up.

So somehow out of all that something profound happened for you at Lucknow?

Right, yes.

Would you like to talk about that?

I don't think I can. There was a subtext all the time. 'This is who you are, this is what you are, accept the delivery of my words and just leave it.' I think that by the beginning of 1997 there was absolutely no reason to talk with him again. There were no more spiritual questions or biographical material I needed. He wasn't in a very good state. I think that after his strokes his capacity to remember was impaired so the stories got even more random. I realised that I'd got all I could and that there was no point in pursuing anymore. I went there every day and touched his feet with the feeling of absolute immense gratitude.

It got really chaotic at the end. Breakfast was still quiet and private. He never talked; he would just come in, stare at his place and drink his cup of tea. There would be a nice, mellow, quiet twenty minutes or whatever. I would just sit there and feel totally complete and satisfied.

He didn't like people to be beggars. He didn't want people to hang around. It wasn't his idea to have a *Satsang* with two hundred people coming everyday saying 'More, more.' His idea of a proper spiritual relationship was that the seeker comes to the guru and says, 'I have got this doubt, this problem. Who am I?' The guru tells him and the disciple experiences it and says, 'Thank you very much,' and goes away. All his idealistic stories, all the best stories from his memory were of people who came from a long distance, got it in a few minutes, left and then never came back. He loved those stories. That's what he really wanted from people; he didn't like them to hang around. It only happened through his later years because he couldn't physically run away. From about 1991 onwards his legs were incapable of taking him anywhere, so he just accepted that he had to stay in one place and he suffered all these people coming. But still he never completely abandoned his idea that the guru was there to transact a single piece of business; the guru was not there to have a long-term relationship.

There was another change one couldn't help noticing. When I first came there in 1992 the Satsang *was very focused on Self-enquiry and gradually he allowed more and more celebration and devotion, and in the last years it was mostly devotion. Was that your impression of what was happening?*

I talked to him on the cusp of this transition and I said, 'When I first came you were really gung-ho on giving *Satsang* and it didn't matter how sick you were. You would crawl on your hands and knees to *Satsang*. You would sit there and everybody that came up you would make them do Self-enquiry. You were like a dog shaking a rag and you wouldn't let go until they got something. Nowadays you have a more hands-off approach and seem mellower towards it.' And he said, 'I have finally realised that no effort is the correct prescription for the guru, not just the disciple. I tried for years to give people experiences, to force them to do Self-enquiry to experience the Self. I can make anyone that comes in front of me, including the cow outside the gate, have this temporary experience, but I can't make it stick. Unless you are ready for the Truth, the Truth will not stay with you. People have these experiences and go away and they lose it and get depressed and then they come back to me. Is it my job to decide about this person and that person and force these people to have these experiences?' He said, 'Whenever I sit in this chair Truth examines every single mind in this hall and the ones that are ready get it immediately. It is not my job to interfere, it is not my job to try and push the process along. But it won't work unless I sit here in this chair every morning. If I stay in bed and don't have physical contact, it is not going to work. It doesn't matter what I do, we can sing songs, and I can tell stories; we don't have to be talking spiritual things. The bottom line is that I have to be there. So long as I am there, this power, this presence, will do the work; it's not my business and I don't have to interfere.' So that was his rationale. He didn't need to go there every morning and make people do Self-enquiry; in fact he didn't need to make people do anything. All he had to do was to turn up and sit there. So things got a lot mellower, he just knew that whatever power came out through him did its work and he didn't need to channel it in any direction.

You said that he admitted that people would get this experience and then lose it. I have heard many times in Satsang *that he wouldn't accept that. When someone would say, 'I've lost it,' he would say, 'You can't have lost something that you never gained.' He would always made it clear to people that it was something that can't be gained or lost.*

He was very hard to pin down on this. This was a major area that nobody got him to make sense of. He said, 'If you got something and lost it, then it wasn't the Self because what you gain or lose can't be the Self, it must be the mind. So what you gained is a mental experience.' On the day that they had the experience he might say, 'Yes, yes, you've got it.' He wouldn't say, 'No, what you have got is a mental state.' He would be very positive on day one, but then when you came back and said, 'It's gone,' then he would say, 'It was your mind. Your mind gave you a state and your mind has lost it again.' So yes, he would say, 'You can't actually lose the Self,' but then he would also say, 'If you got something and lost it, then it wasn't the Self to begin with.'

You actually ended up spending a long time in Lucknow. Was it four or five years?

Five years.

Probably you were there when Papaji left his body?

Yes.

What happened to you then? That must have been a strong moment for you.

It was and it wasn't. I felt that my business with him was done. My relationship with him was never one that needed someone in a physical body. Every day just felt like a bonus, 'He is still here, I will just go and touch his feet today and I will be happy sitting with him.' When he finally did die it wasn't a big shock. I think I was the only person in Lucknow that didn't want to go to Haridwar. Somehow it felt like finished business, so why should I go to Haridwar and drop some ashes in the river? What has that got to do with me? At the last moment someone had a spare ticket, so I thought that I would go. We all went to the Ganga and Surendra, his son, performed the rituals. I think I closed my eyes as the ashes were immersed, Surendra got very upset when I said 'thrown' in the river. He said 'immersed' is the correct word. Surendra immersed the ashes in the river and I closed my eyes and opened them and I actually heard the whole world throbbing like an 'om' or a 'Papaji' and there was an instant knowledge that everything

I saw, that everything I was, was Papaji. It was a very strong rite. Papaji didn't just get immersed in the river – everything I am and everything I can see is Papaji.

In a sense David Godman became immersed in Papaji.

I wouldn't say that. I wouldn't say anything about it. There was knowledge of Papaji being everything, of not being dead of not being the ashes that went into the river. There was this stab of recognition of him being a manifestation. I talked to a couple of people in Lucknow that didn't go, and strangely enough they said that they had the same experience at about the same time of the day that it happened. I don't know how many people felt this. In a way it was a satisfying conclusion – to watch the remains of the body go into the Ganga and at the same time to be given the experience that he is still here and he is still everything and hasn't gone away.

Was that still your experience two years later?

I don't look at the world and hear this throbbing and think that this is all Papaji. Bhagavan said that you don't go around saying, 'I am a man, I am a man' all day. He said that there is an unshakeable knowledge of who you are and if somebody comes along and says, 'You look like a horse,' you can say, 'No, I am not a horse.' There is no need to affirm it; if somebody challenges it you can look at what your experience is and say yes or no. For me there is no continuous thing like that day in Haridwar. It is like a piece of information that was there, given to me, transmitted to me in that moment: This is Papaji, and this is who you are. Don't forget it. It was like a parting message.

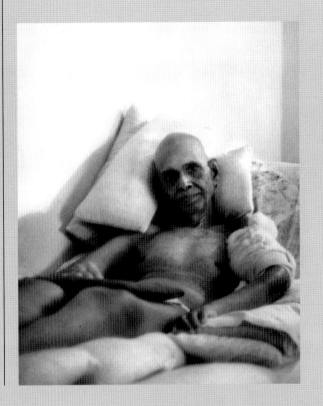

Firm and disciplined inherence in
the self without giving the least
scope for the rise of any thought
except the deep contemplative
remembrance of the Self, does
verily constitute self-surrender to
the Lord.

Sri Ramana Maharshi

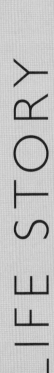

LIFE STORY

Above: Cow statue at the Mother's Shrine

Left: Samadhi Room where Sri Ramana spent his last days

Below: Arunachala from new ring-road south of Tiruvannamalai, west face

Right top: Sri Ramana with a rabbit

Right bottom: Sri Ramana with disciples and ashram cows

CHAPTER 11

James Swartz' Life Story

James Swartz interviewed
by Premananda

James's colourful life story is not totally believable, but,
as he warns us in the beginning that 'his story' finished
with his realisation when he was thirty-one, it doesn't
seem to matter. He splices into his factual account
many important insights and teachings. After living
in the fast lane in his early twenties he tuned into the
psychedelic movement of the 60s and started taking
LSD. He met his master Swami Chinmayananda
when he was twenty-nine and spent two years in
his company studying Vedanta. *An ashram in San*
Francisco followed for a short time, then long years of
trout fishing and living the simple life in a log cabin
in Montana. In the last years, James has returned to
teaching and writing about Vedanta.

Good morning James. You have something you wish to say before we hear your life story?

Is Sri Ramana the Self or is Sri Ramana that little person who had experiences and realised the Self? When you actually realise who you are that little experiencing person isn't really an experiencer any more. From the outside, it looks like you're a person having experiences. It seems like, 'Oh, he's a person who has this amazing life!' But inside, from where you are looking, absolutely nothing is happening, at all. Experience appears but it has no meaning. It does not touch you. There is total peace and stillness.

Are you saying that you don't have a lot of stories to tell us?

Yes. That's right. In fact, in the *Bhagavad Gita*, *Krishna* addresses this issue in the third chapter. He says, 'The one who sees action in inaction and inaction in action is indeed wise.' That means when something's happening, you just don't feel like anything is happening at all. But then, from the relative level there is a story to be told.

You could start with a little background of the wild young James, clothes designer and businessman.

Yes. I was a greedy, self-centered, dishonest, egoic, adulterous, gluttonish, alcoholic, chain-smoking businessman.

So you were a nice guy!

I was definitely not a nice guy! I was a tough guy; I knocked heads with the big guys in Honolulu. I made a lot of money very fast. I got so successful that even the Mafia tried to recruit me. But I had enough brains to realise I didn't want to get involved with those guys. Because my life was based on a lie and contrary to moral rules I was suffering – even though everybody was patting me on the back and telling me how wonderful I was. When you're successful, everybody 'loves' you but they don't really love you. They love your success. But inside I knew very well I wasn't a success. I felt miserable, in fact. Then one night I slept with the wife of one of my colleagues.

I woke up in the morning hung-over, completely worn out, just a mess – but I had to go and get the stores opened. I had three stores in Waikiki Beach. The tourists started coming in between nine and ten in the morning so I had to get the sales staff and the money set up and make sure the displays were alright. On the way I stopped off at the post office to collect my mail.

I've had lots of moments in my life that most people would think were unforgettable – but I've forgotten most of them, simply because I've had such an interesting life. But this day was different. I will never forget it. It was a typical Hawaiian winter day, seventy degrees with the palm trees rustling in the Trade Winds. There had been a light rain the night before, so the pavement was glistening and the tropical flowers were throwing out lovely fragrances. I knew that it was a beautiful day, but I could not feel one thing. I was completely dead, like a stone or an inanimate object.

I was heading into the post office and I noticed a man coming out, a jaunty old fellow wearing Bermuda shorts and an aloha shirt and smoking a corncob pipe. He was reading a letter as he walked, not paying attention. I could see that we were on a collision course: if he didn't look and if I didn't move, we were going to bump into each other. So I decided to step out of the way.

I tried to move and I couldn't. I had lost control completely! The body was on automatic pilot; I thought 'Oh, my God! What's going on here? Am I going mad? Is something happening?' I tried everything, and my body would absolutely not respond. I perceived a powerful energy or force controlling me. We came face-to-face and he looked up at me.

My mouth opened. I did not open it. I had no control over my sense organs at all. A voice spoke that was not my voice. I tell you, that voice was the sweetest, most amazing voice I had ever heard in my life! It was so sweet! It was so pure! It was such a beautiful voice! It said, 'Excuse me, Sir, how old do you think I am?'

I could not believe what was happening. I obviously knew very well how old I was and I couldn't have cared less what he or anybody else thought. I was a big man and a rich successful guy and he was a little nobody so I couldn't have cared less. The voice said, 'Excuse me, Sir, how old do you think I am?' He took it as a straightforward question. He sort of stepped back a little bit, looked me up and down, took a puff on his pipe and said, 'Well, well, Sonny, I'd say you're forty-three.'

That was an eye-opener. I was twenty-six! Being a business man I knew when people lied, because in that world everybody lied. You figured out the truth by the lies. I was successful because I was a good liar. I could see he was lying.

I thought to myself, 'Why is this man lying?' And then it struck me that he was lying because he was a kind man. He didn't want me to think he thought I was older than I really was. So he was shaving off a few years to make me feel good. This got me to thinking for a second. Then the voice said – I didn't speak, I couldn't speak – 'Well yes, thank you very much.' Then suddenly there was a kind of click, a release of the energy, and I got my functions back.

I headed right into the post office. I opened the first door to step into the foyer and suddenly I lost control again. The force was back. The body just turned to the left on its own then turned right and walked into the men's room. There was a big bank of mirrors on the wall over the sinks, and it parked itself in front of them. It just stopped! There was a feeling of 'Ah!' And then to my wonder the room filled with a soft, beautiful, subtle, fabulous, amazing light that permeated everything. And it was accompanied by a powerful, almost tangible silence, so thick you could cut it with a knife or eat it with a spoon. There was so much awareness that the men who were in there immediately flushed the toilets, zipped up and got out. They could feel the power of awareness and were embarrassed by it, I think.

I looked into that mirror and I saw every bit of the sin and corruption that I had become, the foul, disgusting nature of my character. I realised what a useless son of a bitch I was, and I could not get away from this vision. Painful as it was, all the while I was suffused completely in this amazing radiance. I realised that I could not leave until I had completely taken in every bit of this ugliness that I was. As soon as I accepted it completely, the experience stopped.

I walked out, and I knew, very clearly, that there was a benign intelligent deity in this world, that there was a God, and that I had no business being what I was. Within six months I sold my businesses, let my hair grow long, quit drinking, quit smoking and lost sixty pounds. I gave up on married women too. It was the beginning of my spiritual quest.

When was that?

That was in 1967.

There was a lot going on around then.

Yes, there was. I had heard about all of this psychedelic ferment, whatever you like to call it, but I was not involved in it at all; I was just a straight businessman. I didn't really know what it was all about. Then one day I flew to California to open a new store and I got off the airplane, rented a car and headed up to San Francisco to do some business. I had my business clothes on, my attaché case, all my expensive trinkets and a lot of cash. I did a lot of cash business because I wasn't paying taxes. There was a hippie, hitchhiking, and for some reason the car just pulled over on its own. It was unbelievably strange, like the day at the post office. I said, 'Do you want a ride?' I would never ever have considered even talking to a hippie because I was a kind of snooty, upper-class guy. I came from a good background, I spoke nicely. I was arrogant and I had an aristocratic attitude.

But here I am picking up a useless hippie on the side of the road! I start talking, impressing him with the wonder that was me, what an incredible guy I was, what an amazing, powerful, interesting, rich bastard I was. And he didn't seem impressed at all! After I finished talking I said, 'Well, what do you think about that?' And he said, 'Well, man,' – he was very laid back, very California – 'Well, man, I'd say you're one of most fucked up human beings I ever met.' Ordinarily, I'd have got mad and thrown him out of the car, but for some reason his words didn't bother me at all. I said, 'Okay! Fair enough. So what do you think I should do about it?' He reached in his pocket and he took out two tabs of Orange Sunshine LSD and he handed them to me. 'Take these. It might help.' (Laughter)

So it's seventy miles per hour on the Bayshore Freeway; I popped both tabs of acid and washed them down with a cup of coffee. I have no idea where he got out. By the time I got to the Bay Bridge the universe was breathing in and out like a huge lung and the road was springing out and back like it was made of rubber. I could see seagulls leaving *karmic* trails across the sky. I made it up to the top of the Berkeley Hills by the grace of God. In Tilden Park I just drove off the road into a field and opened the door and left everything sitting there in the car. There was five thousand dollars in an attaché case on the front seat, expensive doodads and trinkets, door wide open and the motor running.

I walked out into the fields and I had one of the most extraordinary, mind-blowing, incredible, fantastic trips of my life. I realised at that time that this thing that had happened to me without any drugs, in a men's room in Waikiki, was available through LSD. So I became an acid head.

Is this when you sold the business?

Yes, I sold the business. I collected a bunch of money and started taking LSD. I partied a bit, but basically I used it as a tool for self-discovery. I was able, in a very short time, to purify a huge amount of my negative and unhealthy tendencies simply by observation and analysis. Then one day I was in San Francisco and I bumped into this guy and we had a nice chat. It was a different time then, very cool! When we left he said, 'Here's a couple tabs of mescaline. There's a really great concert tonight across from Seal Rock on Ocean Beach. The Grateful Dead are playing. Enjoy!'

I drove out there, just as the sun was setting, looking forward to some great music, meeting some cute chicks and having a nice time. So I popped open the mescaline and sniffed one cap in one nostril and the other cap in the other nostril, and got my head right. I watched the sunset for a while then wandered into The Family Dog. It was a famous place. It was where Steve Gaskin had his Monday Night Class and it was a gathering spot for the psychedelic crowd.

It was a spiritual place?

Well, it was, sort of. I walk through the door and here's Alan Ginsberg French-kissing some young guy. 'What the hell is this?' I think. And I look on the wall and there's a movie playing, Sai Baba is vomiting up a great big *lingam* out of his guts! A *lingam*, in case you are interested, is a large stone symbol of the Self. 'What the hell is this?' I look around, and the whole place is full of all of these amazing spiritual types! Along one wall are a dozen Californian hippie-surfer-*Yogi* types in different postures with their eyes rolled up. Yogi Bhajan is on the stage. He has a big turban on and you can see this kind of radiant light coming out of his third eye.

One of the beautiful young women came up to me and said, 'Wow, man! You're incredible! You've got amazing energy!'

I said, 'What's going on? I thought this was a rock and roll thing.'

She said, 'Ah! Rock and roll? Are you kidding?'

I said, 'Come on, what the hell is happening? This is really weird.'

And she said, 'It's the holy-man jam, man.' Then she said, 'There's something funny about you. Are you stoned?'

And I said, 'Of course I'm stoned! What do you mean, am I stoned? Isn't everybody stoned?'

She just looked at me, like I was a real jerk. She was one of those prissy, moral, spiritual girls, who was just too good for sex, drugs and rock and roll.

So I said, 'What's wrong with acid?'

And she said, 'Acid is not where it's at.'

And I said, 'Okay. What is where it's at?'

And she says, 'God is where it's at!'

The holy-man jam was a lot of hippies and druggies who had been turned on to God. I found it interesting and stuck around. 'So tell me about this God thing,' I said. By the end of the evening I was sold on God.

That was the end of the sixties?

Yes. I was a little late on the psychedelic thing. LSD gave people a feeling or understanding or experience that there was something beyond this mundane world. LSD is a kind of catalyst or door opener to that dimension if you are suited for it. Those people had moved on and so I thought, 'Well, I'll go to India and find out what it's all about.' So I did. I went to Europe and hitchhiked down to Spain where I caught the boat for Morocco.

A girl picked me up in a small village in the Riff Mountains. She wanted me to take a trip but I was bored with it. She kept insisting. She was an astrologer and said the stars said we had to trip, and we were going to become the divine couple, etc. She was a little light in the loafers. She said we were meant to take this tab of acid at exactly this particular time, and so on. So just to please her and stop her nagging, I popped in a tab of acid and yes, all the same old pyrotechnics started – the colours and lights, and the universe breathing like a giant lung, the whole nine yards.

But you know something? There was an amazing psychedelic experience going on, but it had absolutely no affect on me at all. It was like watching a movie for the twentieth time. I did not change one bit. I realised that I was not who I thought I was. I realised that I was an all-seeing eye of consciousness, that I was completely beyond my mind and that this mind had nothing to do with me at all. I was the all-seeing eye. I was pure awareness.

I realised drugs were over for me so I quit drugs and let my mind and body purify. I just took off and hitchhiked across North Africa. I had amazing out-of-body experiences, I astral travelled and experienced all kinds of psychic and spiritual dimensions. In Libya I levitated. 'I' didn't levitate, but the body levitated, it lifted off the ground without any effort by me.

I travelled over to Egypt where I was interrogated and beaten up by the Egyptian military who thought I was a Jewish spy. I had some of the worst days of my life in Egypt. I ended up on a paddle-wheel steamer going up the Nile River to Sudan. It was an extraordinary trip. I don't think there has been more than a handful of Western people who have ever done this. On the boat were a couple of young Americans – sort of do-gooder, spiritual types – who'd been influenced by Aurobindo and the Mother and this idea of Auroville, a community of people who were going to create the new messianic sort of spirituality.

We chatted at dinner, and they were impressed by my life story and by the wild experiences I had had because they were really quite inexperienced. The husband was so inspired that he got up, ran down to his room and came back with a book, *The Adventure of Consciousness*, by a man named Satprem.

Satprem was a confident of the Mother's. He sat there for ten or fifteen years recording every one of her words, which later became *The Mother's Agenda*, the philosophical foundation for Auroville. I read *The Adventure of Consciousness* and I realised that what was happening to me was commonplace in India, and that there was this amazing spiritual culture awaiting me. There was a wonderful thrill of satisfaction that came from thinking that I was heading to this place where I could gain some understanding of what it was that was actually going on within myself and why all these miraculous things were taking place around me all the time. I'd led such a charmed life. I'd had an amazing life, so far, and it was just starting to get interesting.

After ten days in The Sud, a huge swamp in southern Sudan, I ended up in Juba where a war was going on. I was nearly killed by soldiers but was saved by the Chief of Police. I flew down to Entebbe, Uganda where Idi Amin was eating people, hitchhiked over to Nairobi with a bunch of smugglers who got involved in a gunfight with the customs agents on the border of Kenya. I managed to extricate myself and survive that and made my way to Mombassa where I caught a boat for the Seychelles, Karachi and Bombay.

When I got off that boat and stepped out on the streets of Bombay – I know it sounds like a cliché and I'm sorry to say it – I'd Come Home! India felt remarkably wonderful, a great place to end up.

Could you explain this, because many Western people absolutely wouldn't understand this when you say, 'I'd Come Home!' What is it in India that is so attractive?

Well, if you feel this way you have what are called *purva janma samskaras*. That means you had some sort of birth here in a previous life, and that your soul resonates with the vibrations here. Saints and sages, holy men, fakirs and all kinds of special beings lived here. The dust of the earth is permeated with this vibration of awareness. It felt so comfortable to me. In my previous life I had been a pandit in Kashmir and so I had those *samskaras*. As soon as I stepped on this earth it suddenly just hit me like a ton of bricks: I felt very, very happy! I have a very ironic and perverse kind of nature, and so just the bizarre nature of India struck me and amused me beyond belief!

In a juice shop in Bombay I met a young man named Ravi, who happened to be a disciple of Nisargadatta Maharaj. I started chatting with him and I said, 'Well, what's this guru business?' because I didn't know, I'd never met a guru. He said, 'Come! I'll take you.' So the next day he took me and I met Nisargadatta Maharaj in his little house above his *beedie* (Indian cigarette) stand.

You only met him once?

Yes. I didn't know you were meant to worship gurus. I don't worship people. I don't believe in it. I don't think anybody is better than me or worse than me. We are all the same. He gave me this vision of the Self. I saw the Self without any drugs! Suddenly, as he spoke, somehow, this magic happened and I was back in awareness seeing from the Self's point of view. He said, 'Go to Rishikesh' and I thought, 'Okay, why not?'

I went to Rishikesh and there I fell in with a *Yogi*. He turned out to be a scoundrel and did not acquit himself well, but he was a very attractive and handsome young man with beautiful, black, long, flowing locks and glowing eyes. All these beautiful young women sat around worshipping him with great affection. Somehow he took a liking to me and he used to take me to visit the Maharani. She had a very nice place in Lakshman Jhoola right on the Ganges banks. This was before it became very fashionable for Westerners to be there. The Beatles had come, and that was about it. Rishikesh was still reasonably pure and pristine.

He taught me *Kundalini Yoga*. I was totally sincere about enlightenment because I had had these experiences and I had heard that you could actually gain the experience of the Self through this *Yoga*. So I started practising *Kundalini Yoga*. Oh my God, you wouldn't believe the kind of disgusting things we did to purify our bodies. We drank tons of stuff and swallowed yards of fabric and vomited it up. We did all kinds of weird contortions with our bodies, trying to wake up the spiritual power. It was ridiculous. And nothing happened.

I would chide him. I would say, 'Come on Yogiji! You've got to do better than this! This is not working!' Because actually, I could take a tab of acid and get higher than I was getting from that stuff. I kept pushing him, pressuring him. I said, 'Come on Swami! I want the real thing! Give me some real stuff, man!' He liked me for some strange reason. I don't know why because I was a pretty arrogant and aggressive person. But I had a way with people and I liked him too. I wanted something – and when I want something I can be very nice.

Eventually I started telling him, 'Listen Yogiji. If I don't get some action fairly soon I'm leaving. I want the real thing, now.' To my surprise it worked. He said, 'Okay, I'm going to give you the real thing.'

He taught me a very complicated *Hatha Yoga* routine. It took a few days for him to explain it to me and for me to get clear what I was supposed to do. Then I said, 'I can't remain in the ashram. It's impossible with all the stuff going on here, all these people. Sorry. I'll have to go and find myself some place in the jungle or on the Ganges where I can do this.' So I went up beyond Lakshman Jhoola and found a beautiful cave, which nobody had been in. It was a really lovely place. I started practising with great dedication and concentration. If I want to get results, I get results.

Did you get results?

It turns out I was living in a cave with a four foot cobra! But I was so crazy and so mystical that I thought, '*Shiva* has a cobra around his neck. It must be a good sign!' At night the cobra would go out to hunt. By that time I was sound asleep. I'd get up to do my practices at the crack of dawn and the cobra would be coming in; he'd sleep in the back. So our lifestyles didn't really conflict.

Then one day I was practising there and suddenly: 'Voom!' I just shot completely out of my body. I had an amazing transcendental experience and a vision of *Kali* (goddess of time and change). I realised I was just pure consciousness. I'd had similar experiences many times before – in the men's room in Waikiki, through LSD and at various other times without drugs – and I thought, 'Gee, this is amazing! There is actually a way I can access this state, this wonderful state of consciousness, through this method.' I was so grateful! I decided to thank the *Yogi*.'

I headed off to the ashram thinking the *Yogi* was in the same state. I had so much spiritual power it was amazing. I could look at you and you would wake up. When I showed up I realised that the *Yogi* was just a clever man who had no spiritual power at all. His ego was all wrapped up in the attention he was getting. It was very sad. He had a beautiful body and he'd learned a bunch of *Yoga* stuff and could talk nicely and that was all! He was a complete fraud. He was a smart guy and realised that somehow I'd hit the jackpot with this technique. I was going to prostrate but I realised that he should be prostrating to me. I knew it was all over. I didn't care.

He understood too and he said, 'You know James, I think it's probably best if you leave the ashram. I collected my stuff and left. Of course, a few days later I came crashing down – as one does when one has these extraordinary experiences. You just go back to – what? Picking your nose and worrying about your taxes. Am I going to get laid? Is somebody going to love me? You just go back to being a normal Joe.

Well, you've taken us as far as Rishikesh. What was next?

I met a young hippie woman in Kullu Manali and got a bad case of hepatitis. I ended up an emaciated body on a rope bed in the Punjab with yellow hair, yellow teeth, yellow eyes, broke and weighing a hundred and fifty pounds. Rats were running over my feet. The people there thought, 'Well, another druggie.' They didn't care. They were just waiting for me to die and they'd sweep me up or burn me or throw me somewhere, and that would be it.

Then one day, suddenly I just left the body and became this presence, this peaceful, beautiful awareness. In one corner of my awareness I had a kind of connection with the body, sort of like seeing a second movie in the corner of a movie screen. I wasn't in the body but I could see through it. A crowd started to gather. Nobody had paid any attention to me at all in life. Asians are very accommodating to suffering and death. They don't make a big story about it. They just pass by the body and live their lives and death happens. It is not a big deal. But in death I suddenly became famous because this extraordinary bubble of glowing awareness around the body attracted them. Pretty soon there must have been forty, fifty, sixty people just standing there, reverently, staring at this body which was permeated by the amazing shining light that I am!

And just then a big black Mercedes Benz rolls up. A very beautifully dressed Pakistani gets out and opens the back door for a very elegant, well-dressed man in a tailored suit and Italian shoes, with his hair slicked back just so. He's the man. The crowd parts for him automatically, like the Red Sea for the Israelites. He comes right over to me and squats down. He looks at my body and gently kicks it. No reaction. He kicks it again. Then he leans close to my face and says, 'I can see by the way you bear your suffering that you're a refined man. By the will of Allah I have been sent to take care of you.'

His driver scooped me up and they put me in the back of the Mercedes. We drove through beautiful paddy fields lined with big trees. Suddenly a huge Victorian mansion appeared. It was just like being in a movie, I tell you. The car stopped and immediately a door opened. Everything was completely choreographed. It was absolutely clear that God was taking care of every single thing, right down to the finest detail. On the top of the mansion was a beautiful four-poster bed, under these huge shade trees. There was a mahogany night table with a marble top and porcelain bowl and pitcher. They laid me in the bed.

My host said, 'This is Maskour. He will take care of you. On Thursday afternoon my mistress comes. Then we'll take you out and you can go to the movies.' We became very good friends. He nursed me back to health. They fed me and my energy started to come back. I entered my body again and started to function as a human being. On the seventeenth day, in the early morning, I had a dream. I saw myself sitting in a small ashram in San Francisco. There was a holy man, all dressed in orange with a long beard, giving a talk on *Vedanta*.

As soon as that dream ended I opened my eyes and here comes my host with a packed lunch and a bus ticket. 'By the will of Allah you'll go to Kabul today.' Then he gave me some rupees and two gold rings. I went to Kabul on the bus.

I checked into a guest house and fell asleep. I had a nightmare and screamed out loudly. There was a knock on the door and it was a very good friend I had met in Morocco. He recognised my voice! He looked after me and bought me a ticket to Istanbul. When I got to Istanbul I sold the gold rings and bought two kilos of hashish. I sewed the hash into a vest and caught the Orient Express to Amsterdam where I sold the hash and bought a ticket for California.

When I got to California I decided, 'To hell with this God-damned spiritual thing! This is absolute madness, chasing enlightenment. I'm finished.' That very day I decided to go back to school and finish my degree and be a normal guy, get married and so on.

I'd had all these extraordinary experiences. I haven't told you five percent of the things that happened to me, good and bad, but at the end of the day what did it matter? I was still me.

That very morning I went into the shower. I had a little mirror that I could hang on the showerhead so I could trim my beard when it was soft from the water. I turned on the shower and started soaping up and suddenly I heard an other-worldly sound and the shower stall filled with light just like it had filled the restroom in the post office in Waikiki! A *mantra* (sacred sound) started pouring out of me from the solar plexus. I wasn't chanting it. It was chanting me. *Om namah Sivaya! Om namah Sivaya! Om namah Sivaya!* It had unbelievable radiance and power. I was shaking with joy and happiness.

I looked in the mirror at my face and suddenly a hole about the size of a dime opened up in my forehead, right here, in this space between and just above my eybrows. The flesh in my face and my body became liquid, like water, and it all just – 'Sssssssht!' – flowed into that hole. My whole body went into that hole. And then suddenly it came out on the other side and it just shot up, completely out of the cosmos.

Suddenly, once again, I am the all-seeing eye of consciousness. I am looking out, and I can see the whole universe – the planets, the galaxies, the stars; I can see everything which exists just vibrating in the radiance, in the light of awareness. And in one corner I can see the planet Earth. In that little corner of the planet Earth I can see my body!

The body washes up, towels off, dresses, walks out the door. As soon as the body gets to the street, a car stops. The driver rolls down the window and says, 'Come on! I'll give you a ride!' The energy hits him and suddenly he's awakened. We're just sitting there, one consciousness. The car is driving, everything is happening totally without any kind of conscious control. Everything is suffused in radiant awareness. I am sitting in this huge bubble of awareness – which is me – watching everything unfold on the Earth.

I get out on the streets of San Francisco. I have no idea where I'm going. I have no idea what I'm doing. I know nothing. I do not care what happens. I'm walking up and down the streets through throngs of people. The energy is so powerful that some of them want to come up and touch me, and others are so frightened that they just run off. They have no idea what kind of being is walking down the street. It looks human, but is it?

I could see into every mind, see what they were thinking and feeling. I could see each person's whole life history. This knowledge was being transmitted to me from some unknown source. And through me the Self, God if you want, was healing all these souls. Don't ask me how I knew it, I just knew it. I must have woken up and healed hundreds of people without doing anything. It went on for several hours.

About six-thirty, quarter to seven in the evening, I was walking up Market Street – believe this or not – and an empty city bus pulled up. There was a hippie driver in it who looked a lot like me! 'Hey, you want a ride?' he said. And I said, 'Sure.' He drove me out through Golden Gate Park and out onto the Avenues where he dropped me off.

I thought 'Where am I? What am I doing here?' Then the body started walking up this street for a few blocks. It turned left and it entered a house. There were about fifty people in a room, all sitting silently in meditation. When I came in I was generating so much energy it was kind of disturbing. People looked around and shuffled.

There were two empty chairs and all the rest were filled. My body sat in the one in the second row. I am thinking, 'What the hell is going on here?' But it didn't matter, because I was completely beyond it all. About a minute later, as if the whole thing was completely choreographed, I felt a strong presence and a holy man, a *sadhu* dressed in orange, sits down right in front of me. I can feel him transmitting a greeting to me. The dream I had in Lahore was playing out in real life. I knew who he was and I knew that he knew who I was. A man introduced him as Swami Chinmayananda. He got up and immediately started talking about *Vedanta*.

I tell you, every word was like honey. It was like drinking nectar. It was most extraordinary, so beautiful! The next day I called up my girlfriend and my parents and said, 'Bye-bye.' I sold my car, collected my money and I took off with the Swami. I became his disciple. (Long silence) These are things you can never forget. Everything else is forgotten, really.

So you gave up your life and followed Swami Chinmayananda?

Yes. For two years.

He, in fact, responded to your clear sincerity.

Oh yes, absolutely! There is a saying in the *Vedic* spiritual tradition, *bhakta bhaktiman*. It means the Lord is the devotee of the devotees; the guru is the disciple of the disciples. So the guru gets under you and lifts you up. The guru is there for you. You're not there for the guru. Most people in the spiritual world think that they are there to please the guru, so the guru will give them something. But in this tradition – it's the old tradition, and it's still alive today – the guru is looking for those people who are qualified. It's their *dharma*, their duty, to look after the people who the Lord sends to them. So this was a glorious man, one of those you meet once in a lifetime – like Sri Ramana or Nisargadatta or the Buddha. This guru was the real thing, I tell you. He was one of the most highly respected mahatmas in India in the last half of the last century.

He got his first awakening through Swami Shivananda in Rishikesh. Shivananda was a great mahatma but he was a *Yogi* and didn't have much of a teaching, really. It wasn't satisfactory for Chinmaya. So he moved on and went further up in the Himalayas, to Uttarkashi, where he met a great Himalayan sage named Swami Tapovan who was a pure ascetic. There is a beautiful book written about him, called *Wandering in the Himalayas* that tells his story. He was a very simple man of the highest wisdom and great character. He was not interested in name or fame or anything of the sort. And he had the goods. I mean, he was a pure *Vedanta* man, and a native of Kerala where Swamiji was from, so they had that kind of background together, also. He stayed seven years with his guru.

The guru told him, right up front, 'I only say things once. I don't repeat myself. So you'd better pay attention.' Swamiji was a brilliant man, and highly motivated. That's what he told me, too. He said, 'Just sit down and shut up. Pay attention, and we'll get you out of here as soon as possible because you're taking up space that others can use.' That was his idea. He didn't want me serving him. He said, 'Service to the guru is keeping your mind focused on the Self, keeping your mind fixed on the Self, practising discrimination. That's the real service.' And so he did his part.

Did you live in his ashrams?

He was too famous to stay anywhere. He had centres all over the world. At that time he was doing ten days in one place, and so I went twice around the world with him, to the different centres in India and America and Europe. We'd spend ten days; he'd do a whole spiritual programme from four in the morning until ten at night. And then, in the next ten days, we'd move on to Australia, or to Hong Kong, to California, to Switzerland, back to India. I didn't pay for any food or shelter. I paid for my own tickets and he took care of me. He introduced me to the most extraordinary people.

Swami Chinmayananda was the most famous spiritual leader in India because he created a huge spiritual mission in a matter of fifty years. It's still dynamic and alive today. It's very well known and good too. To my knowledge there's never been one single sex or money scandal in that tradition in the last sixty years. It's holy, pure and sacred.

What about Swami Dayananda? What was his connection with Swami Chinmaya?

Swami Chinmaya designed a two-year *Vedanta* course and Swami Dayananda taught it. Dayananda was in the mission for fifteen years. He was the top Swami. He was groomed to actually take over the Chinmaya mission but opted to go out on his own. He had certain issues with Chinmaya's method of teaching and he didn't want to end up running that huge mission, although he ended up with a pretty big mission of his own, in the end. Because the cream rises to the top. These guys were top guys. They were absolutely impeccable spiritual people who served the truth with total dedication.

What you're saying is that, for you, he was this wonderful man and due to this close association everything became clear.

Well, I just listened to the teachings. And yes, then I had the benefit of his person, of personally being there. We were like brothers. Sometimes I felt like I had been his father before, or something like that. We had a kind of family thing, and very similar character, similar nature.

He was a really tough, no-nonsense businessman type, and I could relate to that. I remember one time in Australia they printed an interview with him in the paper: 'This Swami is no peace-love pussycat! (Laughs) This Swami is a real tiger.' He had amazing love and the purest knowledge. He was the best.

Association with the sages is the root cause of liberation. The scriptures are clear on this. So associate with a sage and you'll definitely become free, if you're qualified. And I was qualified. I had suffered enough and I knew what I wanted. The Lord decided to bless me with this great teacher. So it was really a foregone conclusion. I never worried about it, once I met him. It didn't matter. As soon as I met the guru, I knew absolutely my work was over.

And it was through the teachings that things became clear?

Yes! Absolutely! Because, you see, *Vedanta* is a means of Self-knowledge. It's very scientific. It works beautifully, because it's all set up. It's been working for thousands of years. And if a sage has that inclination to teach, you pick up the methodology along with it and can apply the teachings to your own mind. So basically, for me it was like an enlightenment factory. You just do the spiritual practice, which is listening and reflecting, and slowly your ignorance drops off and you assimilate the knowledge.

The experience of the Self is not going to solve your problems. That was the point! I'd had all these mind-blowing experiences. I knew I was the Self! But why couldn't I remain as the Self?

Because I'd always thought that enlightenment was some kind of experience and I kept trying to get those experiences back, to hold on to them and enjoy this as a big experiential thing, see? And what was wrong with that? I was the experiencer. I was separate from the thing I was experiencing. The experiences were extraordinary. Unbelievable! And the powers, and all the things that came to me as a result of this were amazing.

What was the problem? I thought enlightenment was an experience. Any experience, whether it's a suffering or enjoying experience, is going to change. And as a result of your interaction with the experience, you change – because you're in this impermanent world. So how are you going to have that experience and make it last? Well, you're not going to have that experience and make it last, because you're always experiencing the Self, twenty-four-seven.

The problem is that you don't understand what the Self is and that you are it. *Vedanta* says that this is a nondual reality. And experience is all about the belief that reality is dualistic. The way out of this is to cancel the experiencer by revealing the Self.

What most people think, and what *Yoga* encourages, is, 'I'm going to remain as I am and I am going to get this incredible experience that solves my sense of limitation. I want to add this experience to "me", and that's going to make me happy.' In this case, it's this amazing spiritual experience that's supposed to happen: infinite bliss, tremendous light – however you imagine it.

It happens like this to many people.

Yes. Many, many people have had these incredible, nondual experiences. But what doesn't happen is that the experiencer doesn't get cancelled. That is the problem. And what *Vedanta* does is cancel the experiencer. By 'cancel' I don't mean that it destroys the experiencer so that you cannot experience anymore. You go right on experiencing. It's not a physical destruction that's taking place. The destruction is purely in terms of understanding.

So as soon as you understand, then it's destroyed. But nothing actually is destroyed because it was never there.

Absolutely. I was sitting on the bed in the ashram, staring at the wall one afternoon. And even though I knew it, at that moment it just became crystal clear. It was not a big event. It was a complete non-event. It was just absolutely, totally understood, without any shadow of a doubt. From that moment I was finished. That's why I didn't write any more of my autobiography. What more is there to write? Because the person who had all those experiences ended. That person didn't continue on.

The argument about what happened to Sri Ramana in the cave after enlightenment – it's nonsense! He realised he was the Self at that time. That's called knowledge. That knowledge cancels Ramana. He's only going to be the Self. In which case, there's nothing more to say about it. And he isn't any different from anybody else, ever again! He's not a Ramana. He's everything that is!

But if you have this experiential idea then you think, 'This extraordinary thing happened to this guy; he kept it and he maintained it. It became permanent.' You keep the ego there with this extraordinary accomplishment stuck on top of it. That just sets you up to worship and makes you look tiny and small. 'How could this happen to me? It's only happened to one extraordinary person, ever, in the history of …' You start thinking like this because your view of enlightenment doesn't understand that the experiencer needs to be cancelled.

Sri Ramana is clear about this. He says, '**Only by knowledge will the Self be gained.**' He's very clear. Only by understanding that you are the Self, that this is a nondual reality, do you cancel this experiencer.

That's very beautiful! So you got it, while you were still a young guy.

Well, I was thirty-one.

You were a young, well-educated American man who had this clarity. Did you feel some impulse to share it?

I did not. But my guru told me: 'You will now explode upon the society and bring this knowledge to the people.' Those were his exact words.

I said, 'What to do?'

He said, 'Go sit under a tree in San Francisco, in California.' He told me, 'It will all work out. Don't worry about it.' He actually tried to set me up with a job and various things. He was a very good guy. He cared about me.

You didn't feel to teach then?

I didn't feel to teach but it just happened. I was dead broke when I got back. I had the phone number of this guy who I'd met in Morocco, who had helped me in Afghanistan. He was a merchant seaman and he lived in San Francisco. He just had a little room and he let me sleep in the hallway. We were very close friends, actually. He gave me the money to buy an old car – a Ford Fairlane. I ripped out the back seats and I went around ripping-off old Victorian buildings, stealing junk and selling it. I became a scavenger on the street. I had no money, but within about two years I had a mansion in the exclusive Seacliff area, a business and an ashram. I attracted people like flies – because I was happy.

The hippie thing had cooled down a bit, but there was still a receptive audience. People were still open for knowledge.

Oh yes! The psychedelic movement had turned spiritual. So California was really interested. All the Swamis came over, all the lamas came over. The Zen guys came over. There was a huge spiritual ferment taking place in California at that time. Chogyam Trungpa Rinpoche was there, and so on.

Was that the seventies?

It was the beginning of the seventies. The ashram became a success. I think ten or twelve of the people who came to the ashram realised the Self. But by the middle of the seventies I'd quit. I'd dropped my ashram and moved on! I'd gone up to the mountains in Montana. I didn't want the ashram anymore. It was too much work. I'd proved to myself that I could live up to this teaching work but I didn't want to do it. I was getting a minor bit of fame and quite a bit of power, and I didn't like it. So one day I called a meeting and told everybody, 'Party's over!' I decided to make myself happy instead of all those people.

So you left your ashram, your house and everything?

Yes. I walked away from it all with a 1955 Chevy truck with a small load of antiques and with three grand in my pocket. For seven years of hard work. I got nothing out of it except a kind of satisfaction in doing it. I could have been a millionaire, easy. I could have gone on to be quite rich and quite famous, but I was not interested.

So that was a very important moment.

I suppose. I'm a scientist. I like to make experiments. My life is a big experiment. I try all these things and when I get good at them I walk away. I have no attachment to them. I just want to learn how things work and then make them work. My mind is turned on, it's excited. I have a lot of things in there that I'd like to do in my life, so I just want to learn the essence of things and move on. I learned how to do art, how to write, how to do business. I did house restoration and repair. The ashram supported itself with a very successful antique business. So I knew how to do restoration of antiques and buying and selling.

I knew nothing about the antique trade when we started. We were selling at the flea markets and garage sales and just out of the blue this guy gave me a store. It didn't cost me a dime! We had a very successful store in San Francisco, down on Divisadero Street. Everybody worked like dogs eight hours, ten hours a day.

Anytime you involve yourself with people and money, you've got to work. And I worked! I didn't sit on a throne, you know, acting big. I think the teacher should work just as hard or harder than everybody else. Because you teach by example, not just by precept.

So you carried on with a small antique business?

No. Our family had a beautiful log cabin on a blue ribbon trout stream in the Rocky Mountains, Montana, and I moved there.

You weren't inviting people?

No, I was not inviting people. I'd had enough of it. People are needy, they always want something. They're like children, and spiritual people are no exception. They always want something. That's really not a mature person. A mature person takes care of themselves. I'm kind, I'm generous, I like to help people, I like to give to people. But there's a limit!

Your decision to stop teaching and go and live in the mountains is something very particular that happened in your life.

I'm just selfish! (Laughs) I mean, I've got to look after myself!

Your own teacher was somebody who stayed in selfless service his whole life and you decided at some point to step out of that. But of course, now you're back into that. Maybe you never really left it.

Well, I didn't; but you have to use your discrimination. Just because people want something doesn't mean you should give it to them. You can make a person dependent by helping them, and they won't take care of their own self. One of the qualifications for Self-realisation is *swadharma*, taking care of yourself. If you don't take care of yourself properly, you're not going to have the right thing to give.

But people who wake up are eager to help. It's natural but it's a mistake. You should sit back and think about it. 'Why do I want to help? Why do I need to help? Why can't I let the Lord take care of things?' I should take care of myself, look after myself, see that I'm beautiful, see that I'm holy and pure. This is the biggest help, not running around with a bunch of unresolved stuff trying to enlighten others. I don't need to DO a whole lot of things to make the world better. Just making myself better creates a beautiful thing for the world.

Yes. That's also important.

All of this doership! Look at Mother Teresa. Did you read her papers after she died?

Yes.

She was in agony, total misery. She was tormented like you wouldn't believe. And she never was able to fulfill her spiritual destiny. Five million people came to her funeral because she's a Saint – but when they published these papers it was extraordinary! She spent all of her life trying to live the life of Christ rather than living her own life. She had ten days where she felt that she was connected to God, and that was it. The rest of the time she felt lonely and separate and depressed and cut off from God.

Everything's fine, all the time. You don't have to mess with the world. You don't have to do anything to make this world more beautiful. One of Swamiji's favourite statements was that the Lord or the Self gives us major doses of joy and sorrow to purify our inner equipment, our minds. The joy is there to purify us and the suffering is there to purify us. Just trying to relieve people of their suffering doesn't relieve people of their suffering. You relieve your own suffering when you start to realise the reasons why you're suffering.

I met you probably five years ago, when you had been living simply here in Tiruvannamalai for quite a few years. You were doing your writing and making yourself available for teaching to people who were really interested, but what happened in the other twenty years?

Nothing!

You couldn't have stayed in your cabin for twenty years!

Yes, I did. I'd spend the summers in Montana. It was an idyllic life, just fabulous! I drank out of the stream! I ate rainbow trout everyday, which I caught from the river. I'd shoot a deer for the fall and we'd eat venison. My wife was a cook! An excellent cook and a dancer.

Oh, you had a wife! You have never told me about her. Was she already involved with you in the ashram?

Well, yes. I knew her from California. She was an exotic dancer. I designed the costumes and we'd put together a programme. I managed the whole thing, the money, the costumes and the arrangements. We'd book her into these really classy clubs and collect a lot of cash and then go to India. We'd spend the winter in India, and when it got hot in India it was nice in Montana. We'd fly back to Montana and live in the forest and enjoy. So it was a good lifestyle. I've done that for the last thirty years, more or less.

When you were in India, did you sometimes work with Chinmaya mission?

No, not at all! I don't like groups and organisations. I never, ever, in my life joined one organisation. I like people and I like to be open and free and just sit around. And things happen.

So you work more on an individual basis?

You're much more effective teaching an individual. In *Vedanta* you don't accept anyone unless they're qualified. So it's very easy to help people, to give them *moksha* (liberation). It's very easy for them to finish their *sadhana* (spiritual practise) if it's one-on-one. You just have to sit down and have a few chats.

There was a young man here two or three years ago who'd been knocking around in the spiritual world for years. He was very sincere, very pure; he was really highly qualified. We had maybe five or six meetings and it finished his work. I asked him, 'Well, why didn't it happen with the other teachers?' And he said, 'Well, the problem was, it was all negative teaching. It was very good – I got rid of all my stuff – but they couldn't reveal the Self like *Vedanta* did. *Vedanta* points out directly what it is.'

If you follow the teachings and if you're qualified, you can't miss it. Because you are the Self already. And you know it in some way and you're always experiencing it even when you think you aren't. There is just some slight disconnection in your understanding. What *Vedanta* does is take away that little bit of ignorance. It's not a big deal! It's a very simple thing.

Usually you have to go through maybe ten, twenty, thirty years before you're ready to let go of all your spiritual notions and ideas. Once you are, and you're purified enough, it's very easy to teach somebody.

The best way, and the old style – you'll see it in the *Upanishads* – is a conversational style. The person comes and says, 'Hey! I think you know something. Can I ask you a question?' And the guy says, 'Yes. Ask me a question.'

You live very simply. At the same time you've made yourself available for meetings with people who want to talk. In the last years it seemed that was your joy, in fact.

Yes, but I don't want a bunch of people in my house. You just go out and things happen. It's better to just go out and sit there – and the Lord will send the person who needs to come. Or not. It doesn't matter to me. I'm happy either way.

Right.

Sometimes I run a small class. I just give a regular teaching, and if the people are following the idea they'll have questions. Then we just stop right there and handle the question. If you keep the group small, it's fine. So it works. And with *Vedanta* there aren't that many people who really qualify. When they hear the teaching, even if it's a very high teaching, and they're not ready, you know what happens? They walk out! It's just automatic. They come, they sit, and they don't get it. They think, 'Oh, I don't get this. This is weird! I won't come tomorrow.'

It would be very helpful if you could explain what you mean by 'qualified'.

'Qualified' means you do not expect the world to give you one more thing. You're absolutely fed up! You are not looking for anything in this world. You don't want love, you don't want another girlfriend or a nice job. You're absolutely convinced that none of that's going to do it for you. That's the basic qualification. And if you've got that, and you really desire to be free, then that'll do it.

308

So you could say the qualification is the end of the desire and passion to do something.

Yes. In other words, the desire that formerly went into all that outside stuff goes into freedom. We call that *mumukshutva*, a strong, burning desire for liberation. And if you've got that, you should be dispassionate toward things in the world. And you will be. In other words, you will continue to act and do things, but you'll be indifferent to the results of your actions. So you won't ride high when you get what you want; you won't get depressed when you don't get what you want. You'll just be steady. You'll be able to tell the difference between what's real and what isn't. This world is a tricky place. Everything looks very juicy, sexy and tasty and you just want to grab at it. But inside all those good, tasty things there's a little fishhook that's ready to grab you. And you'd better have good discrimination or you'll get yourself caught up.

So these qualities are necessary: discrimination, dispassion, and a burning desire for liberation. Also forbearance, *bhakti* or devotion, *shraddha* or faith, and so forth. When you have these kinds of qualities then you're ready. And usually you're not qualified until you're in your forties or fifties. You need to go through it!

You need to get disappointed. You need to actually test it out. Try the relationship one more time. 'This time it's the perfect guy; it's the perfect girl! It's just what I want. It'll work this time! It didn't work before, but this time it's different. It's special.' It's not an intellectual thing; it's living your life and seeing that life doesn't work.

And that takes a number of years. You are saying that people usually become qualified when they're middle-aged, that young guys don't get it.

That's right. They keep hoping. When you pop out of the womb there should be a sign like the sign over the entrance to Hades in Dante's Inferno: 'Abandon hope, all ye who enter here.'

To connect your story with the teaching I would like to propose that by the time you were thirty you'd lived what takes most people a hundred years.

309

Yes. I burned it out. I was dead fed up. I knew there was nothing here. I'd tried it all, I'd been successful enough and I said, 'I just don't want to live this life. I'm disappointed with this.' So I had that *mumukshutva*, that burning desire, and that's what caused the teacher to come. And finally – what I thought was very interesting about this – I gave up my spiritual desire too. In other words, that *mantra* and that teacher didn't come until the very day when I gave up all spiritual desire and decided to get off this whole enlightenment thing.

When you decided to go back to college?

Yes. When I decided to go back to university I threw that whole spiritual trip in the waste bin. Then suddenly, the Lord showed me the way.

I think that's a very important point. Isn't there a story about Buddha; didn't he finally give up? Didn't he give up all his practices and his disciples?

That is supposedly what his bodhi tree experience was. He was very weak from doing so much *sadhana* – ascetic practices and weird meditations – and he was trying to get across this little river, the Nagarjuna. Anybody who had any vitality could wade across that river without any problem. He kept falling over and slipping on the rocks and struggling to get across the stupid river! He finally gets across the river, and he's tired. There's a tree there – the apocryphal banyan tree, the enlightenment tree – and he sits down under this tree and he thinks to himself (or this is how the story goes) … 'Jesus! Amazing!' He said, 'If I haven't got enough energy to get across this tiny stream, where is the energy going to come from to get across the whole ocean of existence? Huh? How is that going to work?'

And evidently at that point he realised that you are not going to get it by *karma*, doing things, or by doing charitable works. He realised that only by releasing the notion that there's something to get and that I am the doer are you going to get what you already have.

Your actions will gain something that you don't have. But an action will not get you what you already have. No matter how much you're looking, you're not going to find it by doing. You're only going to find it by understanding. And that's what *Vedanta* does: it just gives you that knowledge which ends the search for knowledge.

Thank you. Is there anything else you'd like to say?

Yes. You can't just hang on and try to wiggle your way through life. You've got to go for it. Whatever you feel, you really should go for it. Don't get stuck in things. Live, and live fully! Eat up your life! Enjoy it!

Yes. It's a benign universe! Nondual means benign.

It means everything here is looking after you. Most people think they are separate from everything and that the world is this big thing that they always have to keep looking out for. They worry about everything they do: 'What will happen now?' And so forth.

This world is the Lord! The whole thing is the Lord! This is a beautiful world! It's what got you here! It gave you all these senses. It gave you all these elements. Look at how it's all working for you! You've got lungs and there's air to breathe. You've got eyes and there are sights to see. It is all taken care of. Every single thing is supplied. Only a thief doesn't offer back to the world.

The best offering you can give to the world is your own enthusiasm, your own joy! Just offer it back. 'Hey! Take it! Take it! You gave me so much! I give to you!' I've got lots to give. I can give forever, because the Self is a gift that keeps on giving, isn't it? There's just no end to it. So get out of this small grasping, greedy, fearful little mind.

The juiciness of your life holds a spectacular lesson, even if it's only a story that never even happened. In the end, it doesn't matter if it's true or not.

Yes. It's all stories. Life is a sea of stories. Ah, here's a nice story to finish with. A few years ago I was reading the paper here in India and I noticed a small headline that said 'Man Turns God'. I thought, 'Man turns God? Only in India will you get a newspaper article that says, "Man Turns God".'

There was this farmer in the Punjab, a very holy, very devout, very disciplined man; a *Yogi* type. He had a little shrine in the corner of his field where he used to meditate every day, and he had a guru and all that. One day – he's about fifty-five – he comes to his wife and he says, 'Amma, thank you very much. Our journey on Earth is finished. God bless you.' And he walked out in the field, took a shovel, and dug his grave. He dug a nice, big grave. Of course, she's thinking, 'Oh, wow! Something's going to happen now!' So she tells the neighbours. And you know how it is in India – the grapevine's faster than the Internet! Pretty soon the whole village is there, a couple of thousand people.

This guy's digging his own grave, and they want to see how this is going to work out. And then he tosses the shovel away, he sits down in a *Yoga* posture, closes his eyes and everyone said they saw his soul – pssht – leave his body! The title was 'Man Turns God'.

So, that's the best story, isn't it? When you merge and discover your oneness with everything. There's no other story like it. It's a beautiful story, and it's possible. I mean if a bozo like me, a redneck from the wilds of Montana can realise who I am, then anybody can!

Your life is a touching story – it's beautiful!

It's beautiful because you're beautiful, Premananda. The beauty's only in you!

Okay. Thank you very much.

No, it's true! It's true! If you see beauty, the beauty's only in you. It's only your own beauty.

Whatever is destined not to happen
will not happen, try hard as you may.
Whatever is destined to happen will
happen, do what you may to prevent
it. This is certain. The best course,
therefore, is to remain silent.

Sri Ramana Maharshi

LIFE STORY

Above: *Sri Ramana's samadhi statue*

Left: *Sri Ramana last days 1950*

Below: *Ramana Ashram Archive Building*

Right top: *Funeral ritual*

Right centre: *Sri Ramana's samadhi*

Right bottom: *Arunachala sunrise*

CHAPTER 12

Premananda's Life Story

*Premananda interviewed by Eddie Blatt 2003
and the latter part by Kali Devi in 2009*

*Premananda describes the longing and chaos of his
twenties and how existence stepped in to lead him from
his temporary refuge in Tokyo to an Indian ashram.
He tells how Osho changed his life from an architect
with a busy mind to a full-time meditator, interested in
awareness and freedom. These years brought peace and
stillness but his second master, Papaji, was able to guide
him to Self-realisation in Lucknow in 1992. Premananda
talks about his years travelling the world sharing his
insights on freedom and about living in the Open Sky
House, a spiritual and creative community near Cologne,
Germany. He tells how Sri Ramana has crept into his
life and talks about his recent books and film.*

Premananda, perhaps we could begin by you describing your early life in England and how you became interested in spirituality.

I was born in December 1944 in Bangor, North Wales. The first year of my life, which of course I don't remember was spent with my mother in a small cottage on a vast, sandy beach. At that time World War II was coming to an end, and my father, who was a doctor in the British army, was in Germany. I didn't have any contact with my father in the first year of my life but I had a close contact with my mother, who I remember as a very soft person. The photographs at that time show me as a cute, blonde, curly-haired baby and my mother as a very lovely looking woman.

I remember that this was a very happy time for me, and at the same time there seemed to be some kind of awareness of the dangerous war situation. My father returned after I was about one year old, and photographs show him as a young, smiling, typical middle-class doctor.

Shortly after that we moved as a family to Ipswich, which is a small town about a hundred kilometres northeast of London, a kind of farming town. We had a house on the edge of the town in the countryside and that is where my brother and sister were born, and later on another brother who was always the 'young brother'. We lived together in that house for about fifteen years and I went through both my childhood and teenage years there.

It was a very typical middle-class house. I was growing up in the 50s. Materially things were quite simple, but as I look back at that time there is always a happy memory. My childhood was a mixture of the influence of my mother, who was a housewife and gave us a lot of freedom and space to play, and the influence of my father. He was working and away from the house during the day. He was an authority figure and rather intellectual. At meal times he often seemed far away in his thoughts. Our family was close knit and we used to sit down together for formal meals. I remember having quite a few friends in that area and because we were in the countryside we were able to play and make adventures outside.

So I guess when we get to the 60s that would be the time that you went to university. Was that in London?

Yes, when I was twenty years old I left the family and moved to London and studied civil engineering. That choice was arbitrary; I really had no idea what I wanted to do. I became a chartered civil and structural engineer but at that moment I started to get some sense of what my true interests were and what I wanted to do.

I was about twenty-three years old. I realised that engineering was far too mechanical and technological for me, so I got a job in a firm that was a mixture of engineers and architects. It's a well-known firm which designed the Sydney Opera House structure and the Pompidou Centre in Paris. It was a big, exciting, international company. I started working there about 1967. The work was challenging and interesting but even from the first days I realised that it wasn't for me. It was a big shock when I went to the first meeting of the chartered engineers. I was looking around the room and realised that I was in the wrong place. I didn't feel any sense of connection with those people.

Did you feel that there was something missing that you had to find?

Ever since the end of my teenage years I'd had a very strong question. When I was a teenager, very often in the late evenings I would end up sitting with my father, and we would have long conversations and debates together far into the night about the world and life and philosophy. I remember those debates as an exploration of life. I was very much into understanding life and people. Out of all of that talking I was left with a question. It was a very strong question, which gradually increased during my early twenties, but I didn't know what the question was and I had no idea what the answer might be.

The question seemed to be about not really fitting in, not feeling 'this is my life and what I want to be'. So when I became an engineer and realised that I didn't want that profession I went through a few years of chaos and confusion while I was looking desperately for somewhere I would fit in.

So that eventually led you to leave your work and to go overseas and travel?

What happened was that finally, after several whiskies, I resigned from my job and went back to university as a mature student to study architecture. I went to a beautiful architecture school. It was an independent school and attracted interesting teachers from around the world. The curriculum was not just about architecture but many other subjects related to architecture and human civilization and culture.

I graduated from that college as an architect and with a longing to explore myself and my relationship with life: What is life and what is it all about?

That question was becoming very strong. When I finished college, I felt that I was in a rut as far as my daily life in London was concerned. I had met some Japanese architects and they were encouraging me to come to Japan. On the spur of the moment I decided to go for three months. I went to Japan and got a job in an architect's office in Tokyo and immediately went into an enormous cultural shock. I had to confront my yuppie, middle-class, English upbringing; very traditional, formal, staid and stiff.

In those days I had gold-rimmed glasses, a goatee beard and wore a white suit. I had a yuppie image, which actually went down quite well with the Japanese. They were very welcoming to me. I met lots of interesting people, mostly architects. But this internal question became even stronger. I went into a 'dark night of the soul'. It wasn't just a night; it went on for several years.

I found myself staying in Japan; I kept postponing leaving, partly because I was intrigued by the different culture, but it was mainly because I was engrossed in an internal dialogue which was provoked by being in an alien culture.

So this time in Japan was very valuable. Although I had many friends I still felt very alone. I met a Japanese woman, a fashion designer, Yoshiko, who later became my wife.

Did she have something to do with your next step on the spiritual path and finding a teacher?

Not really, no.

So how did that come about?

That came about in quite an amazing way. Although I was about twenty-eight years old I still had no idea about the spiritual life. I was beginning with acupuncture and shiatsu, so I was moving in a spiritual direction, but not consciously. Suddenly the destiny of existence took over. I had arranged to meet an architect to speak about Japanese architecture. He was a very interesting man. He was German and a professor at M.I.T. in Boston, America, and was living in Kyoto with his Japanese wife. I was introduced to him because he was an expert in Japanese architecture and I made an appointment and went to see him.

That night we talked almost nothing about architecture. He and his wife made a beautiful dinner. One of his students, a Chinese woman, was also present and we all sat down to dinner in their traditional Japanese house. They started to talk about their spiritual teacher, somebody called Rajneesh. They started to talk about *tantra, Yoga* and meditation. All this was completely new to me. I must have had some interest because we talked through the whole night. It was only when the light came up at dawn that it was suggested it might be time to sleep!

The conversation that night was the big turning point of my life. Although I didn't really understand the significance at that time, it completely changed my life. When they played me a tape the next morning of their spiritual teacher, Rajneesh, I wasn't really interested. I told them, 'I'm sorry, it was a very nice night but I don't think this is really for me.' I remember walking out of the house and them saying, 'You are absolutely ready for this.'

Then destiny really stepped in. It was amazing really. I had taken Yoshiko to England to visit my parents and friends at Christmas. Afterwards we went to Paris for a week on holiday. The plane back to Japan didn't arrive because of a technical problem and the airline put us in a hotel for the night. The next morning we were given a new ticket and we caught the plane, which was Air India. We were flying back to Tokyo via Delhi.

As we were approaching Delhi I suddenly said to Yoshiko, 'Well, why don't we get out in Delhi for a few days and see India?' We decided it on the spur of the moment. The next morning I went to the airline office to confirm our flight and amazingly they told me that we had regular tickets, not cut-rate ones, so if we wanted we could fly throughout India at no extra cost. So I said to my future wife, 'How about having our honeymoon now? We can travel all over India, visit all these places and then go back to Japan a few weeks later.' We agreed, and we had a lovely time.

At some point we got to Bombay and we realised that we were quite close to the ashram of the German professor I had met in Kyoto. Spontaneously we decided to visit the ashram. We took the train to Pune and came to the Rajneesh Ashram. As I walked through the gate, which was called The Gateless Gate, I immediately felt at home. It was incredible. I had always felt that I never fitted in, but suddenly I felt that this was my place, that I was home. The feeling was emotional, powerful and strong and it was without any reason. It was as if the question I'd had for about ten years was suddenly answered. It was an amazing experience.

We went to the morning discourses and heard Rajneesh (who later became Osho) speaking and took part in some of the ashram's workshops and meditations. What was just going to be a couple of days turned into two weeks. By this time I had lost all my work in Japan because Japanese companies don't like you to turn up about a month late! I knew that would happen but I threw everything to the wind because the moment was so powerful. Despite myself, I just had to stay there. That was the big shift in my life.

Did you develop a relationship with Osho and become his devotee?

Not at that time. It was a beginning. I still had a lot of questions because I was a mindy person. We went back to Japan and both decided that we would stay in Japan for a year and earn money, and then we would go back to the ashram on our way back to England where we were going to set up our new married life.

We got married and Yoshiko's family gave her some money, which was exactly the same amount that I earned during that year. So we both had money and we travelled from Japan through China and Asia. We went on a very beautiful journey and ended up at the Pune ashram. We found a nice place to live and settled down. But we were clearly on our way back to England to start our new married life.

What was it about Osho that attracted you to return? Was it the man or his teaching?

I think it was a mixture. It was 1976 and early days for that ashram. There was a tremendous feeling of excitement, love, craziness, wonder and beauty at that time. Osho himself was quite young and his talks were very dynamic. He was talking about things that I had never really thought about and he was challenging all my beliefs. He was pointing strongly to another direction, another possibility for my life. He himself represented the possibility of an internal transformation, which would radically change me and my relationship to the world. And that was very attractive.

So there was something dissatisfying about the way you were living?

Although my family life had been a happy one, when I left home and went into the wider world, it was a world I couldn't easily relate with or didn't particularly want to relate with. In that ashram I found all the ingredients that seemed to be the answer to my dilemma.

How long were you with Osho altogether? Did you stay as a devotee?

After a few months I became a *sannyasin*, which meant that I was initiated directly by Osho and given a new name and a *mala* to wear. I settled into meditation at the ashram and being part of the community. I was already an artist, so my closest friends were painters. There was a painting group. Yoshiko also stayed. There was some resistance from her because she felt my energy moving away from her. It was almost like I had another lover, but my other lover was actually the man called The Master.

She became resistant to the situation and would have been happy if we had left. But a couple of months after me, she also became a *sannyasin* and settled down. We stayed a year together and then she met a man and went back to Europe with him. I decided to stay at the ashram. I stayed another six months. I would have stayed longer but Osho went to America. At that time I had no choice, so I went back to England.

When Osho died, did you want or need to find another guru?

Before he died I spent six months with the Osho community in Oregon, U.S.A. After that I spent another year close to an Osho centre in California. Then when he came back to India the second time, I joined the ashram in Pune again and was there for about three years. I had no thought of looking for another master. There was no question of that. I was totally surrendered to Osho.

I was doing some intense bodywork in those days and previously I had been editing some of Osho's books. I had also been a painter and an architect and in fact worked in the ashram's architecture department. So I had done various jobs in the ashram and was a part of the community there. Suddenly Osho left his body. It was not totally unexpected as he had been ill for a year, but when it actually happened it was a shock. I think I remained there for another year and it was an intense and beautiful time and a lot was happening. I still had no idea to look for another master.

I met a Russian woman in the ashram who was a psychology student from Moscow University and we became lovers. She wanted the bodywork that I was doing to be introduced to her psychology department in Moscow. She invited me to go to Russia. The person who had developed this particular type of bodywork encouraged me to go so I did, and nothing worked out as planned.

It was shortly before the Soviet Union collapsed and changed into Russia. It was a very interesting time as the whole communist way of life was crumbling and wasn't working anymore. People had very little food, and goods weren't available in the shops. Few people were working. There was nothing much happening in the normal way of things. The country was teetering on the brink of collapse. The people had been really starved of contact with Western people and with spiritual nourishment.

I became a sort of travelling guru through a series of amazing accidents. I didn't have any plans to do that but every weekend I found myself teaching meditation workshops, the healing arts that I knew, and giving long talks. Up to a hundred people would turn up, seemingly coming from nowhere. Totally illegally I travelled throughout the Soviet Union. I travelled from Lithuania in the west all the way to Tashkent in the east. I travelled enormous distances very cheaply on the trains. There was a little group of people who travelled with me. It was a wonderful six-month period. I got a taste of sharing Truth with other people, and I liked it very much.

Was something still drawing you back to India?

I left the Soviet Union with another woman who had become my lover, translator and friend and we moved to England. By that time I had been separated for five years from Yoshiko, although we were still friends. The idea was that my Russian friend and I would set up a life in England together. But I had some feeling that my spiritual journey wasn't complete. The feeling was different from the one I'd had inside before. There was a sense of incompletion. I found myself not ready to settle down in England and felt the pull to go back to India. I was still not looking for a master. I was interested in getting that last bit of the jigsaw and I didn't know that I would need another master to do that, so I went back to the same ashram in Pune.

Osho had been gone for about a year by then, and I settled down and continued my own internal search. I got to a nice state, felt inner peace, was at ease with meditation and felt a strong internal focus. So in a way I wasn't really dissatisfied, it was sort of 'okay'. I probably could have continued in that way, but suddenly it was like the wind of existence blew in and I heard about another teacher. The name of the teacher was Poonjaji, known as Papaji. I had read an interview with this man and I had also seen a video. But the real clincher was that I started noticing people who had come back from visiting this Papaji. I saw an amazing transformation in these people. There was a glow and internal smile from them that touched me.

And then a very close friend came back and he started to explain to me something that was very simple. He was explaining about the 'I' and how we had become so conditioned and attached to a certain idea of ourselves.

He tried to show me that if I could see that and let it go, then I was free. He was excited by his realisation and understanding. This was very unexpected and exciting because I had thought of enlightenment as far away and unattainable, and suddenly this close friend was telling me, with a lot of excitement, that it was really attainable right now. All I had to do was see this simple Truth, which I didn't quite see. He tried to explain it to me but I didn't quite get it. But he gave me the final push to go and see Papaji.

Was that in Lucknow, India?

Yes. I was still with my Russian lover. We had been together for about two years. She and I went travelling in Nepal. By then our relationship was a bit rocky, but we were both interested to go and see this master. We went to Lucknow in about April 1992. It was incredibly hot weather and we didn't know how to find this master. We got onto a bicycle rickshaw and told the man to go to a certain area of Lucknow. He went on for what seemed like forever, and when we couldn't stand the heat anymore and our driver was half dead with his cycling, I said, 'Stop! We can't look anymore, so stop!'

Then there was this incredible moment. As I got off the rickshaw my eyes met the name on the gate of the house and it said, 'Poonja'. I thought, 'Wow! This must be the place!' One second later, as I was looking at the house, Papaji himself was walking down towards the gate, and I was walking towards him. We just met totally naturally at the gate. Before I could get my breath or collect my wits, because it was all happening so suddenly, he was saying to me, 'Where are you staying? Where are your bags? What can I do to help you?' So we had this beautiful meeting which was completely unexpected and spontaneous. So I settled in and went everyday to his *Satsangs* (meetings in Truth).

Can you describe the sort of relationship that you had with Papaji? What's the essence of the time you spent with him?

There was an enormous availability. Osho had been the grandmaster, but rather far away. I never had a personal talk with him in the fifteen years I was with him. I had some personal meetings but they were always at a distance. But suddenly Papaji was very available. It was very personal. I remember, after being there for just a few days, going to his house on a Sunday and having lunch in his living room with maybe ten other people. He was sitting there and was tremendously, almost shockingly, available. Shocking because his immediacy confronted me. I had to really look and question, 'What am I doing here?'

In the first three weeks, I sat with him in *Satsang* every day and three times asked him a question. In those days you wrote the question in a letter before *Satsang* and then he would open up the letter and you would go and sit with him. So I had three beautiful meetings. During the third meeting something happened which is hard to describe. You could say that I saw with amazing clarity the thing that I hadn't been able to see with my friend, and which I never understood till that moment. In the fifteen or twenty years of spiritual searching I had never seen this. In that third meeting Papaji showed me with great finality who I was. It was the end of the road.

At the same time as that understanding happened, an enormous energetic phenomenon took place. I can remember sitting in front of him and suddenly not being able to open my eyes. It was physically impossible. When I looked inside there was just whiteness and I couldn't find this person called Premananda. He had been replaced by whiteness, blankness. It went on for quite a long time. At some point I opened my eyes and Papaji started to ask me some simple questions, which later I understood was his way of bringing me back out of this phenomenon into the room again. In a very sensitive way he got me to sit next to him and gave me some water to drink and reassured me, if you like, brought me back to earth again.

When I looked inside it was like I had disappeared into this enormous space and I had the sense of myself spiralling down into a void, into emptiness. The Self had revealed itself and it was seen that this was my true nature, which had always been known.

Would you describe that event as an awakening?

Yes. That meeting marked a total change in my life. It was as if instantaneously the identification with Premananda and the story of Premananda was completely cut. In fact Premananda completely disappeared for some time. From one instantaneous moment to the next there was an enormous shift, which I can only describe as an awakening to the Self.

After your experience you continued in Papaji's company for about five years. So where others had similar awakening experiences and left, you decided to stay?

When I look back, I can't remember. But I think there just simply wasn't a question of leaving. For the next month many spiritual and energetic phenomena happened and I was just present. Then the heat of change became less and I could function in a more everyday, ordinary way. So there was some kind of contact with Premananda again. At that point I decided I would rent a house and settle down and bring my things from Pune. There was so much love for this master and the community it wasn't possible for me to leave.

Eventually Papaji left his body. Was that when you left India?

No, it was not like that. Earlier he had asked me to run a guesthouse and to look after his guests, so I opened quite a large guesthouse, furnished it and became host to people visiting the community and Papaji. I did that year by year and during that time I established a deep internal connection with Papaji.

I didn't spend or have the interest to spend a lot of physical time in his presence, but there was a very strong internal dialogue going on. During that period all of Premananda came back. All of his issues, and *vasanas* (tendancies of the mind) came back to be looked at. I found that they could be looked at dispassionately as I wasn't attached to them or to this Premananda guy anymore. It was very easy to look at different stuff about Premananda's mind. So with Papaji's help, through an internal dialogue, that period of running the guesthouse was also a time of cleaning the mind. After about four years there was the message to leave but I resisted it strongly. Premananda didn't want to leave. I had become rather comfortable. There was this big bubble of love that was rather hard to leave. Eventually things conspired to make it clear that it was time to go. So I packed up the house. I had the choice of going to Australia, where I had never been, or back to England. I couldn't decide but ended up going to Australia. I lived there for five years until the end of 2001.

You have been giving Satsang *since 1997. What does* Satsang *mean and what do you offer people who come to your* Satsangs?

Well, the word *sat,* means Truth, so *Satsang,* means a meeting in Truth. At some point after I arrived in Australia I started working with people, initially teaching meditation and some of the healing arts that I knew. At the same time I saw that I wanted to share this simple insight that my friend had tried to show me and that Papaji finally did show me; I wanted to share it with people.

Initially I thought that everybody would want to know it. I recall my first days in Sydney walking around and feeling that I had a bag of diamonds. I wanted to give away these diamonds and I was amazed to discover that nobody wanted them. I couldn't find people to give these diamonds to. Nobody was interested in this simple Truth; they were far too busy with their lives. I started teaching meditation and other things and gradually students came round and I realised at some point that what I was sharing was my Self, the Self. That gradually became clearer to me, and that even though they weren't consciously interested in having this insight they had been attracted to me.

On the night Papaji left his body, September 7th 1997, I was running a weekend Reiki workshop. When he left his body it was about lunchtime in Australia. I had gone for a walk alone and suddenly had this very powerful energetic happening and an internal message from Papaji that I was familiar with, telling me that I had some work to do. I was incredulous about this message and had trouble believing it even though the messages continued for two days. I didn't know that he had left his body. In a way that was the beginning of Premananda offering *Satsang*. But in another sense it had been happening naturally, very gradually, through the work that I was doing.

In 1997, in Sydney, I remember starting with a few of my meditation students. I told them that I was going to offer them something a little different. So about six people got together in somebody's apartment and I just talked about this simple insight. They were very touched. Things happened quickly. Soon there were twenty and then thirty people coming. Suddenly a building was offered for a small rent. The *Satsang* community painted it and made cushions and set it up as a *Satsang* meeting place. In three months the whole thing got started and my teaching work began.

So you started communicating the Truth, as you understand it. What is this insight? What are you trying to teach people in your Satsangs?

I am just asking people to stop for a moment and become quiet and look and when they look I am asking them to see that for many years they have been saying 'I'. The reference of their lives has been 'I', they see the world from this place of 'I'. I am trying to show them that if they really investigate this 'I', they can't find it. They have the belief that there is an 'I' and a relationship to a world separate from themselves. Their parents and society have reinforced and passed on this belief; the whole society supports it. I try and show people that it is actually not true, that it is a wrong belief. I help people become a little quiet so that they can have a certain space where the story is not so pressing. In that space it's possible to investigate for yourself and see that this belief is in fact not true. Once that is seen clearly then everything changes for that person.

One of the traditional ways of discovering the Truth of the 'I' is Self-enquiry, which is something that Sri Ramana Maharshi spoke about. He was of course Papaji's guru. Can you tell us what is needed for Self-enquiry?

Sri Ramana Maharshi himself said that this was the most direct way to realise the Self. However, there are certain prerequisites for Self-enquiry. There needs to be some work, some time spent to get to know the mind and to quieten it. So whatever technique you use it is important to come to a *sattvic* mind, a clear and peaceful mind. This is a mind that is available to understand the Truth.

Most people have such busy minds and are so identified with their stories that there is simply no space in which Self-enquiry can work. If you do Self-enquiry in that busy state you will go in a circle within the mind. Self-enquiry doesn't work then. If you come to a *sattvic* state, then when you ask yourself the question, Who am I? you start to see that this 'I', the 'I' that is doing things, the 'I', that believes things, and the 'I', that judges things is not true. In the beginning Self-enquiry is a reminder to look deeper. As you start to look deeper you find that this enquiry brings you to stillness and peace. It doesn't bring you to some kind of clever answer.

Is that enquiry essentially an intellectual verbal enquiry or is it a deeper feeling enquiry?

It is not a mental enquiry. Initially it can be a mental enquiry and through that mental enquiry you can come to see the Truth that you are not the mind. But when you start doing it in a *sattvic* state, you find that it takes you to that place inside yourself of peacefulness. When you find that Self-enquiry is bringing you to peacefulness or emptiness you can't believe the mind anymore. You no longer believe this separate 'I', this separate identity. You start to realise that you are part of this oneness, which is called the Self or God.

If Self-realisation is so simple what prevents people from realising the Self permanently?

The thing that prevents people is that the majority are completely conditioned into their story and they live in a society which supports this lack of awareness. The media, friends, families, everybody conspires together. So most people never even consider that there could be some kind of alternative. In my twenties I had this question, so you could say that I never had a choice but to be a seeker. The question had to be answered. But it seems that most people are very content with their lives and they don't ask any questions about truth. A very small group of people do question and become seekers, seekers for the Truth of who they are. This is a very tiny proportion of the population. They find themselves attracted to different teachers, teachings and paths. Some of them find freedom, but many get lost along the way. I am of the strong opinion that a teacher is needed to find freedom. Why are some people drawn to such a teacher? I don't know. I can only really use the word grace. In some people's lives grace is working to bring them to a teacher. When I consider my life I feel incredibly grateful that I was taken first to Osho, who prepared me beautifully, and then to Papaji, who after only a few weeks was able to show me this simple Truth. I feel really blessed. I can't say that Premananda did that, because he didn't!

This is a rather contentious issue, this business of grace. Because if grace occurs spontaneously without one doing anything, is there any need for a spiritual aspirant to practise, or could one simply hang around until it just happens? Is there something a spiritual seeker can do to foster the grace?

This is a very difficult question. The absolute Truth is that you can't do anything, grace works. There is predestiny. Perhaps at that moment grace had me on the list and I was guided very quickly to the right places. Having said that I would also say that there are things that can be done that would put you on the playing field. Be part of a spiritual community, have a spiritual master, he will encourage you to become quiet and look. When you become quiet you start to see this conditioned mind. You start to see how you are so attached to 'my story'. By being in the *Satsang* of a true spiritual teacher, and by true I mean someone who has realised the Self, you can't escape seeing. Being in the presence of a spiritual teacher of that magnitude is never comfortable, that is why few people stay with a teacher and why, for example, often more people come after the teacher has died than when he was alive. This is a common phenomenon. So if there is sufficient honesty and if there is the predestination, the grace working in your support, then in a matter of time you will realise who you are.

That brings us to another contentious issue, the necessity of the guru. I think that all of the great masters have indicated the necessity of the guru. Do you feel the same way?

No doubt. Firstly, real surrender to the teacher gives you a constant reminder that Truth is possible, that there is an alternative, another way of living. He is the constant reminder of that. When you live in society with no contact with a spiritual teacher or a spiritual community, then the whole conditioning, the whole self-hypnosis, returns and you again focus on 'I'. When you are in the presence of a teacher the focus is the Self. This constant reminder is very valuable.

Secondly, the master provides the mirror. Although we can naturally see many of the issues and tendencies, some of the difficult and profound ones often can't be seen and need a mirror.

Thirdly, the master provides this enormous fund of unconditional love. In that love you have the nourishment you need to face some of the old structures, which may be painful and difficult. So the love of the master is very important. The master has two more important tasks. When the fruit is ripe and ready to fall, he knows; so he can just tap the fruit at the right moment. In the Zen tradition there are many stories of how the master does something outrageous to the student just in the right moment, and the student wakes up. The image of the Zen master with his stick. Finally, the master confirms that the awakening has actually happened.

So how do you see yourself with your students, or with the people who spend their time with you? Do you consider yourself to be a guru, a teacher or a friend?

I see myself firstly as a friend. There is no real difference between the master and the student. There is a tiny, small understanding that the master has that the student doesn't have. I am most comfortable as a friend. Guru is there by itself because a friend comes because he is interested in Truth. He comes to someone who is able to show him Truth, so naturally the guru is also there. Guru means someone who brings light to the darkness.

The experience you had with Papaji you called an awakening, and now you are calling a particular event the Self or the recognition of the Self. Is there a difference between an awakening and the Self, and is the process progressive? In other words does someone awake first and then perhaps lose it to some extent, and then over time it becomes deeper and deeper until they realise the Self? Is that how it works?

That has not been my experience. I had done many years of preparation achieving a quiet mind, this *sattvic* state of the mind, but I didn't know it at the time. So when I came to Papaji I was ready, I was prepared. All the work was complete, but there was no understanding. What happened in the meeting with Papaji, in a flash, in an instant, the understanding came. I call that understanding an awakening to the Self.

It happened in 1992 and the contact with the Self has never been lost. The ground of the Self has never left. That moment with Papaji was a dramatic change. Nothing fundamental has happened to that understanding since then, so I would call that an awakening to the Self. What has happened since then, as I have already mentioned, is that many of Premananda's issues, tendencies and patterns of the mind strongly returned. But because there was no identification they could be looked at. Over the years there has been less and less that disturbs the contact with the ground of the Self.

Now, the radiance or clarity of the Self is greater than it was then, not at the exact time of the awakening but two or three months later.

Is this increased radiance because the tendencies or vasanas *have been dealt with and are not as prominent as they used to be?*

I remember when I started offering *Satsang* I felt myself to be very quiet and clear. So at that time I felt myself ready even though I resisted it for some months after that initial message. There would be tremendous bliss and radiance after each meeting, then I would wake up the next day and feel myself right back in the mud with all this stuff around. I remember feeling that this can't be right and that I shouldn't be doing the meetings, that somehow it was not correct.

I was going to stop the meetings when I happened to meet Isaac, who is another spiritual teacher. I talked with him and he said, 'Yes, that is my experience too.' He encouraged me to continue. That doesn't happen anymore. In these last few years the various strong tendencies of Premananda's mind have come up, and by becoming aware of them as unreal they have gone, they have fallen away.

I have one last question. Can the Self be experienced? Is it an experience or is it an understanding? In other words, experiences come and go but the Self never comes or goes.

If 'I' is present then the Self cannot be, and so 'I' cannot experience the Self. However, the 'I' can disappear for a moment revealing the Self. If the mind is silent or quiet the 'I' can disappear. Later the mind can own that experience of the Self. I need to say the Self, when it is experienced, is still within the mind. It is the mind that is experiencing the Self. What I mean when I say 'an awakening to the Self' is different because then there is a deep, inner knowing, 'I am the Self.' In fact, there is no more an 'I' to know the Self. There is just Self beingness. It's just present. I think almost every human being has experienced the Self, that it is

334

a common occurrence. So for example you are walking along in the forest, the sun is shining and a bird flies overhead. The shadow of the bird appears on a rock and in the moment you see the shadow the mind stops and you become aware of the heat of the sun, the smell of the pine forest and the shadow all in an instant. You find yourself totally present, and the Self is revealed. There is this sense of tremendous expansion and peace. This is the Self.

I think it is common for people to meet the Self, but it often goes away quite quickly. Most people never know that they were experiencing the Self because nobody told them 'This is the Self.' Although the experience is common it doesn't necessarily lead people to have a spiritual life. Some people have very strong meetings of the Self. They have maybe hours or even days when they can't function normally and it's so powerful that it forces them to enquire, 'What is this?'

A woman I knew in Sydney was in a supermarket one day buying her groceries. Suddenly she felt herself expanding and becoming as large as the supermarket. She was quite distraught about this. She was feeling incredibly peaceful and in a way ecstatic, but she felt so different she couldn't find herself anymore. The old self, the story – she couldn't find her story anymore. So she was very disturbed and upset and basically wanted to get back to normal. She was brought to have a meeting with me and I could immediately recognise that she was experiencing the Self. She was the Self. We talked together and I tried to encourage her to just accept it as it was. But within a week her desire to be normal and to be the story was so strong that the conditioned self came back. That was a longer meeting with the Self. In fact, it can completely change one's life. Being the Self doesn't fit one's old story; so it forces one to start to find out: What was this? Did I go crazy? Do I need a mental hospital? Do I need a spiritual teacher?

Can that experience be recaptured in any way?

You can't get that experience back or look for that experience, but trying to understand that experience can lead you to find a master. Or in that moment a master comes. In the case of this woman, she became my student. For one or two years she associated with me and then continued with other teachers. In her case it didn't just stop. It was a radical change in her life.

The following section of the interview was conducted in June 2009, in Germany, and covers the years from 2003 to 2009.

What prompted your move from Australia to Europe?

I received a very clear internal message. I was packing up my car in Sydney on my way to a ten-day *Satsang* retreat and the message came that I'm not just packing for a holiday, I'm packing up to leave Australia. It's time to go back to Europe. I was very open to hear this message and so that's really what happened. Just to underline that message, a few hours later my car blew up and on the same day the owner of my apartment wrote to me that he needed it back for his family. So it was very clear that my days in Australia were over and there was a confirmation that it was time to go back to Europe where I hadn't been for eighteen years.

There was some concern about how that was going to work out. I had already planned a trip to India and I found myself staying there in a personal retreat for nearly a year. Then from India I went to Europe. So it was a two-step movement from Australia to Europe via India.

When you came to Europe did you feel guided on your way?

Yes. I already had this message, and then when I got to India it wasn't clear how I would move from there to Europe or where I would go to in Europe. My first idea was to return to England because that's where I'm from, and my second idea was to live near my parents who I hadn't really spent time with for twenty years. But that didn't happen because my parents didn't want it to happen. So that left me not knowing where to go. Then two things happened which always remind me of the workings of destiny. I met a Frenchwoman who wanted to introduce me to a friend of hers in Germany, and about one week before I was actually getting on the plane to go to Germany I met a German man in the street outside Ramana Ashram post office who invited me to come to his town, Leipzig. He'd been to my *Satsangs* in Tiruvannamalai two years before and had been very touched from something I had said. It really helped him. So with these two introductions I came to Europe.

I arrived in a small town in the north of Germany called Wolfenbüttel and stayed with an alternative doctor who had a big, modern house. He was kind enough to arrange some *Satsang* meetings for me in the evenings. That was my beginning in Europe. I then accepted the invitation to go to Leipzig where this contact of mine had arranged a meeting. It was the first meeting of this kind in Leipzig. We had a very energetic evening and out of this evening weekends spontaneously happened. In a way that was really the beginning of what then happened in the next years, because out of that weekend people invited me to other places. So then I was hopping around Germany for the first year, from place to place. I was a kind of *Satsang* gypsy with a large suitcase.

Early in the second year I participated in a spiritual festival in Baden Baden and after a very intensive meeting a farmer came to speak to me. He looked like a Sufi master actually, but anyway he had a horse farm in the Black Forest and he saw that I was quite tired, so he invited me and a few friends to come for a rest. He had built a beautiful meditation room above his stables in a huge old farmhouse and we had a very nice few days there with him. Out of that visit grew the *Satsang* community.

So that was quite a big step, because you were like a gypsy travelling around and suddenly you settled down and had a group of people around you. How was this for you? Had you ever thought about having a community?

I think in the past I had fantasized about people living together with an interest in spirituality, art and such things. But I wasn't really thinking about it at that time. I was more interested in being a *Satsang* gypsy. Again I was aware of the strong workings of destiny, because after this weekend we asked him, 'Well, could we hold a summer retreat on your farm?' It was the first year I'd offered a retreat in Europe so I was not expecting many people, but in fact about fifty people came. During the first few days of the retreat there was a lot of interest in staying on this farm and so the people got together and decided, 'Well, we should have a community.' The farmer was very open and two months later we had about sixteen people living on his farm!

You referred to the community as a 'Satsang' community. What do you mean by this?

We were all interested in freedom, we were all interested in awakening, and we were interested not only to awaken but also to stabilize that and to live that. We didn't quite know what living that meant but that was the beginning idea of the community.

Can you say something more about this change, about living closely with a group of people and about how you see your role as their spiritual master?

In the beginning I didn't really have any idea what it would mean to have a community. And now, five years later, I could say I'm a lot wiser. If I'd known then what I know now I might not have said yes! But having said yes I went along with the evolution of a group of people living together with this intention of awakening and freedom. And now I would have to say that I'm very pleased that I did. We moved from the farm and we're now living in a beautiful seventeenth century mansion on the banks of the Rhine just outside Cologne. It's such a beautiful place that it's encouraged other people to come. Some people left, some people came, and the community has developed not just for *Satsang* but also as a creative place. We have a lot of live music, we have an arts festival every year, we have concerts every Monday night in the house, we have an art studio and a dance studio. We're about to make a recording studio and a woodworking studio and we have space for a pottery. So there's a creative community that's developing alongside the original idea of a *Satsang* community.

How do you see the connection between being free and creativity?

338

When you come to your own stillness, your own silence, your own emptiness, then what you discover is there's nothing to do. 'Okay, so there's nothing to do. Then what?' Naturally out of this emptiness comes creativity, some kind of expression. People have different qualities and there are different expressions of creativity – musicians, singers, photographers, artists – but they all come out of this emptiness. As people in the community are getting quieter they are more ready for this creativity to come. So that's happened naturally over the last five years.

How do you see people benefiting from being in the community? What supports them to get the most benefit from being with you as a teacher?

In the society, when people are working, living, raising a family, they're very busy all the time. This is just the nature of the modern lifestyle. If somebody wants to look at themselves, be with themselves, then this community offers an island, an oasis. The whole effort in the community is to watch what's happening inside.

Today I was talking to a resident who has only been here for two months. He has a very strong structure of totally closing down and then he goes off and stays alone and separates himself. This is very clear to everybody, not just to me, and so there's the possibility that the other people in the community can remind him when this happens. I was joking with him and saying, 'Well, just ask the people to say to you "Box!" because they can see when you're in your box, so that could be an interesting reminder for you not to get lost in your structures.' So that would be an example of the advantages of a spiritual community.

When you first come to the community you come with all your structures and your very busy mind, and then gradually things get easier and easier and more flow happens. People who've been here a longer time tend not to be so much in their old mind structures; they are more in a flow. If you like, there's more love happening and people become less and less interested in their stories. The longer one stays the deeper the understanding that 'I am not my mind.' And so people don't take their minds so seriously and they don't take their ideas and their beliefs so seriously. Then everything becomes much more easy.

Some people who have been here from the very beginning find they are actually enjoying their lives much more. Some of them have transformed incredibly. One woman recently had a visit from her best friend whom she had not seen for four years. She told us that she could hardly recognise her. Working in the office, working in the kitchen, being around the other people, things had changed for her. This doesn't necessarily mean that she's now an awakened person, but it means that for sure transformation has happened and she is able to enjoy her life much more than she could before. So this would be another example of what happens when people come into the community.

In your work as a spiritual teacher do you feel influenced by your masters, Osho and Papaji?

Yes, I think I'm influenced by both of them. Osho was reminding me very strongly to look, to have Self-awareness. His influence encouraged the idea of meditation, to come to a quiet mind, and also the idea of celebration. Be here now and celebrate this moment. Enjoy. Have fun. Spiritual work doesn't have to be serious, it can actually be fun. When I went to Papaji I understood about Self-enquiry and that the difficulty everybody has is the identification or attachment to 'my life', 'my story', 'the story of my life'. So through Papaji's influence and teachings I saw that the important thing was to understand about this identification we have with the 'I'. The things I learned from my masters I now share with the people in the community.

We have regular meditations morning and evening and we have many moments of celebration. Once a week we have a whole evening singing together. Every Monday evening we have a concert with residents or invited musicians. So celebration is happening and at the same time there is constant looking, constant observing of what's really going on. An influence from Papaji is just to be quiet and stay with your Self, the Self being the true nature or the core of who we are.

We're also in touch with the latest technology. Twice a week, Monday and Friday, we transmit *Satsang* live through the Internet, with the possibility of asking live questions. We call it Satsang TV. We also have a Music TV channel for our concerts. It is an incredible new technology which can really create a global village. All you need is a fast Internet connection and our broadcast can be received anywhere in the world.

You mentioned Sri Ramana Maharshi. What is your connection to him?

My connection with him grew out of finding an old photograph. When I was with Osho in Pune I rented some rooms in an old Indian palace and the maharaja of this palace, some thirty years before, had been a direct disciple of Sri Ramana. In the beginning I didn't know who this man in the photograph was, but I was very attracted to the beauty of his eyes, the peace in his eyes, and gradually this photo pulled me in. I put it in a new frame and gave it an important place in my room. I began to find out about him and his teachings, Self-enquiry, 'Who am I?' and gradually, gradually Sri Ramana had more and more influence.

When I went to Papaji I found that he also had a photograph of Sri Ramana. He sat under this photograph to give his meetings. I learned that he had been a direct disciple of Sri Ramana. So with this influence I was drawn to visit Ramana Ashram. It was many years ago now, in 1993, and I became more and more familiar with Sri Ramana's teachings. Now every year for two or three months I am drawn to this small town where he lived in South India, at the holy mountain Arunachala. I would say that after some twenty years of having a connection with Sri Ramana, with Papaji, with Osho, in a very quiet, delicate, gradual way, Sri Ramana has become the most important influence in my life. I feel him guiding me in my work as a spiritual teacher.

When I lived with Papaji, I had the idea for a book about him and the people who came to him. This book has now been published as *Papaji Amazing Grace* and out of the experience of doing this one book, which was the only one I had planned, I now have a number of books which are to do with Sri Ramana and his teachings. *Arunachala Talks* consists of talks given during my annual Arunachala Pilgrimage Retreat. In the last year we published *Blueprints for Awakening* which is interviews with Indian Masters. In the spring of 2010 we'll publish a similar book with

Western Masters, and in-between we're publishing this book. Our small publishing company, Open Sky Press, produces beautiful books in both English and German. All these books have come out of this very subtle connection with Sri Ramana that grew stronger and stronger.

So where to from here in 2009?

After twelve years of constant travelling in response to any invitation, having meetings five evenings a week and an intensive group every weekend, it is time to stay home and develop the community around me. I see that to really make a lasting transformation the community provides the best opportunity, because Western life has become so pressured that most people have no spare time to look, to be aware.

I also value the creativity manifesting around me. Local artists are queueing up to exhibit in our art gallery even though we only exhibit work made from stillness. Muscians love to play in our house even though we only offer small audiences. It is wonderful to bask in the incredible love that has manifest here at Open Sky House.

I am a painter as well as a writer and I am looking forward to transmitting *Satsang* though my paintings. I have many books planned and I see the value of putting them out in the world. Also I have come to see that there are very very few people who really want to live in freedom. Most would just like to squeeze a little spirituality into their existing life. I will always be available for a true seeker. I have so much to be grateful for in my life and I will continue to put back whatever I am able.

Glossary

Advaita	The philosophy that presupposes that the Self or *Brahman* is the sole existing reality. *Advaita* literally translates as 'not two'. Its chief exponent was *Adi Shankara*.
ahamkara	The ego that considers itself as an 'acting I'.
ananda	Bliss; appears as a consequence of experiencing the Self.
Arjuna	Main male figure from the *Bhagavad Gita* who receives instruction from Lord *Krishna* about the nature of being and the meaning of life. *Arjuna* represents the human being caught in ignorance.
Arunachala	Holy mountain at Tiruvannamalai in South India. Considered to be *Shiva*. Sri Ramana Maharshi called *Arunachala* his *guru*. He arrived there aged sixteen and never left.
Arunachaleswara	Hindu temple dedicated to Lord *Shiva*, located at the foot of *Arunachala*, Tiruvannamalai; home of Lord *Shiva* and his wife Parvati. The inner sanctum is more than two thousand years old.
ashram	In ancient India a Hindu hermitage where sages lived in peace and tranquility amidst nature. Today, the term *ashram* is usually used to refer to a community formed primarily for the spiritual guidance of its members, often headed by a spiritual master.
Ashtanga Yoga	Indian system of *Hatha Yoga*. One of the most specified and difficult *Hatha Yoga* systems, where the breath (*pranayama*) is synchronised with physical postures (*asanas*).
atman	The individual aspect of the Self.
Bhagavad Gita	A portion of the *Mahabharata* in which Lord *Krishna*, an incarnation of Lord *Vishnu*, gives spiritual instructions to *Arjuna*.
Bhagavan	Living God. Respectful title for a realised being.
bhajan	Form of worship. Song with spiritual content, which is often dedicated to specific gods.

bhakta	Devotee of God.
bhakti	Devotion, love. Traditionally, one of the principal approaches to God-realisation.
Brahma	The creator. With *Shiva* (the destroyer) and *Vishnu* (the preserver), one of the main Hindu deities.
Brahman	The impersonal, absolute reality – the Self.
Brahmin	A member of the *Brahmin* caste, the first of four Hindu castes, the members of which are priests and scholars of *Vedic* literature.
Buddha	Usually refers to *Gautama Buddha*, the founder of Buddhism, often referred to simply as 'the *Buddha*'. A *buddha* (Sanskrit: awakened) is any being who has become fully awakened.
buddhi	Is 'that, which knows', a wisdom or intelligence.
darshan	Strictly: having the sight of a saint. Though often also used to mean in the company of a saint.
Deepam	One of the oldest festivals of light celebrated by Tamil Hindus on the full moon day of the month of Karthikai (Nov/Dec). Houses and streets are lit up with rows of oil lamps. A huge lamp is lit on the peak of the holy mountain, *Arunachala*, Tiruvannamalai.
dharma	Practice or path of Truth.
gunas	The three qualities of all manifestation: *sattva* (purity), *rajas* (activity) and *tamas* (sluggishness).
Gurdjieff	George Ivanovich *Gurdjieff*, around 1877-1949. Enigmatic, provoking and mystic Greek-Armenian teacher. Invented the *Gurdjieff* dances and founded the 'Institute for the Harmonious Development of Mankind', Fontainebleau, near Paris.
guru	A teacher in the religious or spiritual sense, commonly used in Hinduism and Buddhism. The *guru* is seen in these traditions as a sacred conduit for wisdom and guidance. The one who shows that you are the same as him/her. The importance of finding a true *guru* is given as a prerequisite for attaining Self-realisation.

344

Hatha Yoga	A holistic *Yogic* path to gain enlightenment. The *Hatha Yoga* predominantly practised in the West consists of mostly *asanas* (physical postures) understood as physical exercises. It is also recognised as a stress-reducing practice.
japa	Practice of repetition of the Lord's name or of a *mantra*.
jiva	Living being. The individual soul, which, until liberation, will continue to incarnate. In essence, it is one with the Universal Soul.
jivanmukta	One who is liberated while still alive.
jivatman	The individual aspect of *atman*; the 'opposite pole' is *paramatman*, the absolute aspect of *atman*.
jnana	Knowledge of what is real and what is not real. A principal, traditional path to realisation of the Self.
jnani	One who has realised the Self. One who has and is *jnana*. One who has attained realisation by the path of knowledge.
Kali	A Hindu goddess who represents death, destruction and renewal. The destroyer of the ego and the illusions, cuts through confusion, ignorance and bonds and frees those who strive for the knowledge of God.
karma	Cosmic law of cause and effect, the result of an individual's past actions, which is said to invariably return to him at some point in time. Also: the collective storehouse of merit or demerit from all of an individual's past actions.
Karma Yoga	The *Yoga* of action based on the teachings of the *Bhagavad Gita*. Focuses on the adherence to duty while remaining detached from the reward. It states that one can attain salvation *(moksha)* or love of God *(bhakti)* by performing one's duties in an unselfish manner.
Krishna	Incarnation of *Vishnu*, who is considered the Supreme God. Usually depicted as a young cowherd playing a flute or as a youthful prince giving philosophical instruction. Represents knowledge, bliss and the celebration of life.
Kundalini Yoga	A physical and meditative discipline within the tradition of *Yoga*, to raise up the *Kundalini* energy (spiritual force

or power) from the base of the spine through all the *chakras* (subtle energy centers) to the crown *chakra*.

lingam	A symbol of the Self in the form of a phallus, for the Hindu god, *Shiva*.
Mahabharata	Great epic of the Bharata people. National epic of India. Consists of 106,000 couplets. Existed in various forms for well over two thousand years. It's most famous text is the *Bhagavad Gita*.
Maharaj	Great king. Used as a honorific term for spiritual master.
mahatma	Great soul or man or saint.
mala	*Japa mala* is a circle of 108 beads, like a rosary, often used as an aid for repetition of a *mantra*.
manonasha	Extinction of the mind. Destruction of the illusion of a separate I.
mantra	Sacred sound. In the Hindu traditions a sound from the *Vedas*. Repeated either orally or mentally and used as an aid in bringing concentration to the mind. The most well-known *mantra* is the original sound *om*.
maya	Worldly illusion that makes the unreal world appear to be real.
mithya	Unreal. In Hindu thought, the world as we see it is unreal, is only a projection of God.
moksha	Liberation from *samsara*, the cycle of death and rebirth and all of the suffering and limitations of worldly existence.
mukti	Release. See *moksha*.
nirvikalpa samadhi	The highest state of consciousness, in which the soul loses all sense of being different from the universal Self, but a temporary state from which there is a return to ego-consciousness.
nitya	Forever, eternal, beyond the influence of time.
om	Cosmic, eternal sound.
pradakshina	Going clockwise around a sacred person or place as an act of veneration or reverence.

prakrithi	Essential nature, eternal power.
pranayama	Breath control.
premananda	Unconditional love and bliss.
puja	Worship. Ritual in which offerings are made and prayers said.
punya	Good *karma* created by good thoughts, words and actions. Generated by giving, kindness and *dharma* practice.
purna	Completeness, fullness.
rajas	One of the three *gunas*. Quality of activity, passion, birth, creativity. The fruit is often pain, even though the immediate effect is pleasure.
reiki	Japanese form of healing using the life force energy by laying hands above the body.
rishi	A 'seer' or 'sage' to whom the *Vedas* were 'originally revealed' through states of higher consciousness.
sadguru/satguru	The *guru* who leads one to freedom – Self-realisation.
sadhana	Spiritual practice.
sadhu	A pious or righteous man. Traditionally a renunciate, a wanderer with a bare minimum of possessions, who relies on alms for daily needs.
sahaja samadhi	Highest state of enlightenment. Effortless and permanent.
samadhi	Direct but temporary experience of the Self. The experiencing subject becomes one with the experienced object, the mind becomes still. Also the term to describe the grave of a saint.
sangha	The community or gathering of devotees around a *guru*.
sankalpa	Volition, mental activity, thought, tendencies and attachment.
sannyasin	Renunciate, who, after being initiated by a *guru* or religious superior, is given a spiritual name and takes vows to abandon all ties with conventional society and live with one-pointed attention on God only.

Sanskrit	Ancient language of the *Vedas*. In Hinduism and Buddhism it was regarded as 'the language of the gods'. Nowadays used mainly for religious and scientific discourse. Origin of all Indo-Germanic languages.
sat	Truth.
satchitananda	Truth – consciousness – bliss. The three qualities of the Absolute, *Brahman*.
Satsang	Abiding in the Truth. The gathering of the *guru* with his students.
sattva	Purity, goodness; the highest of the three *gunas*.
sattvic	Pure. Anglicised adjective from *sattva*.
shakti	The power of becoming, the energy of creation; as goddess, the female aspect of *Shiva*.
Shankara	*Adi Shankara*: Indian sage of the 9th century who is considered the most influential figure of *Advaita*.
Shiva/Siva	The destroyer. With *Brahma* (the creator) and *Vishnu* (the preserver), one of the main Hindu deities.
shraddha	Faith and trust.
siddha	A person who has achieved a *siddhi*.
siddhi	Supernatural power, paranormal ability.
sruti	Here the term is used to describe the underlying fundamental drone note which supports singing and almost any instrument.
Swami	Title for religious attainment and scholarship.
tamas	Sluggishness, inactivity, darkness. One of the three *gunas*.
tantra	Asian body of beliefs and practices which works from the principle that the universe we experience is nothing other than the concrete manifestation of the divine energy. It seeks to ritually appropriate and channel that energy within the human microcosm, in creative and emancipatory ways.
turiya	State of pure consciousness similar to *samadhi*.
Upanishad	The concluding portion of the *Vedas* consisting of 108 verses. The *Upanishads* are the texts from which all *Vedic* philosophy is derived.

vairagya	Dispassion, detachment, or renunciation from the pains and pleasures in the material world.
vasanas	Emotional and mental tendencies; habits of action, reaction, and desires one has, which are said to be the product of patterns of living in both this life and past lives.
Vedanta	The philosophy derived from the *Upanishads*, the final section of the *Vedas*.
Vedas	Knowledge. Four collections of scriptures which were channelled by the *rishis*. The ultimate source of authority for Hindus.
vichara	Search, investigation.
videhamukta	One liberated at the fall of the physical body.
Vishnu	One of the principal Hindu deities worshipped as the protector and preserver of the world.
viveka	Discrimination between the permanent and the impermanent.
vrittis	Waves of mental activity.
Yoga	Union. Teaching and practice derived from the ancient *Vedic* philosophy. The practice for and the union with the divine.
Yoga Vasistha	Considered the earliest work reflecting the highest wisdom of *Vedanta*, or *jnana Yoga*. It is the instruction of the sage Vasistha to his pupil, Sri Rama, as recorded by the poet Valmiki in some 62,000 lines. This instruction led Rama to realisation of the Self.
Yogi	One who practises *Yoga*.

Contact Details *and* Book References

This is a list of all books mentioned in *Arunachala Shiva*.
All books published by Sri Ramanasramam are available at:

Ramanasramam Bookshop
Tiruvannamalai, South India
www.sriramana.org

**Aksharamanamalai
(The Marital Garland of Letters)**
Sri Ramana Maharshi, Sri Ramanasramam,
Tiruvannamalai

A Search in Secret India
Paul Brunton, Srishti Publishers and
Distributors, New Delhi, 1934

**Be As You Are – The Teachings
of Sri Ramana Maharshi**
edited by David Godman, Penguin Books,
1985

Blueprints for Awakening
Premananda, Open Sky Press, London,
2008

Call Off the Search
DVD by Jim Lemkin, Avadhuta Foundation,
Boulder

Day by Day with Bhagavan
from the Diary of A. Devaraja Mudaliar,
Sri Ramanasramam, Tiruvannamalai, 2002

Guru Ramana
S.S. Cohen, Sri Ramanasramam,
Tiruvannamalai, 1974 edition

**Garland of Guru's Sayings
(Guru Vachaka Kovai)**
Muruganar, translated by Swaminathan,
Sri Ramanasramam, Tiruvannamalai, 1990

Guru Vachaka Kovai
Muruganar, translated by Dr T.V.
Venkatasubramanian, Robert Butler and
David Godman, edited and annotated by
David Godman, Avadhuta Foundation,
Boulder, 2008

I Am That
Sri Nisargadatta Maharaj, translated by
Maurice Frydman, Chetana Publishing,
Bombay, 1973

Mother's Agenda
Satprem, Institute for Evolutionary
Research, USA, 1993

Nothing Ever Happened
David Godman, Avadhuta Foundation,
Boulder, 1998

Padamalai
Muruganar, edited and translated by
David Godman, T.V. Venkatasubramanian
and Robert Butler, Avadhuta Foundation,
Boulder, 2004

Prior to Consciousness
Sri Nisargadatta Maharaj, edited by Jean Dunn, Chetana Publishing, Bombay, 1999

Sad Darshana Bhashya
translated and compiled by Kapali Sastri, Sri Ramanasramam, Tiruvannamalai, 9th edition, 2006

Self-Enquiry (Vicharasangraham) of Sri Ramana Maharshi
translated by Dr T.M.P. Mahadevan, Sri Ramanasramam, Tiruvannamalai, 1994

Silence of the Heart Dialogues with Robert Adams
Robert Adams, Acropolis Books, Atlanta USA, 1999

Talks with Sri Ramana Maharshi
compiled by Sri Munagala Venkataramiah, Sri Ramanasramam, Tiruvannamalai, 1st edition, 1955

The Adventure of Consciousness
Satprem, Mira Aditi Centre, Mysore, 2000

The Collected Works of Ramana Maharshi
Sri Ramanasramam, Tiruvannamalai, 6th revised edition, 1996

The Last Days and Maha Nirvana of Bhagavan Sri Ramana
Viswanatha Swami, Arthur Osborne and T.N. Krishnaswamy, Sri Ramanasramam, Tiruvannamalai, 1997

The Power of the Presence
David Godman, Avadhuta Foundation, Boulder, Volume One 2000, Volume Two 2001, Volume Three 2002

The 108 Names of Sri Bhagavan (Ramana Ashtothara)
Sri Viswanatha Swami, English translation and commentary by Professor K. Swaminathan, Ramanasramam, Tiruvannamalai, 1st edition 1997

Wandering in the Himalayas
Swami Tapovan Maharaj, Chinmaya Mission, India

Who Am I? (Nan Yar) The teachings of Bhagavan Sri Ramana Maharshi
Sri Ramanasramam, Tiruvannamalai, 22nd edition, 2006

David Godman

For information regarding David Godman

contact:
david_godman@yahoo.co.uk
www.davidgodman.org

David Godman's Publications

Books about Sri Ramana

Guru Vachaka Kovai
Avadhuta Foundation, USA, 2008

Padamalai
Avadhuta Foundation, USA, 2004

Sri Ramana Darsanam
Sri Ramanasramam, India

Be As You Are
Arkana (Penguin Books), 1989

Books about Papaji

The Fire of Freedom
Avadhuta Foundation, USA, 2007

Nothing Ever Happened
Avadhuta Foundation, USA, 1998

Papaji: Interviews
Avadhuta Foundation, USA, 1993

Books about Disciples

The Power of the Presence
parts One, Two and Three
Avadhuta Foundation, USA, 2000

Annamalai Swami – Final Talks
Annamalai Swami Ashram, India, 2000

Living by the Words of Bhagavan
Annamalai Swami Ashram, India, 1995

No Mind – I am the Self
Bhanumathy Ramanadham, Sri Lakshmana Ashram, India, 1986

James Swartz

For information regarding James Swartz' teaching programme

contact:
shiningworld@rediffmail.com
www.shiningworld.com
Phone 001 503-895-5220

James Swartz' Publications

Books

How to Attain Enlightenment
The Vision of Non-Duality

Meditation –
An Inquiry into the Self

The Mystery Beyond the Trinity

Essays on his Website

Self Knowledge

The Gospel of Love

Tattva Bodha –
Knowledge of Truth

Mystic by Default
(Autobiography)

What is Advaita Vedanta?

Symbols of the Self

Vedanta and the Kundalini

What is Neo-Advaita?

The Horse's Mouth

Premananda

To contact the author or for information concerning Premananda's Satsang Meetings

contact:
office@premanandasatsang.org
or visit his website at
www.premanandasatsang.org
Phone +49 2173 4099204

For information concerning Premananda's books and DVDs

contact:
office@openskypress.com
www.openskypress.com
Phone +49 2173 1016070

Premananda's Publications

Books

Blueprints for Awakening
Open Sky Press, London, 2008

Arunachala Talks
Open Sky Press, London, 2007

Papaji Amazing Grace
Open Sky Press, London, 2007

DVDs

Arunachala Shiva
Open Sky Press, London, 2009

Blueprints for Awakening
Wisdom of the Masters
Open Sky Press, London, 2008

Arunachala Talks Series

Authentic Love
Relationships, Love and Sex

Devotion
Surrender and Trust

The Fortress
The Ego and the False Self

The Conditioned Mind
My 'Story' and the False Self

Guru
The One Who Brings Light

Who am I?
Sri Ramana Maharshi's Teaching

A Spiritual Roadmap
Journey to Awakening

ARUNACHALA PILGRIMAGE RETREAT

This Satsang Retreat is an opportunity to live in a community situation for three weeks at the holy mountain Arunachala in Tiruvannamalai, South India. Arunachala has been a powerful place of pilgrimage for two thousand years. We are accommodated in a lovely modern ashram. Our meetings take place on the roof directly overlooking the holy mountain. Each morning there is quiet meditation, yoga and Satsang. We spend the afternoons either alone, in Ramana Maharshi's ashram, or together with the group. Also, we go on a magical five day bus trip of 1500 km that brings us to five wonderful Indian Saints and allows us to see and experience Indian culture and landscapes.

www.india.premanandasatsang.org

Who am I?

open sky house
Be As You Are

The Open Sky House Satsang and Arts Community is housed in a seventeenth century mansion on the banks of the Rhine between Cologne and Dusseldorf, in a small village. There is a regular weekly Satsang and Energy Darshan with Premananda. In addition, regular weekend intensives and retreats are held throughout the year. There is an Arts programme consisting of painting, music, theatre and dance.

The residents work together running several businesses within the house: Open Sky Press, Rhine River Guest House, Flow Fine Art Gallery and Open Sky Seminar. All aspects of work, as well as the ordinary daily life of the community: cooking, childcare, cleaning and personal communication, are used as the background to show the robotic nature of most actions. When there is freedom from habitual reactions and patterns, the mind becomes still.

You are welcome to visit as a Guest or a Volunteer.

www.openskyhouse.org

Be As You Are

OPEN SKY PRESS
Timeless Wisdom

Open Sky Press aims to support people in their search for Truth with a range of publications on Satsang, spiritual awakening, transformation and related subjects.

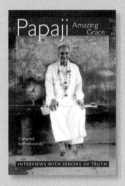

Papaji Amazing Grace is a book of fifteen powerful interviews with people who had an Awakening with their Indian master Papaji (Sri H.W.L. Poonja). They are stories of a housewife, a businessman, even an officer of a nuclear powered aircraft carrier. Each person had the common longing to discover the eternal Truth of who they are.

Arunachala Talks consists of talks given at Premananda's annual Arunachala Satsang Retreat in South India. Premananda lovingly and humorously guides us to see that we are not the experience 'my life', but rather the awareness in which the experience happens.

Blueprints for Awakening is an archive of rare and exceptional video, audio and print material, a marvellous collection of lively, authentic sage wisdom-teaching. British spiritual teacher Premananda uses the teachings of Sri Ramana Maharshi to compose twelve questions which he puts to sixteen Indian Masters. They relate to the major topics which one meets on the spiritual journey.

OPEN SKY PRESS

Tel +49 2173 1016070
distribution@openskypress.com
www.openskypress.com

Preview DVD *and*
Map of Arunachala

Arunachala Shiva offers a map of Arunachala and a Preview DVD of the book's companion film, *Arunachala Shiva*, bringing an extra, vital visual dimension to the contents of this book.

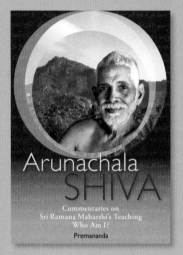

Arunachala Shiva – DVD Film

The Film expresses the important aspects of Sri Ramana's life and teachings. It presents the highlights of the thought provoking commentaries from David Godman, James Swartz and Premananda on Sri Ramana's most important written works. The film contains archive material of Sri Ramana, film of the Ramana Ashram and of course, beautiful footage of Arunachala.

- Film length 90 min.
- Subtitles in German, Russian, Danish, French, Dutch, Spanish.
- Bonus material: High quality photographs.

Map of Arunachala and surroundings including information about the places Sri Ramana lived (in red). This map is a useful tool for all those wishing to visit the holy mountain Arunachala, and for those interested in a detailed picture of Sri Ramana's life. [You find the map in the plastic pocket opposite, behind the Preview DVD]

Film Preview for *Arunachala Shiva*, the DVD Film of this book. You can watch the Preview on your computer or on a PAL system DVD player. Duration: 24 minutes.

Photographs including Sri Ramana's portrait, pictures of Ramana Ashram and Arunachala to view, download and print on your computer.